PORTLAND
FARMERS MARKET
— COOKBOOK —

100 SEASONAL RECIPES
and Stories that Celebrate Local Food and People

ELLEN JACKSON

Photography by Alan Weiner *and* Charity Burggraaf

SASQUATCH BOOKS
SEATTLE

PORTLAND
FARMERS MARKET
— COOKBOOK —

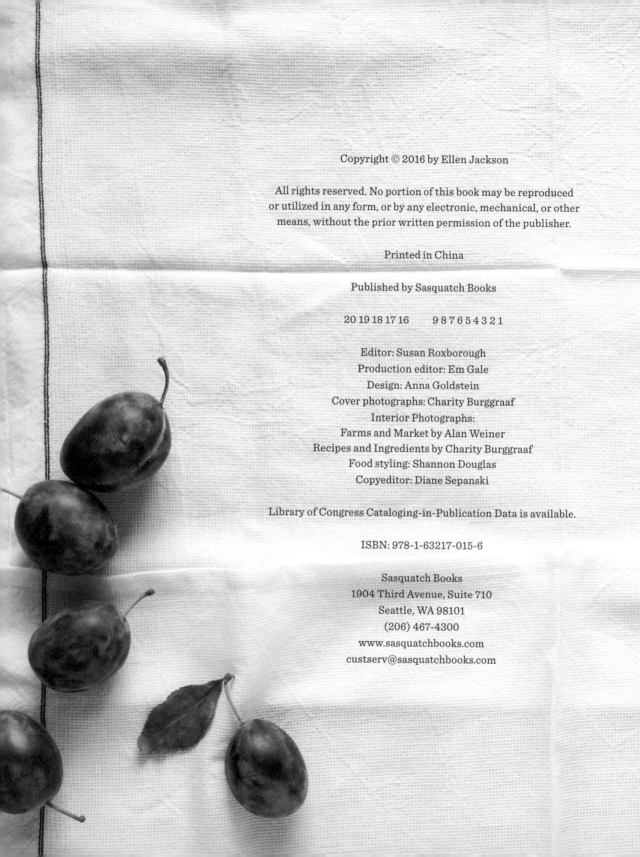

Printed in China

Published by Sasquatch Books

20 19 18 17 16   9 8 7 6 5 4 3 2 1

Editor: Susan Roxborough
Production editor: Em Gale
Design: Anna Goldstein
Cover photographs: Charity Burggraaf
Interior Photographs:
Farms and Market by Alan Weiner
Recipes and Ingredients by Charity Burggraaf
Food styling: Shannon Douglas
Copyeditor: Diane Sepanski

Library of Congress Cataloging-in-Publication Data is available.

ISBN: 978-1-63217-015-6

Sasquatch Books
1904 Third Avenue, Suite 710
Seattle, WA 98101
(206) 467-4300
www.sasquatchbooks.com
custserv@sasquatchbooks.com

To the farmers, foragers, fishermen, ranchers, and food artisans who awaken early and work tirelessly to feed Portlanders

CONTENTS

SUMMER

AUTUMN

WINTER

AND THE BELL RINGS

I'VE HAD THE PLEASURE OF running the Portland Farmers Market for the last five of its twenty-five seasons. Over the years, I've gotten to know our farmers and food artisans, and watched multiple markets spring to life each week. Every time, it feels like a miracle—the transformation from empty parks and parking lots to orderly rows of stalls and tented tables overflowing with fresh food and flowers; once-quiet spaces bustling with shoppers toting bulging bags, families chatting with growers, and market staff and volunteers scurrying about. And then, a few hours later, the markets wind down, vendors pack up their displays and drive home, and the spaces wait serenely until the next market day. I'm in awe of the people who produce our food, and I think we all should be.

Though operating for only a handful of hours each week, Portland's farmers' markets make a lasting impact. The seven markets we operate contribute about $8 million each year to Oregon's economy. Of equal importance is the incredible, immeasurable joy they bring to the shoppers, eaters, growers, home cooks, and restaurant chefs and owners who support them and to whom we offer this book. Ellen Jackson, a longtime member of our board of directors, dreamed for years about using her culinary know-how to pen a Portland Farmers Market cookbook. As we approached our silver anniversary, she suggested that now was the time. Thank you, Ellen, together with our recipe contributors: I hope we've created a fitting tribute to our local food culture, our market vendors, and the community that celebrates them.

Farmers are at our core—they are our reason for being. In 1992, thirteen of them set up shop in a parking lot beside the Willamette River, flanked by the historic Albers Mill and the now defunct *River Queen*, a ferryboat turned floating restaurant. What activists and market founders Craig Mosbaek, Ted Snider, and Richard Hagan started has grown and flourished year upon year to represent the 250-plus farmers and food artisans who currently sell at our markets. Some would say they sparked a movement with their intention to support local farm families and small food entrepreneurs, as now our region is home to more than forty independently run markets, and Portland's food scene, barely on the radar in 1992, is internationally famous.

From that single-market beginning, Portland Farmers Market added vendors and new locations slowly and thoughtfully, one every few years to arrive at today's seven. With markets in three downtown locations and four close-in neighborhoods, we span the city center and welcome seven hundred thousand shoppers each year. And not just during the summer. We opened a winter market in downtown Portland in 2012. Our growers have tackled the challenges of winter production in order to create a source of year-round income, and shoppers have come out in droves to support them. Since 2014 we have operated year-round under the shelter of giant elm trees in the center of the Portland State University campus.

The success of our vendors is measured in numbers—of market shoppers and dollars spent—but Portland Farmers Market acts as a business incubator as well. Our markets are invaluable venues for new food businesses to sample and market products, gather loyal customers, and grow to scale. More than fifty vendors have used our markets as springboards to open restaurants, bakeries, and wholesale businesses. Some have literally grown up in—and right out of—the market.

Guided by their graciousness and our policy, prepared-foods vendors are required to source at least 25 percent of their ingredients locally, ideally from their fellow Portland Farmers Market farmers and ranchers. Many reach much further and build their reputations on the high quality and fresh flavors that are the unmistakable hallmark of using local ingredients.

For shoppers, a trip to the farmers' market is authentically Portland. For example, we've gone beyond recycling and composting: when you purchase a meal at one of our larger markets, you get it on a real plate with real silverware, which you then return to a central location. Prepared-foods vendors collect the dirty dishes and silverware at the end of the market and take them back to their kitchens, where they wash them for use the following week.

People come to our markets to fill their bellies and shopping bags, but they also come for fun—live music, vibrant programming, and engaging events. Local chefs are invited to shop the market for the ingredients to prepare a simple meal, which they create in front of an audience of devoted onlookers, eager to observe—and taste—something new. Children busily assemble the ingredients for recipes designed just for them in Saturday-morning Kids Cook classes. In fact, many of the recipes in this book come from chefs who have stood on our stage and shared their tips and tricks for using the abundant veggies, fruits, meats, and cheeses available at the market.

In 2009 we opened the King neighborhood market and the seed of something greater was planted: a group of volunteers and contributors started Fresh Exchange, a cash matching program for the market's shoppers who receive SNAP (food stamp) benefits. The program has prospered, both locally and nationally. Today, Portland Farmers Market operates the Farmers Market Fund, our companion charitable organization, and runs the SNAP matching program (Double Up Food Bucks) at more than forty-five farmers' markets in the state of Oregon.

Our strength is measured by our success at accelerating prosperity among our vendors. It is only by realizing that vision that we secure our position in the community, better establish our brand, and ensure our solid financial future. Every decision we make considers the benefits to, or impact on, our farmers who painstakingly plant and care for the astonishing variety of fresh foods they grow. Artists and scientists in their (literal and figurative) fields, they are the same people who pick, clean, pack, and haul what they grow to our marketplaces. When you bring the fruits of their labor home to your kitchen, you're getting vital nutrients and glorious flavor. Both are critical to our well-being, and both are at their peak in farm-fresh food.

To our regular shoppers and visitors, thank you for loving Portland Farmers Market as much today as you did twenty-five years ago; you've helped our PSU market to be frequently ranked among the top ten on the planet! And with deep gratitude to the farmers, food artisans, and chefs who vend at our markets—you make it everything that it is.

Trudy

—**TRUDY TOLIVER,** executive director, Portland Farmers Market

INTRODUCTION

I HAVE BEEN SHOPPING AT the Portland Farmers Market almost as long as it's been around. I moved to Portland in 1994 to join Cory Schreiber and the team who opened Wildwood Restaurant and Bar. It was a special bunch of people, many of whom still live and work in Portland, having gone on to help shape our local culinary landscape. Together we have watched the once-quiet city blossom into a unique destination for diners, celebrated one another's milestones, and supported each other in the ways that Portlanders in the food business do. Several new waves of talent have since emerged, with protégés of the city's early influential kitchens opening restaurants of their own and mentoring their own eager cooks. (Look no further than Cory Schreiber, page xxii, and Adam Sappington, page xxiii). The pioneering spirit that defined Portland in the mid '90s is very much intact.

Portland is frequently named among America's best food cities, and now the rest of the world knows us not only for our coffee and beer, but also for Chinook salmon and Hood River strawberries, chanterelle mushrooms and huckleberries, pinot noir and wild game, truffles and marionberries. James Beard famously described Oregon's bounty in 1964: "No place on earth, with the exception of Paris, has done so much to influence my professional life." Portlanders know they are lucky to call this place home. Portlanders who make their living from the land and who love to cook and eat feel doubly blessed.

For me, writing a Portland Farmers Market cookbook represented an opportunity to capture both the agricultural glory of the Pacific Northwest and the pride of place we share as Portlanders. Nowhere is that ethos more evident than at our farmers' markets. For twenty-five years, Portland Farmers Market has informed our way of thinking about how food is grown and sourced, cooked and eaten, and its vendors have played a key role in contributing to the remarkable food our culinary professionals serve to an appreciative and receptive audience. As a member of the board of directors nearing the end of my six-year term, this project came to me at the best possible time, overlapping with our twenty-fifth anniversary. I appreciate the staff and board entrusting me with paying tribute to one of the city's shiniest jewels; it has been an honor and privilege.

Oregon boasts an abundance of superlative, sustainable ingredients, and the recipes in the *Portland Farmers Market Cookbook* are informed by the flavors, colors, and textures of the region. Many of the book's one hundred ingredient-driven recipes come from cooks and chefs whose simple, seasonal styles are inspired by their relationships with the foragers, farmers, and fishermen who deliver their wares—usually from within one hundred miles of the city—to our markets and the kitchen doors of our restaurants. The balance of the recipes come from those same foragers, farmers, and fisherman, arguably the individuals best equipped to advise us in our preparation of the ingredients they foster from seed to fruit.

A veteran of Portland restaurant kitchens, I've always felt a special kinship with the people who grow our food. I was fortunate to work in kitchens and with chefs whose priorities around food sourcing and policy reflected my own—Cory Schreiber, Greg Higgins, Vitaly Paley, and Scott Dolich are just a few. Sustainability, seasonality, supporting local growers, and economies—these are the issues that continue to matter most to me. Now working from my home kitchen, the impact I can make with my purchases is reduced from feeding hundreds in an evening to two, but my ambition is and always has been to empower others to make good decisions about what they eat and to get them into the kitchen.

In addition to operating markets, Portland Farmers Market serves as a leader of the local food movement, a source of education, a culinary focal point in the community, a cultural destination, an economic engine for entrepreneurs, and a beacon for Portland's sustainability movement. The care and standards applied to selecting vendors and choosing a product mix are an important reason why the Portland Farmers Market brand is synonymous with quality, integrity, and authenticity. Area residents and chefs trust Portland Farmers Market to provide access to the best and freshest local food available; in return, they reward the market with their patronage and loyalty.

I hope that we can reward that devotion with this collection of seasonal recipes from market vendors, chefs, and shoppers, along with the vibrant photos and profiles of beloved food producers. If the *Portland Farmers Market Cookbook* manages to capture the essence of our market experience and transform it into something you'll take into your own kitchen, dog-ear its pages, and use in good health, I'll consider my part in it a success.

WHY SHOP AT FARMERS' MARKETS?

In addition to being fun for the family, farmers' markets frequently offer musical entertainment, educational programming, samples of food, and special events. Here are some more compelling reasons to shop at farmers' markets:

· Food plucked fresh from the earth at peak ripeness and nutrition just plain tastes better—and is better for you and the environment.

· At farmers' markets, you can meet and speak directly to the people who grow, raise, bake, preserve, prepare, and forage for your food.

· Purchasing directly from local farmers and food producers boosts the local economy and creates jobs.

· Unusual and heirloom varieties not available at supermarkets are often available at farmers' markets.

· Studies show that you're ten times more likely to have a meaningful conversation at a farmers' market than a grocery store!

BE A SAVVY FARMERS' MARKET SHOPPER

· Eat seasonally and buy produce at the peak of the season when supply is plentiful.

· For the best prices, be flexible with your shopping list and consider buying "seconds" or in bulk.

· Bring cash—more and more vendors accept credit cards, but everyone takes cash.

· Come early for the best selection or later in the day when vendors may offer discounts rather than taking unsold produce home.

· Talk to your farmers if you have questions about their growing practices or how to cook a new or unfamiliar ingredient.

· Reduce plastic consumption by bringing reusable bags.

THEN

WHEN I RETURNED TO PORTLAND in 1994 to open Wildwood Restaurant & Bar, the Portland Farmers Market was two years old. In an empty parking lot on the banks of the Willamette River in the shadow of the Broadway Bridge, farmers were selling some of the most incredible tasting fruits and vegetables I had ever tried, right underneath a large faded sign for the historic Albers Mill. I was home.

I was drawn back to Portland, in large part, by the quality of local products that would become the mainstay of Wildwood's menu. At that time, it was not common for a Portland chef to procure ingredients directly from farmers, ranchers, fishers, and cheese makers, let alone mention a food source or producer by name on a menu. What a difference twenty-five years can make!

Wildwood, and my vision for it, was dependent on the direct purchase of the local products that inspired its menus. Even the restaurant's tag line, "cook from the source," was a nod to the region's bounty. Along with other Portland chefs in the 1990s—Cathy Whims, Vitaly Paley, and Greg Higgins, to name a few—I forged close relationships with the region's food producers, and together we began to define the cuisine of the Pacific Northwest.

Since that time, Portland has matured into one of America's great food cities. The direct distribution of local food products to the public is something we take for granted now, but it was absolutely critical to our food culture's evolution. Portland Farmers Market has also played a critical role, by drawing thousands of shoppers to its bustling markets, and creating opportunities for residents and tourists alike to experience Oregon's bountiful agriculture firsthand on almost any day of the week, throughout the calendar year.

I am thrilled that the market has chosen to celebrate twenty-five years of hard work with a cookbook. From the thirteen original vendors to the two hundred–plus who currently sell at the markets, it is clear that Portland Farmers Market is thriving. And without the individuals who have contributed countless hours of their time and energy on the farms, at the booths, and behind the scenes, this success would not be possible. This cookbook is a testament to their work. Now get started! Go cook from the source; you'll eat well.

—CORY SCHREIBER, chef and former chef/owner, Wildwood Restaurant

NOW

I LOVE TO EAT. I love the community that gathering around the table to share food, drink, and stories creates. I love the satisfaction that comes from selecting the sweetest bundle of peas, the juiciest tomato, and the most fragrant melon. Such discoveries demand nothing more than the simplest of preparations—those that allow the produce to be the star of the show. That's what cooking in Oregon has taught me.

When I moved to Portland from landlocked Missouri, Portland Farmers Market was one of my first stops. I'll never forget seeing that first Oregon-grown strawberry. I'd never had anything like it and couldn't wait to eat it! I believe this book encapsulates the magic—the same sense of wonder that I met with when I arrived—that chefs and shoppers alike experience every Saturday when they visit the tree-covered South Park Blocks to shop at the Portland Farmers Market.

The recipes in this book tell a story, and not just Portland's story. This is a book about Oregon and how Portland, now recognized nationally as a food city, was built on the independent spirit for which the state is known. Our farmers, fishers, and foragers play a pivotal role in that story, the story of why we cook. From gathering heirloom seeds to reconditioning the land for sustainable planting and ranching, these folks are the embodiment of independence and self-reliance. They are the very definition of our state motto: "She flies with her own wings." And for me, that's what it means to be a cook in Portland. That independent spirit is what they—and we—stand for, and it's the reason the community here and beyond has taken notice of what's happening in Portland.

Wherever you live, from the smallest of towns to the biggest of cities, I'm fairly certain there's a farmers' market or fresh produce stand close by. Seek it out. Let the farmers tell you their stories. Sample the freshly picked fruit or vegetables, still warm from the sun. Then use this book. Get it dirty, take notes in its margins, make the recipes your own. That's why it was written.

—**ADAM SAPPINGTON**, chef/owner, Country Cat Restaurant;
former chef de cuisine, Wildwood Restaurant

SPRING

EAGERLY ANTICIPATED SIGNS OF SPRING weather can be slow to arrive in the Pacific Northwest, but the season's edible harbingers are everywhere: green garlic, chervil, slender leeks, asparagus, tiny green peas. Foragers comb forest and field, and search along riverbanks for morels, fir tips, and nettles. Farmers look ahead and ready their beds for summer crops. Backyard gardeners plant radishes, an impatient grower's secret weapon for jump-starting spring. We're all waiting for tender green shoots to push up through the earth, uncoil, and reach for the light.

There is a perceptible shift at Portland's flagship farmers' market too. Beneath blossoming cherry trees, the market fills its expansive South Park Blocks footprint on the campus of Portland State University, two hundred vendors strong. Customers fondly greet favorite growers, inquire after their families, and exchange stories about the season that's passed.

Following a winter filled with long-simmered stews, rich braises, and savory roasts, spring invites us to lighten up with delicate cooking methods: salads and unfussy sautés, blanching, steaming, and cooking as simply as possible to let the natural flavors shine through. We yearn for foods that are fresh and uncomplicated. Under the market's peaked canopies, farmers are happy to indulge us.

Brassicas and sturdy root vegetables are pushed to one side to make way for pale bulbs of fennel, chives with their blossoms, tart sorrel, and delicate pea tendrils. And as they wait for the agreeable excess of summer and fall, fruit fans satisfy their appetite for sweets with stalks of ruby-red rhubarb, luscious strawberries, and the first glossy cherries—not exactly a hardship. And so another market season begins.

DECK FAMILY FARM

JOHN AND CHRISTINE DECK AND their five children raise nearly every protein you can put on your table: beef, pork, lamb, and poultry, including ducks and turkeys. They also keep twenty dairy cows that supply a raw-milk co-op, and a collection of farm dogs, cats, and horses.

For nearly a decade they've pastured this mix of livestock in Junction City, Oregon, on a bucolic 320 acres of organic Willamette Valley farmland. The land supports 900 laying hens, 160 beef cows, and 300-plus hogs, but Christine likes to say that they're in the business of raising grass. Everything they do is about improving the management-intensive grazing systems used to control the spread of invasive plants: grazers are moved every two to three days to nibble on a plot until most of the vegetation is trimmed down. Then the plot is given time to replenish itself for the next grazing cycle.

John and Christine met at the University of California, Davis, and immediately bonded over a shared love of agriculture. Motivated by Christine's desire to return to her roots and help reestablish farming as a viable economic endeavor, they started to look for land. When they realized they couldn't afford to farm in California's Central Valley, the couple ventured north, where they purchased their current property from a family who raised cattle there for sixty years, using mostly conventional systems. John and Christine knew the road to returning the soil to health would be long: restoring its unique make-up of deep alluvial deposits, seabed sediment, and eroded basaltic lava.

After phasing out the use of chemicals and fencing off creeks contaminated by run-off from animals and synthetic fertilizers, the couple reseeded the soil with native grasses and planted more than forty thousand trees to prevent soil erosion and water pollution. They implemented new methods and healthy inputs to manage the restored land, and selected multiple animal species to graze it. Christine explained, "Not unlike planting a variety of crops, grazing multiple species interrupts the life cycles of parasites that build up with any monoculture, animal or plant."

They chose the mix of livestock with responsible management of their land in mind, but recognized that offering a good product mix was also crucial to meeting the demands of a diverse customer base. Once the first and only meat vendor at the market, Deck Family Farm now has more competition. But they have learned, as all farmers do, to be responsive to the economic intersection between sustainably-minded farmers and avid local shoppers. They're seeding arable land with grain crops, and planting fruit trees. Their long-term goal is to offer a whole diet of diverse organic foods for shoppers. Given their successes thus far, they're sure to achieve it.

SMALL PLATES

Tartine of Shaved Baby Artichokes with Goat Cheese 7

Chicken Liver Mousse with Rhubarb
Chutney and Watercress Salad 10

White Gazpacho with Razor Clams and Ramps 12

Nettle and Olive Oil Flan 14

Roasted Asparagus on Morel Toasts 16

Miso-Lemon Deviled Eggs 18

Radish, Mâche, and Arugula Salad with Nettle-Cashew Cream 21

Spinach and Strawberry Salad with Roasted Shallot Vinaigrette 23

English Pea and White Bean Salad
with Spring Herb Chimichurri 24

Fava Bean and Gem Lettuce Salad with
Arugula Pesto and Favanade 25

Roasted New Potatoes and Baby Carrots
with Lavender Cream Sauce 28

TARTINE OF SHAVED BABY ARTICHOKES
with Goat Cheese

CORY SCHREIBER, CULINARY ARTS INSTRUCTOR, ART INSTITUTE OF PORTLAND

Artichokes lend themselves to a surprising number of preparations. This rustic yet elegant open-faced sandwich—the French call it a *tartine*—takes a bit more time to prepare than simple steamed artichokes, but the result is a different flavor and texture than you're likely to have experienced in past encounters with the vegetable: tender, bright, and grassy, best paired with a soft, tangy goat cheese. Prep the rest of the ingredients before you start cleaning the artichokes, so they aren't sitting in water overly long.

Makes 4 to 6 servings

1. Slice the baguette diagonally into ½-inch-thick slices. In a shallow, wide pan with a heavy bottom over medium heat, warm ¼ cup of the oil. When the oil is hot, put as many slices of bread in the pan as you can without crowding. Brown the bread until it is golden and crispy on one side, 2 to 3 minutes. Remove the slices to a baking sheet and season the crispy side of each toast with salt. Set the baking sheet aside and keep it in a warm spot or a low-temperature oven while you toast the remaining bread.

2. Using a sharp knife and a cutting board, cut each artichoke in half and lay it cut-side down. Using a knife or mandoline, slice each half lengthwise as thinly as possible. Place the sliced artichokes in a bowl, squeeze some juice from one of the lemons over them to prevent discoloration, and repeat with the remaining artichokes. Drain the sliced artichokes and pat them dry. Zest and juice the remaining lemon. Finely chop the zest. Set the lemon juice and zest aside.

3. In a heavy, thick-bottomed pan large enough to hold the ingredients in a single layer without crowding over medium heat, warm 3 tablespoons of the oil. Add the artichokes and season them with salt. Sauté the artichokes until they begin to color lightly, about 2 minutes. Add the shallots and garlic, continue to sauté for 2 minutes, then add the spinach and another pinch of salt. When the spinach has collapsed, add the lemon zest and half of the juice, and season with salt and pepper. Remove the pan from the heat and allow the flavors to continue to commingle in the pan.

1 baguette, loaf of ciabatta, or country-style bread

½ cup extra-virgin olive oil, divided

Kosher salt and freshly ground black pepper

10 baby artichokes, cleaned and held in acidulated water (see Preparing Artichokes for Cooking on the following page)

2 lemons

2 large shallots, halved and thinly sliced

2 garlic cloves, finely minced

1 bunch spinach, roughly chopped

4 ounces fresh soft goat cheese or goat's milk feta

CONTINUED

4. Spoon some of the artichoke mixture onto each piece of toast, top with a dollop of the goat cheese, and, if desired, warm slightly to serve. Drizzle lightly with the remaining 1 tablespoon oil and lemon juice and serve immediately.

HOW TO CHOOSE AND STORE ARTICHOKES

Over the years artichokes have become plentiful at our farmers' markets. The cool marine air of Oregon's north coast is ideal for growing the thistles, but over time, artichokes have also adapted to thrive in spring and fall in Willamette Valley climes. Customers are now even accustomed to finding them in different varieties and sizes.

Whether large or small, purple or green, tulip- or globe-shaped, artichokes should be selected using the following criteria: they should be heavy and firm, with fat stalks (indicating a large heart) and closed petals that don't have any black spots. Though they'll keep for a few weeks, store artichokes in the refrigerator and use them within a few days for the best flavor and texture.

PREPARING ARTICHOKES FOR COOKING

· Cut 2 lemons in half and squeeze the juice from one into a large nonreactive bowl filled with cold water.

· Using a serrated knife, cut off and discard the pointy top third of the artichoke.

· Pull back the dark outer leaves and snap them off at the base until you get to the tender, pale-green inner leaves.

· Trim away the stem if it is dark or very small. Otherwise, use a vegetable peeler to remove the tough outer layers around the stem, stopping when you reach the pale layer underneath.

· Use a small paring knife to trim away any remaining tough or dark-green parts around the edge and underside of the artichoke.

· Rub the trimmed artichoke all over with one of the cut lemons and submerge it in the lemon water while you clean the rest.

CHICKEN LIVER MOUSSE
with Rhubarb Chutney and Watercress Salad

KAT LESUEUR, CHEF/OWNER, COCOTTE BISTRO & BAR

This recipe is a crowd-pleaser. Delicious and decadent, it's been known to convert even picky eaters who claim not to like liver. And it's easy to whip up in advance for entertaining the following day: make the mousse and chutney up to several days ahead and assemble the other components immediately before serving. In France, a small salad is usually served as an accompaniment to charcuterie or cheese, as a contrast to its richness. Here, spring's watercress, sugar snap peas, and radishes add brightness and crunch, while tart rhubarb chutney is a foil for the creamy mousse; both the salad and chutney ingredients can be adapted for the season. Slices of crusty baguette complete the plate.

The addition of heavy cream to the mousse, while optional, makes it soft and creamy for spreading, but slightly more challenging to unmold. If you use it, note that the cream should be added before the butter, to minimize the risk of breaking the emulsion.

Makes 6 to 8 servings

1 pound chicken livers, rinsed in milk and patted dry

Kosher salt and freshly ground black pepper

3 tablespoons canola or other neutral-flavored oil, plus more if needed

2 large shallots, thinly sliced

3 tablespoons cognac or fortified wine

¼ cup heavy cream (optional)

2 cups (4 sticks) unsalted butter, cubed, at room temperature

About 1 tablespoon sherry vinegar

1. If you are planning to unmold the mousse, prepare a terrine mold, loaf pan, or other container by spraying it with cooking spray. Line the inside with a piece of plastic wrap large enough to hang over the edges of the pan. Set aside.

2. To make the mousse, make sure the livers are very dry and season them liberally with salt and pepper. In a large sauté pan over medium heat, heat the oil (add another tablespoon if 3 isn't enough to coat the bottom) until it ripples but isn't smoking. Gently add the livers to the pan and reduce the heat slightly. Cook the livers until they are nicely caramelized on one side, 5 to 7 minutes, then turn them over and add the shallots to the pan. Cook the two together for about 3 minutes before carefully adding the cognac—stand back from the pan as you pour, as it will flame. After the alcohol burns off, reduce the liquid in the pan until it is thick enough to coat the back of a spoon.

3. Immediately transfer the contents of the pan to a blender or the bowl of a food processor. Add the cream, and pulse a few times to incorporate. With the machine running, add the butter cubes one at a time, completely incorporating each one before adding the next. When all the butter has been incorporated, add the vinegar. Taste and check the seasoning, adding another tablespoon of vinegar if necessary; it should offset any metallic flavor from the liver and add brightness. Pass the mousse through a fine-mesh sieve into the prepared terrine mold or a serving dish. Cover the dish with plastic wrap and refrigerate the mousse for at least 6 hours.

4. Meanwhile, make the chutney. In a large nonreactive saucepan, combine the rhubarb, orange juice, brown sugar, vinegar, honey, cinnamon, and cloves. Bring the mixture to a simmer over medium-high heat, then reduce the heat to medium-low and cook until the rhubarb is mushy and the liquid is syrupy and caramelized, 50 to 60 minutes. The volume will reduce by about 75 percent, leaving you with about 1¼ cups of chutney with a jam-like consistency. Season to taste with salt and pepper and refrigerate the chutney until you are ready to serve the mousse.

5. About 30 minutes before serving, make the salad. In a large bowl, toss together the watercress, radishes, and snap peas, and set them aside while you make the vinaigrette. In a small bowl, whisk together the vinegar, shallot, and salt. Let the mixture sit for 5 minutes to soften the flavor of the shallot, then add the mustard and, while whisking, drizzle in the oil in a slow stream until it is emulsified. Stir in the tarragon.

6. Unmold the terrine or remove the serving dish from the refrigerator. Toss the salad lightly with the dressing. Slice the mousse and serve it with a spoonful of the chutney and a handful of the salad. A generous smear of spicy Dijon mustard on the side sets off the dish.

FOR THE CHUTNEY:

2 cups rhubarb (from about ¾ pound), cut in ½-inch dice

2 cups freshly squeezed orange juice

1 cup lightly packed light brown sugar

½ cup apple cider vinegar

1 tablespoon honey

½ teaspoon ground cinnamon

⅛ teaspoon ground cloves

Kosher salt and freshly ground black pepper

FOR THE SALAD:

1 large or 2 small bunches watercress

1 bunch French Breakfast radishes, trimmed and thinly sliced

¼ pound sugar snap peas, shucked (keep a few whole and split one side open to reveal the peas, for garnish)

2 tablespoons champagne vinegar

1 tablespoon minced shallot

½ teaspoon salt

½ teaspoon Dijon mustard, plus more for serving

6 tablespoons extra-virgin olive oil

2 teaspoons finely chopped fresh tarragon

WHITE GAZPACHO
with Razor Clams and Ramps

WILL PREISCH AND JOEL STOCKS, CHEFS/CO-OWNERS, HOLDFAST

This take on a classic gazpacho that reflects Spain's Arabic past has a delightful, unexpected Northwest twist: the silky-smooth soup is finished with a salad of razor clams, ramp greens, and pickled ramps. In the words of chef Will Preisch, "Pretty dang Holdfast-y." We agree.

Pickled ramps are addictive—you'll find yourself putting them in and on everything—and a good way to keep them around after they disappear from the market. Make a big batch and save the leftover greens for pesto; follow the Sorrel Pesto recipe (page 39), substituting ramp greens for the sorrel leaves.

Makes 4 to 6 servings

2 cups blanched sliced almonds, divided

1 head garlic

½ cup plus 2 tablespoons extra-virgin olive oil, divided, plus more for drizzling

Kosher salt

¼ baguette, crust removed

2 tablespoons sherry vinegar

Reserved greens from the Ramp Pickles

½ to ¾ pound razor clams, cleaned

1 recipe Ramp Pickles (recipe follows)

1 lemon

1. Preheat the oven to 300 degrees F.

2. Spread the almonds in a single layer on a baking sheet with sides. Cut the head of garlic in half around the equator, and lay the halves in a small baking dish cut-side up. Drizzle each side with 1 tablespoon of the oil and sprinkle with salt, then cover the dish tightly with aluminum foil. Toast the nuts until they are aromatic, 10 to 15 minutes. Roast the garlic at the same time, until the cloves are golden brown and tender, about 50 minutes.

3. While the garlic is roasting, cut the bread into ½-inch cubes and spread them in a single layer on a baking sheet. After removing the almonds and while the garlic is in the oven, toast the bread cubes until the bread is dry and lightly golden, about 15 minutes.

4. Allow the ingredients from the oven to cool completely. In a large bowl, combine 1¾ cups of the almonds and the bread with half of the roasted garlic, reserving the remaining garlic for another use (such as adding to vinaigrettes, sauces, or salsas). Add the bread mixture, in batches, to a blender with a total of 4 cups of water, adding a portion of the ½ cup of oil to each batch last. Blend until very smooth and strain through a fine-mesh sieve. Stir in the vinegar, season to taste with salt, and set the gazpacho aside.

5. Slice the reserved greens from the ramps into 1-inch pieces. In a medium sauté pan over medium-high heat, warm the remaining 1 tablespoon oil. Add the greens and cook briefly, no more than 1 minute. Set the pan aside and heat a large cast-iron pan over high heat. Season the clams with salt and, when the pan is smoking, add them to the pan. Cook the clams for 10 seconds on one side only. Slice the charred clams into bite-size pieces and put them in a large bowl, along with the ramp pickles and greens. Season the salad to taste with salt and freshly squeezed lemon juice and toss to combine.

6. To serve, place a small mound of the clam mixture in each bowl and pour the gazpacho around it. Garnish with the remaining toasted almonds and a drizzle of olive oil.

RAMP PICKLES

Makes ½ pint

1. In a large bowl, place the ramp bulbs. In a small nonreactive saucepan over medium-high heat, combine the sugar, vinegar, fennel seeds, coriander seeds, mustard seeds, bay leaf, and salt. Bring the mixture to a boil, then remove the pan from the heat and pour the pickling liquid over the ramp bulbs. Let the liquid cool at room temperature, then refrigerate the pickled ramps. Once cool, slice the bulbs into coins.

8 ounces ramp bulbs (reserve the greens for the salad)

1 cup sugar

1 cup white wine vinegar

1 teaspoon fennel seeds

1 teaspoon coriander seeds

1 teaspoon mustard seeds

1 bay leaf

1 tablespoon kosher salt

RAMPS

Ramps (also known as wild leeks) are a fleeting seasonal treat. One of only a few plants that are truly wild-harvested, they're found at higher elevations in heavily wooded deciduous forests east of the Great Plains. They can be propagated, as they are by Portland Farmers Market vendor Temptress Truffles, but must be sown from seed. They are heavily dependent on weather patterns during their six- to eighteen-month germination window, and can take up to seven years to mature.

NETTLE AND OLIVE OIL FLAN

CATHY WHIMS, CHEF/OWNER, NOSTRANA, OVEN AND SHAKER, AND HAMLET

Each December, six-time James Beard Award–finalist chef Cathy Whims celebrates Italy's harvest of newly pressed olive oil by bringing the *olio nuovo* into Nostrano just one week after the first pressing. This nettle flan was created to celebrate its arrival. It can be made throughout the year using different greens from the market—fava and pea tips, sorrel, spinach, Tuscan kale—but the delicate flavor and gorgeous color when it's made with the young, tender tops of nettles are the kitchen's favorite. This deserves the best olive oil you've got. Herb blossoms are available when nettles, fava and pea tips, and sorrel are in season; substitute the delicate leaves during the rest of the year.

Makes 8 six-ounce flans

8 ounces nettle tops
(about 8 cups packed)

2 cups heavy cream

4 eggs

1 teaspoon fine sea salt

¼ cup extra-virgin olive oil,
plus more for serving

Fleur de sel, for garnish

Chervil, sage, or chive
blossoms, for garnish

1. Preheat the oven to 275 degrees F.

2. Cook the nettles according to the instructions on the opposite page, then coarsely chop them; you should have about ⅔ cup. Set them aside. Butter 8 small (6-ounce) ramekins, place them in a roasting pan or deep baking dish, and set them aside.

3. In a blender or the bowl of a food processor, add the nettles, along with the cream, eggs, and salt. Blend until the mixture is smooth, then add the oil in a thin, steady stream with the blender running. Taste for seasoning, adding more salt if necessary. Divide the mixture among the prepared ramekins, add warm water to the pan to reach halfway up the ramekins' sides, and bake until just set, about 1 hour.

4. Remove the pan from the oven and let the dishes sit in the water bath for about 10 minutes. When they are cool enough to handle, run a small, thin-bladed paring knife around the insides of the ramekins and invert each onto its own plate. To serve, drizzle olive oil around each flan, sprinkle it with *fleur de sel*, and garnish with herb blossoms.

HOW TO BLANCH NETTLES

Fresh nettles, aka stinging nettles, are covered in tiny needles. If you accidentally brush against the plant's pale-green stem or saw-toothed leaves, you won't soon forget the sensation! Use care—and wear gloves—to avoid touching them with your bare skin.

To eat them, nettles must be cooked so they lose their sting; blanching—immersing vegetables briefly in boiling water and then plunging them in ice water to stop the cooking process—is the easiest way to do that.

Prepare an ice bath by filling a large bowl with cold water and several handfuls of ice. Bring a large pot of generously salted water to a boil over high heat. Using tongs or gloves, add the nettles to the water for 2 minutes for delicate tops and leaves, or up to 3 minutes for larger, more mature leaves. Drain immediately and plunge them into the ice bath. When the nettles are cool, squeeze them dry using a tea towel to remove as much moisture as possible. Now they're ready to use in your recipe.

ROASTED ASPARAGUS
on Morel Toasts

CANDACE SMITH, OWNER, OUTBACK FARMS

Of the long list of perfect unions born of spring, few are more beloved than earthy morels in the company of grassy asparagus. Here, sautéed morels finished with cream are spread on crusty bread and topped with crisp-tender roasted asparagus. Roasting the asparagus at high heat coaxes deep flavor and a complexity that is sacrificed when it is grilled.

Makes 6 servings

1 loaf ciabatta or baguette

¼ cup extra-virgin olive oil, divided, plus more for brushing the bread

1 large shallot, finely minced (about 2 tablespoons)

1 tablespoon unsalted butter

½ pound fresh morel mushrooms, wiped clean and cut in ¼-inch dice

1 cup heavy cream

2 gratings whole nutmeg

Kosher salt and freshly ground black pepper

2 bunches asparagus

Fleur de sel or flaky finishing salt, for seasoning the asparagus

Finely chopped zest of 1 lemon

Finely chopped fresh chives and chive blossoms, for garnish

1. Preheat the oven to 300 degrees F.

2. Cut the bread into ¼-inch-thick slices; depending on the size of your loaf, you should get about 18. Lightly brush the slices with oil, put them on a baking sheet, and bake until they are lightly browned and slightly crisp, 10 to 15 minutes. Remove the bread from the oven and increase the temperature to 500 degrees F.

3. In a medium sauté pan over medium-high heat, warm 1 tablespoon of the oil. Add the shallot and cook, stirring occasionally, until softened and translucent, about 3 minutes. Add the butter to the pan. When it is foamy, add the morels and sauté until they are lightly browned and fragrant, about 5 minutes. Add the cream, reduce the heat to medium-low, and simmer the mixture until the cream thickens, about 10 minutes. Add the nutmeg and season to taste with salt and pepper. Set the pan aside, keeping the contents warm.

4. Snap the tough ends off the asparagus, leaving 8 to 10 inches of tender stalk. Spread the stalks on rimmed baking sheets in a single layer and lightly drizzle them with 2 tablespoons of the oil. Roast the asparagus until it is bright green and crisp-tender, 5 to 8 minutes, depending on the thickness of the stalks. Remove the baking sheets from the oven, cut the asparagus stalks in half, and generously sprinkle with the remaining 1 tablespoon oil, *fleur de sel*, lemon zest, and more pepper.

5. To serve, spread each toast with a tablespoon of the morel mixture. Top with several asparagus pieces and garnish with the chives and chive blossoms.

HOW TO CHOOSE AND STORE ASPARAGUS

Grassy and herbaceous, asparagus should have firm stalks and tight tips. Fat stalks tend to be sweeter and more flavorful, good for roasting, grilling, and shaving raw for salads. Skinny, pencil-thin spears have a delicate flavor that is best preserved by quickly steaming or broiling.

Purple asparagus is said to be exceptionally sweet. You're unlikely to taste the difference if you close your eyes, but then you'd miss the exceptionally beautiful deep-green color the spears take on when they're cooked.

Buy as much asparagus as you will use over 3 to 4 days, and store it in the crisper drawer, loosely wrapped.

MISO-LEMON DEVILED EGGS

LIZ CRAIN, FOOD WRITER AND COOKBOOK AUTHOR

Everyone loves deviled eggs, and when they're made with bright-orange yolks from fresh pastured eggs, they're as beautiful as they are delicious. In this twist on the picnic staple, the flavors are accented with *shichimi togarashi* ("seven-flavor chili pepper"), a Japanese condiment found online or at Japanese groceries. If you can't find it, garnish your eggs with *gomasio* (sesame salt, another Japanese condiment) or a red, black, or smoked finishing salt. Pickled beets, spicy pickled peppers such as Mama Lil's, or a julienne of radish will also do the trick.

Red miso is typically made from soybeans fermented with barley and can be found in well-stocked groceries and natural foods stores. Its deep umami flavor stands up to the fish and chili sauces, which would overwhelm the milder yellow miso.

Note: Fresh eggs are more difficult to peel, so refrigerate them for several days before boiling.

Makes 1 dozen deviled eggs

6 large pastured eggs

¼ cup mayonnaise

1 tablespoon red miso

1 teaspoon freshly squeezed lemon juice

½ teaspoon fish sauce (aka *nuoc mam*)

½ teaspoon chili sauce, such as Sriracha

Fine sea salt and freshly ground pepper

Shichimi togarashi (optional), for garnish

1. Put the eggs in a single layer in a medium saucepan with a tight-fitting lid. Add cold water to cover the eggs by 1½ inches and bring it to a rolling boil over high heat. Remove the pan from the heat, cover it, and let the eggs stand for 14 minutes.

2. After 14 minutes, pour off the hot water and run the eggs under cold water until they are cool to the touch. Peel the eggs, halve them lengthwise, and carefully transfer the egg yolks into a bowl by pushing and lightly twisting the whites. Mash the egg yolks with a fork until they are finely crumbled and no large lumps remain. Place the whites on a plate.

3. In a small bowl, whisk together the mayonnaise, miso, lemon juice, and fish and chili sauces. Add the mixture to the egg yolks, using a fork to combine the two until you have a smooth, creamy consistency. Season to taste with salt and pepper. (Note: The saltiness of both store-bought miso and fish sauce varies greatly; be sure to taste the filling before adding additional seasoning.) Spoon or pipe the yolk mixture into the whites and sprinkle with *shichimi togarashi* before serving.

FARMERS' MARKET EGGS

Fresh eggs from free-roaming hens who feast on bugs and grubs, and peck at dirt and field grains, are among the best and most popular items at the market. It's difficult to imagine a less expensive, tastier way to add protein to your diet.

Eggs are somewhat seasonal, and spring is when they are most plentiful. Hens don't lay as much in hot weather or when temperatures drop and the days (and amount of daylight) shorten. Though you'll find them at all of our markets throughout the year, you might want to arrive at the market a bit earlier for eggs in the winter!

Bonus: Eggs purchased at the farmers' market are super fresh and will keep for at least six weeks refrigerated; most grocery store eggs are at least that old by the time they get to the market (60 days is the average). Stock up when you see them.

RADISH, MÂCHE, AND ARUGULA SALAD
with Nettle-Cashew Cream

SASHA DAVIES, CHEF/CO-OWNER, CYRIL'S AT CLAY PIGEON WINERY

This salad pairs sweet mâche with peppery arugula and radishes in three hues for a vibrant taste of spring. Chinese green radishes are shaped like a daikon, but with bright-green flesh. Watermelon radishes are green on the outside, with striking magenta flesh, and are also related to daikon. The idea here is to make your salad colorful, so Easter Egg and French Breakfast varieties are options too if green or watermelon radishes aren't available.

The nettle-cashew cream is a rich and tasty dairy-free alternative to cream cheese or sour cream. You'll definitely have some left over: it's delicious served over pasta, as a dip or spread, or thinned slightly to make a sauce.

Makes 4 to 6 servings

1. Preheat the oven to 400 degrees F.

2. In a small bowl, toss the green and globe radishes with 2 tablespoons of the oil and a pinch of salt. Spread the radishes in a single layer on a baking sheet and roast until just tender, 10 to 15 minutes.

3. Meanwhile, in a small nonreactive bowl, whisk the yuzu juice with the remaining ¾ cup oil until combined. Season to taste with salt and set aside. In a large bowl, toss the watermelon radishes, mâche, and arugula with a pinch of salt. Add the warm green and globe radishes to the bowl with the salad greens, pour on the yuzu dressing, and toss to combine. Season to taste with additional salt.

4. To serve, smear a generous tablespoon of cashew cream on each plate, or the entire amount on a large platter. Divide the salad among the plates or arrange it on the platter, on top of the cream, and serve immediately.

CONTINUED

1 to 2 green radishes, trimmed, peeled, and cut into ¼-inch cubes (about 1 cup)

1 bunch red globe radishes, trimmed and quartered (small ones left whole)

¾ cup plus 2 tablespoons extra-virgin olive oil, divided

Kosher salt (Davies likes the pure kosher sea salt from Portland's Jacobsen Salt Company)

¼ cup yuzu juice or freshly squeezed lemon juice (from 2 medium lemons)

1 to 2 watermelon radishes, trimmed, halved, and cut into ½-inch thick wedges

1 bunch mâche

½ bunch arugula

½ cup Nettle-Cashew Cream (recipe follows)

NETTLE-CASHEW CREAM

Makes 1¾ cups

½ cup raw cashews

8 ounces nettle leaves
(about 8 cups, packed)

2 to 3 tablespoons freshly
squeezed lemon juice

2½ teaspoons kosher salt

1. In a small bowl, add the cashews and cover them with plenty of water. Let them sit overnight at room temperature, covered with a kitchen towel.

2. The next day, cook the nettles according to the instructions in How to Blanch Nettles (page 15); you should have about ⅔ cup, tightly packed.

3. Drain the cashews and place them, along with ¼ cup water, in the bowl of a food processor. Process until the cashews are very smooth and creamy; this may take a few minutes. Add the nettles, lemon juice, and salt, and continue to blend until the cream has the consistency of a spreadable paste. Taste and check the seasonings, adding more salt and lemon juice if needed.

SPINACH AND STRAWBERRY SALAD
with Roasted Shallot Vinaigrette

KATHY UNGER, CO-OWNER, UNGER FARMS

A version of this salad had its moment in the 1980s. Now it's back, with a new dressing (no more poppy seeds!) and more refined than ever. The combination of ingredients creates a pleasing variety of flavors and textures: crisp, fresh spinach; the subtle sweetness of strawberries and slowly cooked shallots; the nuttiness of walnuts and Parmesan. There's a reason this classic salad is still around.

Makes 6 servings

1. In a small saucepan over medium heat, warm the oil with the shallots. Reduce the heat to low and cook the shallots until they have softened but not browned, 5 to 8 minutes. Add the vinegar and mustard, whisking to emulsify. Season to taste with salt and pepper and keep the dressing warm.

2. In a large serving bowl, place the spinach and season it with salt and pepper before adding 1½ cups of the strawberries and the walnuts. Add half of the vinaigrette, toss well to coat the spinach leaves, then add more, 1 tablespoon at a time, until the ingredients are dressed to your liking. You'll probably have some vinaigrette left over.

3. Use a vegetable peeler to shave the Parmesan over the top of the salad and garnish with the remaining strawberries. Serve immediately.

½ cup walnut oil

½ cup thinly sliced shallots (2 to 3 small shallots)

3 tablespoons red wine vinegar

2 teaspoons Dijon mustard

Kosher salt and freshly ground black pepper

2 bunches spinach (about 8 cups, loosely packed)

1 pint strawberries, hulled and thinly sliced, divided

½ cup coarsely chopped toasted walnuts

2 ounces Parmesan or other hard grating cheese

ENGLISH PEA AND WHITE BEAN SALAD

with Spring Herb Chimichurri

KATHERINE DEUMLING, OWNER, COOK WITH WHAT YOU HAVE

More and more regional farmers are growing dry beans. When combined with shelling peas, whose season is somewhat fleeting, they make a robust salad. Mortgage Runner is a variety of white bean that is particularly good for this salad, although it isn't widely available. Cannellini, navy, Tarbais (aka Tarbesque), Zolfino, and Purgatorio beans are good choices too.

The beans and peas' sweet, creamy starchiness is a lovely foil for a bright, herb-based *chimichurri* dressing, modeled on the Argentinian sauce of the same name. Feel free to experiment with the ratio of herbs according to what's in season, your preferences, and what you have on hand. This salad holds up well and is a good choice for potlucks, picnics, and lunch the next day.

Makes 4 to 6 servings

½ cup extra-virgin olive oil

⅓ cup red wine vinegar

1 cup finely chopped fresh flat leaf parsley leaves

½ cup finely chopped fresh cilantro leaves

2 to 3 tablespoons finely chopped fresh oregano

½ teaspoon ground cumin

¼ teaspoon red pepper flakes

Kosher salt and freshly ground black pepper

2 pounds English peas (about 1½ cups shelled)

3 cups cooked and drained white beans

4 green onions, (white and green parts) trimmed and thinly sliced

1. In a small bowl, whisk together the oil, vinegar, parsley, cilantro, oregano, cumin, and pepper flakes. Add a big pinch of salt and whisk to thoroughly combine it. Season to taste with pepper and more salt—the dressing should have a good vinegary kick and plenty of salt. Set it aside.

2. Bring a small pot of lightly salted water to a boil over medium-high heat. Add the peas and simmer just until they are tender and bright green, about 5 minutes. Drain, rinse the peas thoroughly with cold water, and drain again.

3. In a large bowl, toss the peas, beans, and green onions with about three-quarters of the dressing, then taste it and adjust the seasonings, adding more dressing if needed. Serve the salad at room temperature.

FAVA BEAN AND GEM LETTUCE SALAD
with Arugula Pesto and Favanade

SCOTT DOLICH, CHEF/OWNER, PARK KITCHEN AND THE BENT BRICK

In this salad, fresh fava beans are the perfect expression of late spring/early summer, when the weather is still cool enough for arugula and lettuces to thrive. Look for Little Gem lettuce, a smaller, sweeter version of romaine. Drag a forkful of salad through the thick smear of favanade, a creamy hummus-like puree made from fresh fava beans, on the bottom of the plate for the full experience: creamy, bitter, crunchy, tart. This salad's got it all.

Slather leftover favanade on toast, stir it into pasta or rice, or put a spoonful in a bowl with warm new potatoes.

Makes 4 servings

1. Slice the lettuce crosswise into thick ribbons and put them in a large bowl; you should have about 6 cups. Crumble the toasted bread over the lettuce into pea-size croutons. Add the fava beans and 2 to 3 spoonfuls of the pesto, the lemon juice, and a pinch of salt.

2. To serve, thickly spread 2 tablespoons of favanade on each plate, or the entire amount on a large platter. Divide the salad among the plates or arrange it on the platter, allowing a little of the favanade to show from underneath. Shave some cheese over the top using a vegetable peeler.

CONTINUED

4 to 6 heads gem lettuce or lettuce hearts, depending on size

2 (½-inch-thick) slices open-crumb bread, such as ciabatta, toasted

1 cup blanched, peeled fava beans (from about 1 pound)

¼ cup Arugula Pesto (recipe follows)

2 tablespoons freshly squeezed lemon juice

Flaky sea salt

½ cup Favanade (recipe follows)

Pecorino Romano or other favorite hard grating cheese

CHOOSING AND PREPARING FAVA BEANS

Fresh fava beans are easily identified by their slightly bulbous, downy pods. The 7- to 9-inch pods are a medium shade of grassy green and separate easily. Overly thick or yellowing beans are past their peak. Inside, a cottony white lining cradles large seeds resembling lima or butter beans encased in husks.

Shell fava beans as you would pea pods: pierce the skin with your thumbnail and squeeze the beans out. You can eat the thin, opaque skin or plunge the beans in boiling salted water for 2 minutes, rinse them under cold water, and slip them out.

FAVANADE

Makes about 1⅓ cups

1. Bring a large saucepan of generously salted water to a boil over medium-high heat. While the water comes to a boil, prepare an ice bath by filling a large bowl with cold water and several handfuls of ice. When the water is boiling, add the fava beans and cook for 2 minutes. Drain and transfer them immediately to the ice bath. When they are cool enough to handle, break open the outer membrane and squeeze the bean out. You should have about 1 cup of shelled beans.

2. In a small sauté pan over medium-low heat, warm the oil. Add the shallot and garlic and cook, stirring often, until the shallot is soft and translucent, about 3 minutes. Remove the pan from the heat and set it aside to cool.

3. In the bowl of a food processor, combine the fava beans, cooled shallot and garlic, ricotta and Pecorino cheeses, salt, pepper, and pepper flakes. Puree until smooth, scraping down the side of the bowl as needed; the texture should resemble that of tapenade. Taste for additional seasoning, then cover and refrigerate until ready to serve. This puree tastes best the day it is made.

1 pound fava beans, peeled (for peeling instructions, see Choosing and Preparing Fava Beans on page 25)

2 tablespoons extra-virgin olive oil

4 teaspoons finely chopped shallot

1 teaspoon finely minced garlic

1 cup Homemade Ricotta Cheese (page 174) or store-bought

2 tablespoons grated Pecorino Romano, Grana Padano, or similar hard grating cheese

1½ teaspoons fine sea salt

½ teaspoon freshly ground black pepper

⅛ teaspoon red pepper flakes

ARUGULA PESTO

Makes about 1½ cups

1. In the bowl of a food processor, pulse the arugula leaves with the hazelnuts, cheese, garlic, and lemon zest until combined. With the machine running, add the oil in a steady stream and process to a smooth paste. Season to taste with salt and pepper.

2¾ cups loosely packed arugula

3 tablespoons coarsely chopped toasted hazelnuts

2 tablespoons grated Pecorino Romano, Grana Padano, or similar hard grating cheese

1 small garlic clove, smashed

2 teaspoons finely chopped lemon zest

¾ cup canola oil

Kosher salt and freshly ground black pepper

ROASTED NEW POTATOES AND BABY CARROTS
with Lavender Cream Sauce

LUCIE GOUIN & ARTHUR POULOS, OWNERS, LA TERRA VITA

Lucie and Art blended their backgrounds (French and Greek, respectively) with a shared love of farming and settled in Oregon in 2004. They chose Scio for their integrated family farm, which uses biodynamic methods to raise organic heirloom vegetables for farmers' markets and their CSA.

Late spring is the only time of year when both new potatoes and baby heirloom carrots are in season. Use organic new potatoes and carrots if you can find them, and leave their delicate skins on, as they are full of nutrients. Consider serving this alongside white fish, which pairs beautifully with the lavender cream sauce—you'll want to make extra sauce if you do.

Makes 4 to 6 servings

¼ cup (½ stick) unsalted butter

3 tablespoons extra-virgin olive oil, divided, plus extra for finishing

1½ teaspoons coarse sea salt, such as Maldon

2 pounds new potatoes, preferably organic

1 pound heirloom baby carrots, preferably organic, tops and tips trimmed

12 garlic cloves, peeled

5 sprigs fresh organic lavender, with or without flowers, leaves stripped from the stems

1. Preheat the oven to 450 degrees F.

2. Thinly slice the butter into 8 to 10 pats and distribute them in the bottom of a 13-by-9-inch roasting tray or baking dish. Rub one of the pats across the bottom of the pan to prevent the vegetables from sticking. Drizzle the pan with 1 tablespoon of the oil and sprinkle with the salt.

3. Cut the potatoes in half (or quarters if they are large) and arrange them cut-side down in the pan. Evenly distribute the whole carrots among the potato halves, along with the garlic cloves and lavender buds. Drizzle the remaining 2 tablespoons oil over the vegetables and place the pan on the middle rack in the oven. Roast the vegetables for 50 minutes or until caramelized and tender, stirring after 15 minutes and again after another 20 minutes, to coat them with the melted butter and oil and prevent the potatoes from sticking to the bottom. (Rearrange the potatoes so that they remain cut-side down after you stir them.)

4. Meanwhile, make the cream sauce. In a small saucepan over medium heat, bring the half-and-half to a simmer. Remove the pan from the heat, add a pinch of salt, and set it aside, keeping it warm.

5. In a small saucepan over low heat, melt the butter. Stir in the flour, increase the heat to medium, and cook, stirring constantly, until the mixture begins to foam, about 5 minutes. When the froth begins to subside, and what's underneath resembles dark melted butter, stir the roux together and scrape it into the pan of warm milk.

6. Return the pan with the milk to a simmer over medium heat and vigorously whisk the roux into the milk until smooth. Continue to simmer, stirring frequently, until the sauce thickens, about 8 minutes. Remove the pan from the heat and season the sauce to taste with salt and pepper. Add the wine, 1 tablespoon at a time, to give the sauce an additional floral note and some brightness.

7. To serve, stir the lavender into the cream sauce. Arrange the roasted vegetables, including the garlic cloves, on a platter and pass the lavender cream sauce so guests can serve themselves.

FOR THE CREAM SAUCE:

1½ cups half-and-half

Sea salt

2 tablespoons unsalted butter

1 tablespoon unbleached pastry flour

Freshly ground black pepper

3 tablespoons pinot gris or lightly fruity white wine (optional)

Buds from 3 sprigs fresh organic lavender, finely chopped (about 1 tablespoon total)

LARGE PLATES

French-Style Scrambled Eggs with Morel-Chive Cream Sauce 31

Dandelion-Ricotta Gnocchi with Spicy Orange Brown Butter 32

Pan-Roasted Chinook Salmon with Polenta and Raab 34

Grass-Fed Strip Loin with Porcini Bread
Salad and Pickled Rhubarb 37

Grilled Chicken with Sorrel Pesto 39

Swiss Chard–Spinach Pies with Fennel and Sumac 40

Grilled Halibut with Fiddleheads, Pea Tendrils,
and Green Garlic Vinaigrette 41

Keema Matar (Ground Lamb with Fresh Peas) 44

Fried Cauliflower "Rice" with Farm Eggs and Bacon 45

FRENCH-STYLE SCRAMBLED EGGS
with Morel-Chive Cream Sauce

TODD KOEBKE, CULINARY ARTS INSTRUCTOR, SABIN-SCHELLENBERG CENTER

After the cold and rainy winter, Portlanders flock to the market in great numbers on sunny spring Saturday mornings. If they don't find breakfast from one of the many vendors, they might, like Todd Koebke, find inspiration for a late breakfast when they arrive home.

This recipe is full of springtime favorites: meaty morel mushrooms, pastured farm eggs, fresh chives, and warm brioche. Add your own inspirations to your market-basket breakfast: roasted asparagus, sautéed spinach, or fiddlehead ferns would all be at home on this plate.

Makes 4 servings

1. In a medium bowl, lightly beat the eggs. Add the milk, whisking gently to combine. In a medium sauté pan or cast-iron skillet, warm the butter over medium heat until foamy. Add the eggs, stirring gently with a heatproof spatula until they are lightly set. If they are cooking too quickly or begin to get any color, move the pan back and forth, off the heat. They should be very soft and creamy. Season to taste with salt and pepper.

2. To serve, divide the eggs among 4 plates or transfer them to a warm serving platter. Spoon the sauce over the top, making sure to include plenty of mushrooms. Garnish with the chives and serve the toasted brioche on the side.

8 large eggs

¾ cup whole milk or heavy cream

3 tablespoons unsalted butter

Fine sea salt and freshly ground black pepper

1 recipe Morel-Chive Cream Sauce (recipe follows)

Chopped fresh chives, for garnish

4 slices fresh brioche, toasted

MOREL-CHIVE CREAM SAUCE

Makes about 1¼ cups sauce

1. In a large sauté pan over medium heat, melt 2 tablespoons of the butter. Add the morels and garlic, and sauté until the mushrooms are tender and the liquid they release (it will be a fair amount) has evaporated almost entirely, about 6 minutes. Add the cream and continue to reduce the sauce until it lightly coats the back of a spoon, about 8 minutes. Add the remaining 1 tablespoon butter and the chives, and continue to reduce until the sauce thickens slightly, 1 to 2 minutes more. Season to taste with salt.

3 tablespoons unsalted butter, divided

2 cups small morels, cleaned (see Cleaning Foraged Mushrooms, page 153, for instructions)

2 garlic cloves, finely minced

¾ cup heavy cream

¼ cup finely chopped chives

Sea salt

DANDELION-RICOTTA GNOCCHI
with Spicy Orange Brown Butter

ERIC JOPPIE, CHEF, BAR AVIGNON

These green-speckled dumplings are a bit like ravioli without the pasta. Spring dandelion greens offer welcome bitterness, accenting the ricotta's richness and the nutty brown butter. Late-season citrus (try Cara Cara oranges) and red pepper flakes round out the dish with sweetness, acidity, and bright spice.

Don't hesitate to experiment with other seasonal flavors: spinach, nettles, or kale can be used in place of the dandelions, with blood oranges or Meyer lemons standing in for the citrus. If you don't have time to make your own ricotta, try to find one of the extra-smooth, superfine styles sometimes found in specialty food stores.

The cooked gnocchi will keep in the refrigerator for twenty-four hours. Make them the day before you want to serve them, then make the brown butter right before serving.

Makes 6 servings

3 bunches dandelion greens (about 1 pound)

3 ounces (1½ cups) grated hard cheese, such as Grana Padano or Parmigiano-Reggiano, divided

2 eggs

2 oranges, zested and cut in half

1 pound (about 1¾ cups) Homemade Ricotta Cheese (page 174) or store-bought

1 teaspoon kosher salt

1⅓ cups all-purpose flour

¾ cup (1½ sticks) unsalted butter

1½ teaspoons red pepper flakes, or more to taste, divided

1. Bring a large pot of generously salted water to a boil over high heat. While the water comes to a boil, prepare an ice bath by filling a large bowl with cold water and several handfuls of ice. Cut any tough ribs or stems from the dandelion greens (though the greens available at the market in spring are usually delicate, with thin, tender stems). Cook the greens until tender, about 30 seconds, then drain and plunge them into the ice bath. When they have cooled completely, squeeze the greens dry with your hands and coarsely chop them. You should end up with 1 packed cup of coarsely chopped greens.

2. Put the greens in the bowl of a food processor, along with ½ cup of the cheese, the eggs, and orange zest. Process the ingredients until smooth, pulsing in bursts of 30 seconds to 1 minute. Add the ricotta and salt, and process until combined. Add the flour ⅓ cup at a time, pulsing just until combined to make a very thick batter (or a very wet dough).

3. Transfer the dough to a generously floured work surface and bring it together gently with floured hands until it is cohesive enough that it can be lifted into a piping bag fitted with a ⅝-inch plain tip (#8). (If you don't have a piping bag, use a ziplock bag and snip off a corner, leaving a ¾-inch opening.) Let the dough rest in the piping bag for at least 15 minutes to allow the flour to continue to absorb the liquid.

4. Bring a large pot of generously salted water to a boil over high heat. Twist the bag so that the dough is compact and sits in the bottom. When the water is boiling, hold the bag in one hand and a small, sharp knife in the other. Hold the tip of the piping bag several inches above the boiling water. Squeeze the bag and twist, cutting the dough at 1-inch intervals as it comes out of the bag. (This will become less awkward with practice.) Try to cut 15 to 20 dumplings per round. Cook them until they float to the top, then wait 30 seconds before using a slotted spoon to remove the gnocchi to a baking sheet. They will be delicate when warm but will become sturdier as they cool. Boil the dumplings in batches until the dough is gone; you should get about 84. Reserve a cup of the cooking liquid.

5. To serve, heat a large, wide skillet over medium-high heat. Add 4 tablespoons of the butter, swirling it in the pan until it smells nutty and is lightly browned. Add ½ teaspoon of the pepper flakes and a third of the gnocchi, and sauté until the gnocchi are nicely browned on all sides. Squeeze the juice from one of the orange halves into the pan and take the pan off the heat. Toss the gnocchi with ⅓ cup of the remaining cheese and set them aside to keep warm. Repeat 2 times with remaining gnocchi, butter, pepper flakes, orange juice, and cheese, adding each new batch to the warm finished gnocchi. When all of the gnocchi have been browned, serve immediately.

PAN-ROASTED CHINOOK SALMON
with Polenta and Raab

GREG HIGGINS, CHEF/OWNER, HIGGINS RESTAURANT AND BAR

James Beard Award–recipient Greg Higgins is a pioneer of Northwest cuisine and an early and influential national voice for sustainability in the food industry. He arrived in Portland in the late 1980s and continues to define and reinvent a style of cooking that has its roots in Northwest soil.

Spring is when glorious Chinook salmon head into our rivers to spawn. The ingredients in this recipe pair wonderfully with one another: succulent muscular salmon, crisp and bittersweet raab, creamy polenta. Pair it with an Oregon pinot noir to complete this spring feast.

Makes 4 servings

1 cup coarse polenta, such as Lonesome Whistle Farm's Abenaki Corn Polenta

1 tablespoon finely minced garlic

1 cup grated Pecorino Romano or Parmigiano-Reggiano cheese

Kosher salt and freshly ground black pepper

Zest and juice of 2 medium lemons

½ teaspoon ground turmeric

1 tablespoon sugar

¼ cup extra-virgin olive oil

2 tablespoons minced fresh dill

4 (6-ounce) Chinook salmon fillets

4 tablespoons vegetable oil

1 bunch raab, any variety, trimmed and blanched for 2 to 3 minutes

1. In a medium saucepan combine the polenta and garlic with 4 cups of water and gradually bring it to a low boil, stirring frequently. Stir and cook the polenta until it thickens, 20 to 30 minutes. Remove the pan from the heat, stir in the cheese, and season to taste with salt and pepper. Set the polenta aside in a warm spot, loosely covered, stirring it occasionally.

2. Finely mince the lemon zest and add it to the lemon juice, turmeric, and sugar in a small pan. Bring the mixture to a simmer over low heat and gently simmer until it has reduced to a light syrup, 2 to 3 minutes. Remove the pan from the heat and allow the vinaigrette to cool. Whisk in the olive oil and dill, then taste and adjust the seasoning as needed. Set the vinaigrette aside.

3. Preheat the oven to 400 degrees F.

4. Season the salmon fillets with salt and pepper. In a large heavy skillet, warm the vegetable oil just until it begins to smoke. Sear the fillets skin side up until they brown nicely, 2 to 3 minutes, then flip them over. Arrange the raab around the fish and place the skillet the oven. Roast for 5 to 7 minutes, or to your preferred doneness. Serve the roasted salmon and raab on the polenta, drizzled with the lemon-dill vinaigrette.

RAAB

Raab, rabe, rapa, rapini: all are names for the budding shoots of brassicas family members (including arugula, kale, collards, cabbage, and turnips) that have "bolted," or gone to seed, sprouting naturally after overwintering in the ground. The slim stalks sport saw-tooth edged leaves with tight clusters of buds on top, and taste slightly different depending on the mother plant. They share the tendency to be delicate and sweet, which is the result of winter frosts that convert the plants' starches into sugar.

GRASS-FED STRIP LOIN

with *Porcini Bread Salad and Pickled Rhubarb*

NAOMI POMEROY, CHEF/OWNER, BEAST

Springtime porcini mushrooms are unique to the Pacific Northwest, where they can usually be found from late May through June. Lightly nutty, and milder and firmer than fall porcini, which have a deep earthy flavor, they are the perfect companions for other favorites of the season: rhubarb, asparagus, and spring onions.

Makes 4 to 6 servings

1. Preheat the oven to 400 degrees F.

2. In a large bowl, toss the bread with the melted butter and oil. Season it generously with salt and pepper. Spread the bread out in a single layer on a baking sheet and toast until it is golden brown in spots, but still chewy, 8 to 10 minutes. Remove the pan from the oven and set it aside. Leave the oven on to roast the strip loin.

3. To make the strip loin, in a large heavy ovenproof pan or cast-iron skillet over medium-high heat, warm the oil. When the oil is hot, season the meat on all sides with salt and pepper and add it to the pan. Warm it briefly by cooking for 3 to 4 minutes, or just before it begins to brown. Add the butter and once it has melted, baste the beef with it, using a large spoon. After basting for 2 to 3 minutes, add the thyme sprigs, turn the beef over, and roast it in the oven until an instant-read thermometer registers 120 degrees F for rare, 7 to 10 minutes. Remove the pan from the oven, put the meat on a plate, reserving the pan juices, and loosely cover it with foil. Allow the meat to rest for 20 minutes.

4. Meanwhile, prepare the mushrooms. Trim the bottoms and soak the whole mushrooms in 4 cups of water with the sea salt for 10 minutes to remove any dirt or bugs from the crevices. Rinse and dry the mushrooms, and slice them ¼ inch thick. (Trim the gills if they are yellow colored.) Melt the butter in a large heavy skillet over medium-high heat. When the butter is foamy, increase the heat to high, add the mushrooms, and season

CONTINUED

FOR THE BREAD SALAD:

½ loaf (about 8 ounces) chewy, open-crumb, peasant-style bread, such as ciabatta, torn in 1½- to 2-inch pieces (about 6 cups)

2 tablespoons unsalted butter, melted

2 tablespoons extra-virgin olive oil

Kosher salt and freshly ground black pepper

———————————

2 tablespoons extra-virgin olive oil

1¾ pounds grass-fed New York strip loin, trimmed of silver skin

Kosher salt and freshly ground black pepper

3 tablespoons unsalted butter

2 sprigs fresh thyme

1 pound (5 to 6) small porcini

1 tablespoon fine sea salt

3 tablespoons unsalted butter

8 stalks asparagus, woody ends trimmed and sliced on the bias as thinly as possible

1½ cups Pickled Rhubarb and Spring Onions (recipe follows)

1 cup lightly packed flat-leaf parsley leaves, or 1 small bunch arugula

3 ounces hard sheep's milk cheese, such as Ancient Heritage Dairy's Heritage or Hannah

them generously with kosher salt. Sauté the mushrooms, stirring them frequently, until they have released their liquid, softened, and turned golden, about 8 minutes. Set them aside.

5. To assemble the salad, in a large bowl, combine the toasted bread, asparagus, and mushrooms. Add the reserved meat juices and toss to combine. Add the pickled rhubarb and spring onions and toss well, then taste and adjust the seasoning as needed with salt, pepper, or some of the rhubarb pickling liquid for acidity. Add the parsley and use a vegetable peeler to shave the cheese over the salad. Toss once more and arrange on a platter. Slice the beef into 1½-inch-thick pieces and serve it alongside.

PICKLED RHUBARB AND SPRING ONIONS

Makes about 4 cups

¾ cup white wine vinegar

1½ cups sugar

4 teaspoons kosher salt

3 stalks rhubarb, thinly sliced on a strong bias (about 3 cups)

2 small spring onions, thinly sliced (about 1½ cups)

1. In a large nonreactive saucepan, combine the vinegar, sugar, and salt with ½ cup water. Bring the mixture to a boil over medium-high heat. Add the rhubarb, then reduce the heat and simmer it briefly, until the rhubarb softens slightly without falling apart, 3 to 5 minutes. Remove the rhubarb from the pickling liquid and spread it in a single layer on a baking sheet to cool. Let the pickling liquid cool as well. Once both are cool, add the rhubarb back, along with the onions.

CHOOSING, CLEANING, AND STORING PORCINI MUSHROOMS

Look for firm, dense porcini mushrooms without pinholes. Store them in the refrigerator in a brown bag and use within a day or two. Brush them clean with a damp brush before using, and trim away any damaged spots you find. You can also give them a quick soak in salted water to draw out any dirt or bugs from their crevices.

GRILLED CHICKEN
with Sorrel Pesto

DIANE MORGAN, COOKBOOK AUTHOR AND PORTLAND FARMERS MARKET SHOPPER

James Beard Award–winning cookbook author Diane Morgan makes this pesto in the springtime, when fresh sorrel turns up at the farmers' market. Similar in appearance to spinach, sorrel has a bracing, lemony bite that beautifully accents the flavor of grilled items. But don't skip over this recipe just because you've missed sorrel's fleeting season: baby arugula and watercress are acceptable substitutes, and every bit as gorgeous on the plate.

Makes 4 servings

1. Prepare a medium-hot fire in a charcoal grill or preheat a gas grill to medium-high. Trim any pieces of fat clinging to the chicken breasts and put them in a shallow baking dish or bowl. In a small bowl, combine the cumin, salt, and pepper. Rub the chicken breasts on both sides with oil, followed by the spice rub. Set the chicken aside.

2. When the grill is ready, oil the grate. Place the chicken breasts directly on the hot grill and sear on one side, about 4 minutes. Turn and sear on the other side until the juices run clear when the thickest part of a breast is pierced with a knife or an instant-read thermometer registers 165 degrees F, about 4 minutes longer.

3. Put each chicken breast on a warm plate and drizzle with the pesto. Serve immediately and pass the remaining pesto.

4 boneless, skinless chicken breast halves

2 teaspoons ground cumin

1½ teaspoons fine sea salt

1½ teaspoons freshly ground black pepper

Extra-virgin olive oil, for the spice rub and oiling the grill

About ½ cup Sorrel Pesto (recipe follows)

SORREL PESTO

Makes about 1½ cups

1. In the bowl of a food processor, pulse the sorrel, garlic, Parmesan, pine nuts, lemon juice, and salt until finely chopped, stopping once or twice to scrape down the sides of the bowl with a rubber spatula. With the machine running, drizzle in the oil and process until the pesto comes together. Stored in a jar with a tight-fitting lid, this pesto will keep for up to 3 days in the refrigerator or up to 3 months in the freezer.

2½ cups lightly packed roughly chopped sorrel

2 large garlic cloves, coarsely chopped

⅓ cup freshly grated Parmesan cheese, preferably Parmigiano-Reggiano

¼ cup lightly toasted pine nuts

1½ teaspoons freshly squeezed lemon juice

½ teaspoon fine sea salt

⅔ cup extra-virgin olive oil

SWISS CHARD-SPINACH PIES
with Fennel and Sumac

HODA KHOURI, CHEF/OWNER, HODA'S MIDDLE EASTERN CUISINE

Fatayer, or Lebanese spinach pies, are the inspiration for these savory treats, which make use of market greens. A second-generation Portland restaurateur who grew up in Beirut, chef/owner Hoda Khouri has served them at her Southeast Portland restaurant since the day it opened. The dough can be rolled in different sizes to make large calzone-type turnovers or little bite-sized pies. They freeze well, so roll up your sleeves and make a big batch.

Sumac is a Middle Eastern spice made from dried, ground sumac berries, which are slightly fruity and pleasantly astringent; purchase it at well-stocked groceries.

Note: Save the chard stems for soup making or pickling.

Makes 16 large or 32 small pies

1 bunch Swiss chard, stemmed

1 bunch spinach, large stems removed, washed well

1 small onion, cut into ¼-inch dice (about 1 cup)

¼ cup finely diced fresh fennel bulb

¼ cup extra-virgin olive oil, plus more for brushing the pies

Juice of 3 lemons (about ⅔ cup)

3 tablespoons ground sumac

1½ teaspoons fine sea salt

1 teaspoon freshly ground black pepper

2 (1-pound) balls pizza dough, homemade or store-bought

3 ounces fresh mozzarella cheese

1. Cut the chard and spinach leaves into ¼-inch ribbons; you should have about 8 packed cups of greens. In a large bowl, using your hands, toss the greens with the onions, fennel, oil, lemon juice, sumac, salt, and pepper, very lightly massaging to incorporate everything. Let the greens sit for about 2 hours, during which time they will soften and the various flavors will mingle.

2. When you're ready to make the pies, preheat the oven to 375 degrees F and lightly oil 2 baking sheets. Set them aside.

3. Use a sharp knife to divide each dough ball into 8 portions, about 2 ounces each. Lightly dust a work surface with flour and roll each portion into a small round about 5 inches in diameter. Use your hands to lightly squeeze any extra moisture from the filling, then use a slotted spoon or a fork to place about 3 tablespoons of filling in the center of each round. Top the filling with a little piece of mozzarella.

4. To form the traditional triangles, think about each round as having 3 sides. Lift 2 of the sides, bring them together in the center over the filling, then lift the third side. Pinch them together at the top, and then pinch down the loose edges to make a raised ridge. When you're finished, you'll have a Y-shaped seam on top of the triangular pastry.

5. Place the pies on the prepared baking sheets and lightly brush the tops with oil. Bake the pies until they are light golden brown, 15 to 20 minutes.

GRILLED HALIBUT
with Fiddleheads, Pea Tendrils, and
Green Garlic Vinaigrette

PAUL LOSCH, CHEF/CO-OWNER, RUDDICK/WOOD

A springtime favorite that lends itself to a variety of uses, green garlic makes an exquisite vinaigrette, visually arresting and full of flavor. With the spring halibut season coinciding with the appearance of early-spring vegetables, including that tasty seasonal telltale, fiddlehead ferns, this light dish is welcome after a long, wet Pacific Northwest winter. Use the leftover vinaigrette on grains, salad greens, grilled vegetables, chicken, and poached eggs.

Makes 4 servings

1. Bring a medium pot of generously salted water to a boil over high heat. Prepare an ice bath by filling a bowl with cold water and a few handfuls of ice cubes. Drop the fiddleheads into the boiling water all at once and cook for 1 to 2 minutes after the water returns to a boil. They should retain a small amount of crispness and crunch. Drain and transfer them immediately to the ice bath. When they have cooled completely, drain and set them aside.

2. In a medium sauté pan, heat the oil over medium-high heat. Add the onions to the pan and season them with salt and pepper. Sauté the onions until they are soft and some of the edges begins to brown, 5 to 6 minutes. Set them aside.

3. Prepare a medium-hot fire in a charcoal grill or preheat a gas grill to medium-high. Lightly brush both sides of the halibut with oil, and season with salt and pepper. When the grill is ready, oil the grate. Place the fish directly on the hot grill, flesh side down, rotating the pieces 90 degrees after 2 minutes, to mark the flesh (a step that's nice but not necessary). After another 2 minutes, turn the fillets over and repeat.

4. While the halibut is grilling, return the pan with the onions to medium-high heat. When the onions are hot again, add the fiddleheads and cook for 2 more minutes. Remove the onions and fiddleheads to a large bowl containing the pea tendrils. Toss them with half of the vinaigrette and season the vegetables to taste with salt and pepper. To serve, arrange the vegetables on a serving platter, or divide among 4 plates. Top with the halibut and drizzle with more vinaigrette. Serve immediately.

1 pound (about 4 cups) fiddlehead ferns, cleaned (see How to Clean Fiddlehead Ferns, page 43)

2 tablespoons grapeseed oil, plus more for brushing the halibut

1 small sweet onion such as Walla Walla, thinly sliced

Kosher salt and freshly ground black pepper

4 (6-ounce) halibut fillets, skin on

2 ounces fresh pea tendrils (about 3 cups, lightly packed)

½ cup Green Garlic Vinaigrette (recipe follows)

CONTINUED

GREEN GARLIC VINAIGRETTE

Makes about 1 cup

2 to 3 stalks green garlic

½ cup plus 2 tablespoons grapeseed or other neutral-flavored oil, divided

¼ teaspoon Aleppo pepper

Kosher salt

1 small shallot, coarsely chopped

2 tablespoons white wine vinegar

2 tablespoons freshly squeezed lemon juice (from 1 medium lemon)

¼ cup extra-virgin olive oil

1 tablespoon honey

1. Prepare a medium-hot fire in a charcoal grill or preheat a gas grill to medium-high. (A hot cast-iron pan can be used in lieu of a grill, to scorch the garlic.)

2. Trim any tough greens from the garlic and toss it in a small bowl with 2 tablespoons of the grapeseed oil, the pepper, and a pinch of salt. When the grill is ready, place the garlic directly on the hot grill. Grill the stalks until they begin to char lightly and become limp and tender, 3 to 5 minutes. Transfer the garlic to a plate and let it cool.

3. Once the garlic is cool, chop the stalks into 1-inch pieces and add them to a blender with the shallot, vinegar, and lemon juice. Puree in bursts until smooth. With the machine running, slowly add the remaining ½ cup grapeseed oil and the olive oil in a steady stream until the vinaigrette is emulsified and creamy. Taste the vinaigrette; there should be a balance of sweetness (from the grilled garlic) and acidity from the vinegar. Add a little honey as needed to pull the flavors together. Store leftover vinaigrette in the refrigerator for 3 to 5 days.

HOW TO CLEAN FIDDLEHEAD FERNS

To clean fiddleheads, trim the bottoms (the "necks") and remove any loose dirt or debris from the "heads." Put the ferns in a bowl of cold water, agitate them to remove any remaining debris, and let them sit for 5 to 10 minutes before using a slotted spoon to lift them out of the water onto a clean tea towel to dry.

KEEMA MATAR

(Ground Lamb with Fresh Peas)

LEENA EZEKIEL, CHEF/OWNER, THALI SUPPER CLUB

This classic North Indian dish is traditionally made with ground beef or lamb and fresh green peas. When fresh peas are no longer available, use frozen ones (harvested from your garden or purchased at the market in season) or chickpeas, for a more robust dish not unlike an Indian version of chili.

Serve *keema matar* with hot steamed basmati rice or Indian flatbread such as naan, chapati, or roti. To balance its spicy flavor and soothe the palate, a cucumber and yogurt salad, or another main dish featuring potatoes, such as *tari aloo*, are good choices.

Makes 6 to 8 servings

2 tablespoons canola, grapeseed, or other neutral-flavored oil

2 red onions, cut into ¼-inch dice (about 3 cups)

1 tablespoon finely chopped garlic

1 tablespoon peeled, finely chopped gingerroot

2 pounds lean ground lamb, preferably pastured

2 teaspoons ground cumin

2 teaspoons garam masala

1 teaspoon ground turmeric

½ teaspoon cayenne pepper

2 cups finely diced tomatoes, preferably home-canned

2 cups fresh shelling peas

Sea salt

Cilantro leaves, for garnish

1. In a large, wide sauté pan, heat the oil over medium-high heat. When it is hot, add the onions and fry, stirring occasionally, until they are golden brown, 5 to 7 minutes. Add the garlic and ginger and cook, continuing to stir, until fragrant, 2 to 3 minutes. Increase the heat to high, add the lamb, cumin, garam masala, turmeric, and cayenne to the pan, and cook, stirring constantly, until the lamb is no longer pink and the liquid has evaporated, about 5 minutes. Add the tomatoes, stir well to incorporate them, and cook the mixture for 5 minutes before adding the peas. Reduce the heat and simmer the mixture for 5 more minutes. Season to taste with salt, garnish with cilantro leaves, and serve immediately.

FRIED CAULIFLOWER "RICE"

with Farm Eggs and Bacon

ALLISON JONES, DIGITAL AND HEALTH EDITOR, *PORTLAND MONTHLY MAGAZINE*

Necessity being the mother of invention, Paleo enthusiasts and those on restricted diets have been inspired to transform a humble head of cauliflower into tiny grains of "rice" that can be dressed up nearly any way you please. Once you've got the food-processor part down, the possibilities are endless—imagine cauliflower risotto, paella, or bowls of cauliflower rice as a base for curries and stir-fries, or tucked into lettuce wraps with steak.

Here, the vegetable is transformed into an easy and satisfying meal for brunch or those nights when you feel like breakfast for dinner. Add some chopsticks and a dash of tamari, and you'll be convinced it's takeout.

Makes 4 to 6 servings

1. In a food processor, pulse the florets in batches until the cauliflower resembles grains of rice. You'll need to process it in several batches so as not to overfill the food processor and puree the cauliflower. You should end up with about 9 cups. (You can also use a knife to dice the florets, which will easily break into very small pieces as you go.) Set the cauliflower aside.

2. In a large skillet or wok over medium heat, cook the bacon until just crispy. Use a slotted spoon to remove the pieces from the pan and place them on a plate lined with paper towels to drain. Reserve the bacon grease in the pan.

3. Whisk the eggs in a small bowl with a generous pinch of salt and pepper to taste. Set them aside.

4. Warm the bacon grease over medium-high heat. When it is hot, add the onions and cook until they have softened, 5 to 7 minutes. Add the cauliflower and oil to the pan with more salt and pepper to taste. Sauté the cauliflower until it is tender, about 6 minutes, then it push to the edges of the pan. Add the eggs, stir to combine, and continue to stir until the eggs are cooked, about 8 minutes. Stir in the bacon and garlic chives. Serve immediately with tamari and hot sauce on the side. For extra-hungry diners, add a fried egg on top!

1 large head cauliflower (about 3 pounds), cut into florets

8 slices bacon, diced

8 pastured eggs

Kosher salt and freshly ground black pepper

1 medium white onion, finely diced (about 2 cups)

1 tablespoon toasted sesame oil

⅔ cup finely chopped garlic chives, parsley, or combination of other favorite herbs

Tamari or soy sauce, for serving

Hot sauce, for serving

SWEETS, SIPS, AND CONDIMENTS

Fresh Strawberry Coffee Cake with Rhubarb Sauce 47

Rhubarb-Chocolate Ganache with Sichuan
Peppercorns and Mint 50

Strawberry Pavlova with Tarragon and Mascarpone 53

Bing Cherry Clafouti 55

Spring Herbal Tonic 57

The St. Pauli with Homemade Sour Cherry Vodka 59

Quick Radish Kimchi with Kale 60

FRESH STRAWBERRY COFFEE CAKE
with Rhubarb Sauce

LINDSEY MIDDLETON, NEW CASCADIA TRADITIONAL BAKERY

Coffee cake is really just an excuse to eat cake for breakfast. And what's wrong with that? The fresh flavors of late spring—strawberries, basil, and rhubarb—complement one another perfectly in this morning treat.

Most major groceries now carry the ingredients to make New Cascadia's flour mix, from companies such as Bob's Red Mill, or look for them online. If you don't have issues with wheat, the recipe can be made with 2¾ cups of regular cake flour; eliminate the xanthan gum.

Makes one 12-cup Bundt cake

1. Preheat the oven to 350 degrees F and lightly grease a 12-cup Bundt pan with butter or vegetable oil.

2. In a medium bowl, whisk together the gluten-free flour, baking powder, xanthan gum, baking soda, and salt. Set the dry ingredients aside.

3. In the bowl of a stand mixer fitted with the paddle attachment, beat the butter and brown sugar on medium speed until well combined and lighter in color, 2 to 3 minutes. Add the eggs, one at a time, incorporating each one before adding the next. Add the vanilla and lemon zest, followed by the sour cream. Mix until just combined.

4. Toss the strawberries with the dry ingredients to coat them with the flour. Add the flour, berries, and basil to the mixing bowl, reduce the speed to low, and mix for several rotations, or until there are no flour streaks. Scrape the batter into the prepared pan and bake until a cake tester inserted in the tallest part of the cake comes out clean, about 90 minutes. Remove the pan from the oven to a wire rack to cool for 15 to 20 minutes before inverting the cake onto a serving platter.

5. While the cake cools, make the rhubarb sauce. In a small nonreactive saucepan, toss the rhubarb with the sugar. Cook over medium heat until the rhubarb is mushy, about 20 minutes, stirring occasionally and breaking the pieces up with a wooden spoon. Spoon the rhubarb over the cooled cake before serving.

2½ cups New Cascadia Gluten-Free Cake Flour (recipe follows)

2 teaspoons baking powder

1¼ teaspoons xanthan gum

1 teaspoon baking soda

2 teaspoons fine sea salt

1½ cups (3 sticks) unsalted butter, at room temperature

1½ cups lightly packed light brown sugar

6 eggs

2 teaspoons pure vanilla extract

2 teaspoons finely chopped lemon zest (from 1 medium lemon)

1½ cups sour cream

2 cups hulled and roughly chopped fresh strawberries (from 1 pint)

4 teaspoons coarsely chopped fresh basil

FOR THE SAUCE:

1 to 2 stalks rhubarb, cut into ½-inch dice (about ¾ cup)

¼ cup sugar

CONTINUED

NEW CASCADIA GLUTEN-FREE CAKE FLOUR

Makes 4½ cups

3 cups brown rice flour

1 cup potato starch

½ cup tapioca flour (also called tapioca starch)

1½ teaspoons xanthan gum

1. In a large bowl, whisk all the ingredients together thoroughly. Store in a cool, dry place; the flour will keep for up to 6 months.

> ## VARIATIONS
>
> This versatile breakfast cake can be made with a range of fruits in season (try raspberries with lemon, or apples with cinnamon). When winter rolls around, put together a decadent Oregon version of a peanut butter cup: eliminate the strawberries, lemon zest, and basil; substitute ¾ cup of hazelnut butter for the same amount of sour cream; and add 1 to 1½ cups of chocolate chips. You might decide to have it after dinner instead, with a cup of coffee.

RHUBARB-CHOCOLATE GANACHE
with Sichuan Peppercorns and Mint

DAVID BRIGGS, OWNER/CHOCOLATIER, XOCOLATL DE DAVÍD

Though often paired with strawberries, doesn't rhubarb deserve a spotlight all its own—or at least an occasional new partner? Here, it's chocolate. The ganache can be made the day before serving and covered with plastic wrap once the individual containers have cooled. Its optimal serving temperature is slightly cooler than room temperature, and its texture should be similar to ice cream. Pickled strawberries are, ideally, a two-day process, but can be made in one day in a pinch. Because it's a bit fancy, you might want to pair this dessert with a glass of sparkling wine, another wonderful combination.

Note: Sichuan peppercorns are fairly easy to find and are sometimes labeled "prickly ash." Check an Asian market if you're having trouble locating them.

Makes 6 servings

12 ounces Rhubarb Juice (recipe follows)

12 ounces bittersweet chocolate (65 percent or higher), chopped into small pieces

Fleur de sel or flaky sea salt

1 teaspoon Sichuan peppercorns, for garnish

6 tablespoons Pickled Strawberries (recipe follows)

1 small sprig fresh mint

1. In a small nonreactive pan over medium heat, bring the rhubarb juice to a simmer. Meanwhile, put the chocolate in a mixing bowl with a pinch of *fleur de sel*. When the rhubarb juice simmers, pour it over the chocolate and let the mixture stand for 1 minute before gently whisking the two ingredients together to make a smooth mixture.

2. Divide the ganache among 6 shallow bowls, parfait glasses, or small mason jars and refrigerate them for at least 3 hours before serving, or until the mixture is set.

3. Remove the ganache from the refrigerator 1 hour before serving. Grind the peppercorns in a spice grinder or using a mortar and pestle, and set them aside.

4. To assemble, sprinkle a small pinch of *fleur de sel* over the ganache in each container. Place a generous tablespoon of pickled strawberries on one side of the ganache and sprinkle them with a tiny pinch of Sichuan peppercorns. Garnish with a fine chiffonade of mint and serve.

RHUBARB JUICE

Makes about 6 cups

1. In a large bowl, toss the rhubarb with the sugar.

2. Fill a large pot with 2 quarts of water. Add the rhubarb and sugar, and bring the contents to a boil over high heat. When it comes to a boil, reduce the heat and simmer the ingredients for 20 minutes. Remove the pan from the heat and strain the rhubarb juice through a fine-mesh sieve into a clean bowl, using the back of a spoon to press as much liquid as you can from the rhubarb pieces. Allow the juice to stand for 30 minutes, during which time any remaining sediment should fall to the bottom of the bowl. Store the juice in an airtight container in the refrigerator for no longer than overnight.

10 ounces rhubarb, sliced crosswise into ½-inch pieces (about 2 cups)

1 tablespoon sugar

PICKLED STRAWBERRIES

Makes 2 cups

1. Quarter the strawberries and, depending on their size, cut each quarter into 2 or 3 pieces. In a medium bowl, toss the berries with the sugar, then let them sit in the refrigerator for at least 4 hours, or up to overnight, to macerate.

2. The next day, strain the juice from the berries into a small, nonreactive saucepan with the vinegar and salt. Bring the liquid to a simmer over medium-high heat, then pour it over the strawberries and add the mint. Let the pickled strawberries cool to room temperature, remove the mint, and store them in an airtight container in the refrigerator for up to 2 weeks.

1 pint (about 2 cups) fresh strawberries, hulled

2 tablespoons sugar

2½ tablespoons rice wine vinegar

Small pinch of kosher salt

1 small sprig fresh mint

STRAWBERRY PAVLOVA
with Tarragon and Mascarpone

ELLEN JACKSON, COOKBOOK AUTHOR AND BOARD MEMBER,
PORTLAND FARMERS MARKET

According to legend, famed Russian ballerina Anna Pavlova's 1920s tour of Australia and New Zealand inspired the pavlova dessert. A more spectacular—or simple—finish to a meal is difficult to imagine. This one just takes some planning ahead, because the meringue bakes in a low, slow oven. If you make the meringue and infuse the cream the day before you plan to serve it, this dessert is a cinch, yet every bit the showstopper.

Makes 6 to 8 servings

1. Place a rack in the center of the oven and preheat it to 200 degrees F. Line a baking sheet with parchment paper and trace around the edge of a 12-inch cake pan or a dinner plate to mark a circle on the parchment. Set the baking sheet aside.

2. In the clean, dry bowl of a stand mixer fitted with the whisk attachment, beat the whites with the salt on medium speed until foamy. Add the cream of tartar and increase the speed to medium-high. With the mixer running, add 2 tablespoons of granulated sugar until the whites form soft peaks. Gradually add the remaining granulated sugar, 2 tablespoons at a time, until the whites are stiff and glossy. Add the vanilla and mix one rotation to combine.

3. Sift the confectioners' sugar over the whites and use a spatula to gently fold it in just until combined. Scrape the whites out of the mixing bowl into the middle of the circle on the parchment paper. Using the back of a large kitchen spoon, spread the meringue out to fill the circle, creating a slight indentation in the center and some spiky irregularities.

4. Bake the meringue for 2 hours without opening the oven door. After 2 hours, it should be very lightly browned and firm to the touch. You can check the center for doneness with the tip of a small paring knife; it's okay if it's a little bit sticky. If it's ready, turn off the oven and leave the meringue inside to cool for another 1½ hours. Once it is completely cool, store the meringue in an airtight container until you're ready to assemble the pavlova.

6 large egg whites, at room temperature

Pinch of fine sea salt

½ teaspoon cream of tartar

¾ cup superfine granulated sugar

1 teaspoon pure vanilla extract

1 cup confectioners' sugar

FOR THE CREAM:

½ cup lightly packed fresh tarragon leaves, plus more for garnish

1¼ cups heavy cream

—————————

3 pints (about 6 cups) fresh strawberries, hulled

¼ cup superfine granulated sugar, divided

2 teaspoons freshly squeezed lime juice

½ cup mascarpone cheese

CONTINUED

5. In the meantime, make the tarragon cream. Bruise the tarragon leaves by lightly crushing them in your hands or gently tapping them with the back of a wooden spoon to release their aromatic oils without chopping them. In a small saucepan over medium-high heat, bring the cream to a boil, stirring occasionally to prevent it from scalding. When it comes to a boil, immediately add the tarragon. Remove the pan from the heat and cover it tightly. Let the tarragon steep for 30 minutes, then taste the cream. If the flavor is to your liking, strain the cream into a clean bowl, pressing on the leaves to extract their flavor. Chill the cream until it is very cold, at least 5 hours and preferably overnight.

6. To serve, slice the strawberries lengthwise, about ¼ inch thick (or halve the berries if they are small). In a medium bowl, toss the berries with 3 tablespoons of the sugar and the lime juice and set them aside to macerate at room temperature for 15 to 20 minutes.

7. Just before serving, whip the tarragon-infused cream with the remaining tablespoon of sugar and the mascarpone until soft peaks form. Place the meringue on a serving platter and fill in the indentation with the cream. Top with the berries and their juices, and garnish with tarragon leaves.

BING CHERRY CLAFOUTI

DAVE ADAMSHICK, DIGITAL MEDIA CONSULTANT, PORTLAND FARMERS MARKET

Late-spring brings cherries—sweet and sour—to the market, and a clafouti (pronounced cla-foo-TEE) is among the best ways to enjoy them. A traditional custardy cake from rural southern France, it's made with a simple, light batter (more crepe than pancake) that lets the flavor of the fruit shine through. Look for early-season Bing, Chelan, and Lambert cherries, and Vans to make this again in the summer.

Some recipes claiming to be authentic insist on using cherries with their pits, for the subtle almond flavor they (and other stone-fruit pits) impart. But unless you're willing to gamble on an after-hours visit to the dentist, use almond liqueur or pure almond extract instead. If you're feeling really ambitious, save the pits to make a custard sauce to accompany your clafouti. We like to serve this with a glass of chilled cherry cider.

Makes 6 servings

1. Preheat the oven to 375 degrees F.

2. Generously coat the inside of a 10-inch ovenproof skillet or pie pan with the butter.

3. In a large bowl, combine the flour, granulated sugar, and salt and make a well in the middle. Add the milk, eggs, and amaretto. Stir the mixture together with a wooden spoon until well combined; the consistency of the batter will be similar to heavy cream.

4. Cover the bottom of the buttered pan with the cherries, pour the batter over the top, and bake on the middle rack of the oven until the clafouti is firm, 35 to 45 minutes. Remove the pan to a wire rack to cool for 10 minutes before dusting the clafouti with confectioners' sugar. Serve warm.

1 tablespoon unsalted butter

⅔ cup all-purpose flour

½ cup granulated sugar

½ teaspoon fine sea salt

½ cup whole milk, slightly warm

4 eggs, lightly beaten

2 tablespoons amaretto, or 1 tablespoon pure almond extract (optional)

1 pound Bing or other sweet, dark cherries, stemmed and pitted (see Cherry-Pitting Hack below)

Confectioners' sugar, for dusting the clafouti

CHERRY-PITTING HACK

If you don't have a bona fide cherry pitter, this method has the distinct advantage of not pushing the pit out and puncturing both the top and bottom of the fruit. Round up a large paperclip and the cork from last night's wine. Bend the paperclip back and forth until it breaks into two open loops. Push the smaller loop in one end of the cork until it protrudes no more than half an inch. Plunge the loop into the stem end of the cherry, using the cork for leverage, hook the pit, and ease it out.

NORTHWEST CHERRIES

Cherry trees came to Oregon in 1847, and the delicious, dark, sweet-tart Bing cherry was king for many years. Easily harvested and packed, the plump cherry originated in Milwaukie (yes, our Milwaukie) where, legend has it, horticulturalist Seth Lewelling and Ah Bing, a Manchurian orchard worker, propagated it. Lambert, Lapin, Van, and Chelan are other black cherries found locally.

Rosy-cheeked Royal Anns were once the only white cherry (only by comparison to black cherries) grown in the Pacific Northwest. The entire crop of butter-yellow fruit was sold for maraschinos. To sell them fresh, Royal Anns were promoted as Golden Bings, but their light coloring showed every bruise caused by shipping. More for us!

Like their mountain namesake, Rainiers are snowy white, with a soft pink blush, the consequence of crossing the Bing and the Van in hopes of extending the short growing season. With up to 24 percent sugar content, Rainiers are the sweetest cherries in the orchard and are prized in Japan, where they command up to eighty-five cents apiece and have been successfully imported since 1992.

The Pacific Northwest has become the most important cherry growing region in the country. And for that, we owe thanks to Seth Lewelling's brother Henderson, who sported a chinstrap beard that today's Portlanders would admire. Had he not loaded his family, seven hundred saplings, and innumerable seeds and hauled them across the Oregon Trail in an ox-drawn cart, we might not have a Bing cherry clafouti in the oven right now.

SPRING HERBAL TONIC

MADELYN MORRIS, OWNER AND HERBALIST, MICKELBERRY GARDENS

Made from fresh springtime herbs and early market greens, this tea is a delicious tonic that helps acclimate your body as it emerges from the cold and dark of winter.

The young tips of nettles (*Urtica dioica*) grow in rich soils and are harvested before the plant begins to flower; packed with vitamins, minerals, and trace elements, they are reputed to have a gentle detoxifying effect. Vitamin-rich bitter dandelion greens are excellent for digestion. Their strong flavor is complemented when combined with members of the mint family: uplifting peppermint and relaxing lemon balm. Full of vitamin C, Douglas fir tips (the fresh needle growth) round out the tea, along with raw honey, which provides the sweetness of flowers, preserved by honeybees.

Makes 4 servings

1. In a large pot over medium heat, bring 8 cups of water to a gentle boil, then remove the pot from the heat and add the mint, nettles, dandelion, lemon balm, and Douglas fir. Gently stir the leaves to submerge them, and cover the pot with a tight-fitting lid. Steep the leaves for at least 15 minutes—the longer they steep, the stronger the flavors will be. (Covering the pot contains the steam vapors, which are full of volatile oils that flavor the water.)

2. When the flavor is to your liking, filter the herbs from the tea with a strainer and allow the tea to cool to a drinkable temperature. Stir in the honey. (Adding the raw honey to the tea once it has cooled slightly helps preserve its delicate enzymes.) Serve immediately or refrigerate and consume within 24 to 36 hours.

1 cup lightly packed fresh mint leaves

½ cup lightly packed fresh nettle tips

¼ cup lightly packed fresh dandelion leaves

¼ cup lightly packed fresh lemon balm leaves

Handful of Douglas fir tips

Raw local honey

THE ST. PAULI

with Homemade Sour Cherry Vodka

AMY BENSON AND CHRIS ROEHM, OWNERS, SQUARE PEG FARM

Amy and Chris created The St. Pauli on a hot July afternoon, when they were hanging out with friends Clare Carver and Brian Marcy of Big Table Farm. Having just returned from the annual Fourth of July St. Paul Rodeo with plenty of tales to recount, they were a few rounds in when Clare pronounced the concoction delicious and named it after the event that inspired its consumption.

The sour cherry vodka recipe was born out of another recipe for cherries soaked in bourbon, a combination you'd be hard pressed to find fault with. However, vodka's distinct lack of flavor makes it the best vehicle for preserving the flavor of summer as relayed by sour pie cherries.

Makes 1 cocktail

1. Fill a tall glass with ice, add the vodka and lemon juice, and top off the glass with club soda. Garnish with a lemon twist and some vodka cherries.

3 ounces Sour Cherry Vodka (recipe follows)

1 tablespoon freshly squeezed lemon juice

Club soda

Lemon twist and vodka cherries, for garnish

SOUR CHERRY VODKA

Makes 2 quarts

1. Prick each cherry with a toothpick and divide them evenly between 2 half-gallon jars with tight-fitting lids. Add ½ cup sugar and 4 cups vodka to each jar, cover, and refrigerate the jars. Invert the jars occasionally during the first few weeks to ensure that the sugar dissolves completely. Then they just need to sit.

2. Be patient and leave the jars in the refrigerator about 6 months, or until the winter solstice. At that point the cherries are ready to be enjoyed in cocktails or spooned over ice cream. Use the vodka to make refreshing St. Pauli cocktails when rodeo season rolls around 7 months later.

4 pounds sour pie cherries (about 12 cups), stemmed, but not pitted

1 cup sugar

8 cups vodka

QUICK RADISH KIMCHI
with Kale

MATT CHOI, CO-OWNER, CHOI'S KIMCHI COMPANY

This recipe is reminiscent of *geotjeori* (loosely translated as "fresh kimchi salad"), a refreshing and easily prepared kimchi that is ready to eat instantly because it isn't fermented. Its fresh finished texture, which contrasts nicely with soups and protein-based entrées, means you can use any kind of radish available. Swap out the kale for another cabbage-family member, such as bok choy or collard greens, if you're inclined.

Korean red chili flakes, or *gochugaru*, are perhaps the most important ingredient in making kimchi; find them at Korean and international groceries, or substitute dried red pepper flakes.

Makes 2 to 3 cups

2 large or 3 small kale or cabbage leaves, cut into 1-inch pieces

8 ounces radishes (daikon or any variety you prefer), julienned

1 green onion (white and light-green parts), split lengthwise and cut on the diagonal into 2-inch pieces

2 tablespoons white vinegar

2 tablespoons soy sauce

2 tablespoons sugar

2 tablespoons Korean red chili flakes (*gochugaru*)

1 tablespoon kosher salt

¾ teaspoon finely minced garlic

1. In a large nonreactive bowl, combine the kale, radishes, and green onion. In a small glass bowl or measuring cup, whisk together the vinegar, soy sauce, sugar, chili flakes, salt, and garlic. Pour the liquid over the vegetables and toss well. Serve immediately. Store the kimchi in an airtight container in the refrigerator for up to several weeks.

THE DAY AFTER MEMORIAL DAY, summer is officially within reach. The remainder of the school year is measured in days, not weeks, and the remnants of spring—sweet peas, strawberries, and squash blossoms—are joined by mounds of tender green beans, zucchini, and raspberries.

The sights and smells of summer's first fragrant peaches and plump tomatoes have been known to weaken the knees of even the most seasoned shoppers. Our heads fill with visions of inspired meals and impromptu barbecues, picnics, and preserving. Maybe we even panic a little, not wanting to miss a single sunny bite. "Do I have enough canning jars for pickling *and* preserving?" we ask ourselves. "Is there space in the freezer for berries?" The goal: capture a slice of summer that can be pulled from the pantry and savored when it's cold and rainy again.

Oregon's summer abundance can be overwhelming. Blackberry brambles know no boundaries; plum tree limbs overhang sidewalks and fences; and fig trees form the buds that will become Brown Turkeys, a variety grown in backyards throughout the city. U-pick fields inspire trips to gather berries, pie cherries, sweet corn and peaches, dahlias and zinnias. It's a collection of so many wonderful things to eat that it's difficult to choose. Market outings (you can shop six days a week at one of Portland Farmers Market's seven venues) offer the same dizzying array of fruits and vegetables. We resist the urge to buy everything in sight, yet few shopping bags go unfilled.

The best of summer cooking is about thinking ahead, preparing food in the cool of the early morning to eat later. It's tough to commit to a full meal when temperatures rise, and we crave food that's light, refreshing, and easily prepared—salads, gazpacho, ceviche. Heat urges us to eat alfresco at every opportunity, to stock up on vitamin D and memories of shared meals that we will call on later. And we barbecue! Grilling, that hallmark of summer, serves up the smoky flavors and crusty textures that flatter soft stone fruits, vegetables, and meats.

Farmers' market produce is picked at the peak of freshness and ripeness, an option that isn't available if it has to travel across the country—or even the region—to its final destination. Local means farmers and orchardists can grow a certain variety of tomato or strawberry for no other reason than that it tastes unbelievably good. Eighty percent of Portland Farmers Market vendors come from within one hundred miles of Portland; "long-haul" and "fourteen-wheeler" are not in their vernacular. Many market vendors offer the best value too, with deals on bumper crops and large quantities, the spoils of summer.

PERSEPHONE FARM

PERSEPHONE FARM SITS IN THE transition from Willamette Valley to the Cascade Mountain foothills, nestled between the meandering Santiam River and a forested hillside. The fifty-five acre organic farm is owned and operated by Jeff Falen and Elanor O'Brien, self-taught farmers who fled academia and the city life to make a living from the land.

During thirty years of farming on twenty-two arable acres, their operation has shifted dramatically. The couple began with just five crops grown exclusively for a wholesaler. They also kept a small "home" flock of hens whose eggs they sold at farmers' markets. Encouraged by demand, they grew the flock, housing the birds in mobile chicken coops that they moved every few days to give the chickens access to fresh grasses, bugs, and grubs. They soon learned that selling eggs laid by pastured hens wasn't a good business proposition: it simply didn't pencil out at the prices shoppers were willing to pay. Still, like most farmers, they keep chickens because they offer symbiotic—and delicious—benefits: reducing the need for fertilizer, helping with weed and pest control, and bringing diversity and balance to plant-dominated soil.

And so much depends on the soil! When the ground is fallow, cover crops like rye, clover, and vetch are sowed to fortify the stubborn clay soil. To mitigate the risk of disease and pests, crops are rotated, and fields are taken out of food production once every four years, to regenerate. Trialing crop varieties for heartiness and "shelf life" (how well and how long they can be stored) is crucial to their ability to bring an array of interesting crops to the market throughout the year.

It is widely accepted that varietal characteristics like cold or heat tolerance, rate of maturation, water requirements, and pest resistance are especially critical to the success of organic farmers. Trialing is a good risk management strategy that also offers one of the joys of farming: experimentation. Identifying interesting new varieties is one way that Persephone differentiates themselves in the marketplace and attracts new customers.

Jeff and Elanor's commitment to sustainability and their decision not to use non-recyclable products like plastic mulch and hoop houses drive their practices. They rely on warm autumn days rather than hasten or extend the natural growing seasons with plastic covers or supplemental heat and light; plants grow in their own time. These choices, when combined with cool wet spring weather, can mean Persephone's first harvest is later than other farms. Being nimble and staying true to their principles has allowed Persephone to build a beloved following in their twenty-five years as market vendors and to discover the true meaning of seasonality.

SMALL PLATES

Grilled Peaches with Blue Cheese and Blackberries 69

Watermelon-Tomato Gazpacho with Pickled
Strawberries and Raspberry Ice 71

Albacore Ceviche with Zucchini Guacamole
and Cherry Tomato Salsa 72

Heirloom Tomato Salad with Dill and Tonnato 74

Salted Cucumbers with Ricotta, Red Onions, and Basil 76

Green Bean Salad with Blackberries and Creamy Sweet Onions 77

Fire-Roasted Artichokes with Lemon Aioli 79

GRILLED PEACHES

with Blue Cheese and Blackberries

TREVOR BAIRD, BAIRD FAMILY ORCHARDS

Peaches are able to straddle that line between sweet and savory, showing their best selves whether paired with raspberries or bacon. Here, grilling the fruit over a flame lightly caramelizes its natural sugars and intensifies its juiciness. It isn't necessary to peel the peaches for the grill, and the skin works to contain the fruit and juices. If you're not a fan of blue cheese, fill the peaches with ricotta, goat, or any soft cheese of your choosing. Or substitute savory charred Padrón peppers, pancetta, or prosciutto for the sweet berries.

Makes 4 servings

1. In a small sauté pan over medium heat, simmer the vinegar until it has reduced by half and is syrupy, about 10 minutes. Stir in the honey, season with pepper, and set the pan aside.

2. Prepare a medium-hot fire in a charcoal grill or preheat a gas grill to medium-high. Clean and lightly oil the grill grate.

3. In a large bowl, toss the peaches with the oil and sprinkle generously with salt and pepper. Place the peach halves on the grill grate, cut side down, and cook until the flesh is caramelized, about 4 minutes. Use tongs to flip the peaches over, and fill each cavity with about ¼ ounce or generous tablespoon of the cheese. Continue to grill until the peaches brown and soften on the bottom without falling apart, 3 to 4 minutes.

4. To serve, place 2 peach halves on each of 4 plates, garnish them generously with blackberries, and drizzle the balsamic syrup over the top.

½ cup aged balsamic vinegar

1½ tablespoons honey

Freshly ground black pepper

4 medium peaches, firm but ripe, halved and pitted

2 tablespoons extra-virgin olive oil

Flaky salt

2 to 3 ounces soft blue cheese or other soft cheese such as Ancient Heritage Dairy's Adelle

2 cups blackberries

HOW TO CHOOSE PEACHES

As with most fresh produce, it isn't the shape or size, the color of the skin, or the tint of its blush, but rather the perfume that leads you to choose the best, ripest items for your market basket. This is especially true with peaches—the nose knows. Choose fruit with a fragrant aroma and flesh that yields slightly when gently pressed.

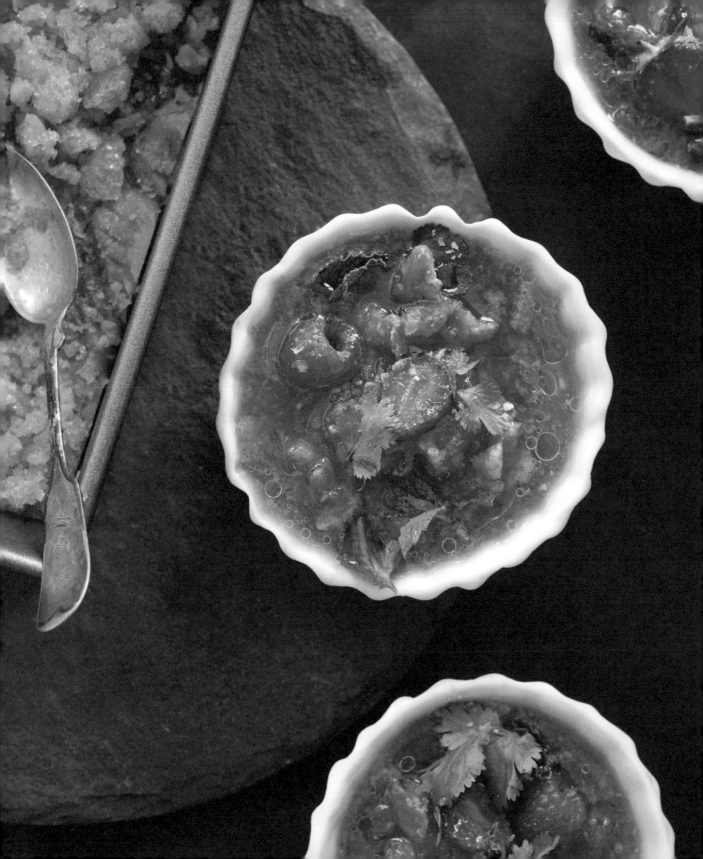

WATERMELON-TOMATO GAZPACHO

with *Pickled Strawberries and Raspberry Ice*

GREGORY GOURDET, EXECUTIVE CHEF, DEPARTURE

Cold soups satisfy in summer. Refreshing and light, this one is a bowlful of luscious tomatoes, juicy melons, and bright berries, an easy and elegant way to start a meal. You'll find that the flavors become more complex and full if you prepare it one or more days before serving.

Makes 4 servings

1. Core the tomatoes, cut them in half horizontally, scoop out the seeds and reserve them. Roughly chop the remaining flesh. Put the seed pulp in a fine-mesh sieve over a bowl and press lightly with the back of a spoon to extract all of the juice. In a large bowl, toss the tomatoes with the watermelon, jalapeño, garlic, ginger, vinegar, salt, and sugar. Add the tomato juice and, working in batches, puree the ingredients in a blender until completely smooth. Chill until cold.

2. To make the raspberry ice, combine the raspberries in the jar of a blender with 1¾ cups water, the candied ginger, sugar, and salt. Blend until smooth and strain through a fine-mesh sieve into a shallow pan. Place the pan in the freezer and freeze until the mixture is firm, 4 hours to overnight. Stir the ice with a fork every 30 minutes or so to prevent it from freezing into a solid block.

3. To make the pickled berries, in a medium nonreactive bowl, combine the strawberries and raspberries. In a small bowl, whisk the maple syrup with the vinegar, add the chili, and pour the pickling liquid over the berries. Gently stir to coat the berries with the liquid, being careful not to crush the raspberries.

4. To serve, break the ice up with a fork, so that it has a flaky, feathery texture. Pour the chilled soup into 4 bowls, garnishing with almost the same amount of raspberry ice. Add some pickled berries with a few drops of their juice. Drizzle each bowl with some oil, add a sprinkle of sea salt, and garnish with plenty of cilantro and mint. Serve immediately.

1 pound red heirloom tomatoes

1 pound watermelon, peeled, seeded, and roughly chopped

1 small red jalapeño, coarsely chopped

1 small garlic clove, smashed

2-inch knob gingerroot, peeled and thinly sliced

2 tablespoons rice wine vinegar

2 tablespoons fine sea salt

1 tablespoon sugar

FOR THE RASPBERRY ICE:

2 pints (about 4 cups) raspberries

2 tablespoons candied ginger

⅓ cup sugar

1 teaspoon fine sea salt

FOR THE PICKLED BERRIES:

1⅓ cups hulled, sliced strawberries

1 pint (about 2 cups) raspberries

½ cup maple syrup

½ cup rice wine vinegar

½ small hot red chili, thinly sliced

———————————

Extra-virgin olive oil, for drizzling

Flaky sea salt, for sprinkling

Fresh cilantro leaves, for garnish

Fresh mint leaves, for garnish

ALBACORE CEVICHE
with Zucchini Guacamole and Cherry Tomato Salsa

KELLY MYERS, EXECUTIVE CHEF, XICO

When combined with Oregon albacore (or any raw fish), the citric acid naturally found in lime juice "cooks" the fish without changing its flavor, causing it to become slightly more firm and opaque—ceviche. Served with guacamole to which a puree of raw zucchini is added, salsa made with sweet cherry tomatoes, warm tortilla chips, and margaritas, this can even be a refreshing light summer meal.

Note: All of the items should be made and consumed the same day. The guacamole and salsa go together easily while the albacore marinates.

Makes 4 to 6 servings

1 pound albacore tuna, cut into ½-inch cubes

Juice of 3 limes

1 tablespoon extra-virgin olive oil

¼ teaspoon dried oregano, preferably Mexican

Sea salt

1 recipe Zucchini Guacamole (recipe follows)

1 recipe Cherry Tomato Salsa (recipe follows)

Tortilla chips, for serving

1. In a nonreactive bowl, toss the albacore with the lime juice. Cover the bowl and marinate the tuna in the refrigerator, checking every 10 minutes, until the pieces are opaque and slightly firmer. If you're uncertain if it is ready, cut a piece of tuna in half; the flesh should be opaque and white on the outside, and rosy pink on the inside. Drain the tuna through a fine-mesh sieve, discarding the lime juice. Put the fish in a bowl, add the oil and oregano, and season to taste with salt.

2. Spoon the albacore over the guacamole, and serve the salsa on the side with tortilla chips.

ZUCCHINI GUACAMOLE

Makes about 2 cups

1. In a small bowl, toss the zucchini with ½ teaspoon of the salt until the salt is well distributed. Set the zucchini aside for 30 minutes to soften. Transfer the contents to the bowl of a food processor. Blend the zucchini into a smooth puree, scraping down the sides of the bowl as needed. You should have about ½ cup of puree.

2. In a small nonreactive bowl, stir together the onion, chili, cilantro, and lime juice. Remove the mixture to a cutting board and sprinkle it with the remaining ½ teaspoon salt. Chop everything until it becomes a dark-green, wet paste (see the technique for making garlic paste for Lemon Aioli in step 1, page 80). In a medium bowl, mash the avocados. Stir in the paste and the zucchini puree. Taste and check for seasoning, adding more salt if needed.

1 small zucchini, cut into ½-inch cubes

1 teaspoon fine sea salt, divided

2 teaspoons finely minced white or spring onion

1 small Serrano chili, seeded and finely minced

1 tablespoon coarsely chopped fresh cilantro leaves

1 teaspoon freshly squeezed lime juice

2 firm but ripe avocados, peeled and pitted

CHERRY TOMATO SALSA

Makes about 2 cups

1. In a medium bowl, combine all the ingredients and set the salsa aside for 20 minutes for the flavors to develop. Before serving, taste and check for seasoning, adding more salt if needed.

1 pint (2 cups) cherry tomatoes, stemmed and halved

2 tablespoons extra-virgin olive oil

1 small Serrano chili, seeded and finely minced

¼ cup coarsely chopped fresh cilantro leaves

1 tablespoon finely minced white or spring onion

Sea salt

HEIRLOOM TOMATO SALAD
with Dill and Tonnato

JENN LOUIS, CHEF/CO-OWNER, LINCOLN AND SUNSHINE TAVERN

Tomatoes, a paragon of summer, express a certain urgency to be eaten when they are so ripe that they are straining against their own skin. When that time arrives, make this salad. Tonnato is a smooth, creamy sauce made with tuna and anchovies.

Makes 4 servings

2 large heirloom tomatoes, cut into ¼-inch-thick slices

Sea salt

8 ounces (about 3 to 4) pickling cucumbers, thinly sliced

1 large shallot, thinly sliced (about ¼ cup)

20 Taggiasca or Niçoise olives, pitted and halved

2 tablespoons plus 2 teaspoons coarsely chopped fresh oregano leaves

4 teaspoons finely chopped fresh dill

12 fresh basil leaves, torn

4 green onions (green parts only), thinly sliced on the bias

¾ cup Citrus Vinaigrette (recipe follows)

½ cup Tonnato (recipe follows)

1. Lay the tomato slices on a plate or in a nonreactive pan in a single layer and season lightly with salt. Set aside.

2. In a small bowl, toss the cucumbers, shallot, olives, oregano, dill, basil, and green onions. Lightly season with salt, toss again, then add enough vinaigrette to generously coat and flavor the salad.

3. To serve, place about 2 tablespoons of tonnato on each of 4 plates and arrange a quarter of the tomato slices on top. Pile a quarter of the cucumber salad on the tomatoes and serve immediately.

EXTENDING THE TOMATO SEASON

Summer is about nothing if not the joy of eating fresh tomatoes every day, sometimes warm from the vine. Or in a BLT. Or a caprese salad. The easiest way to enjoy the flavor of ripe tomatoes after the growing season is over is to freeze them whole. Place unwashed, unpeeled, ripe tomatoes of any size on a baking sheet in the freezer. Once they're frozen, put the tomatoes in ziplock bags and pull them out for soups and sauces. The skins will slip off easily when rinsed briefly.

CITRUS VINAIGRETTE

Makes 1⅓ cups

1. Zest the orange and coarsely chop half of the zest. Juice the whole orange and measure out ¼ cup juice. In a blender, combine the orange zest and juice, preserved lemon rind, garlic, vinegar, grapeseed oil, lemon juice, and honey. Puree the ingredients until they are smooth and well combined. With the blender running, slowly drizzle in the olive oil until it is emulsified. Season to taste with salt and pepper. The vinaigrette can be made ahead and stored in the refrigerator for up to 5 days.

1 orange

¼ preserved lemon, rinsed, pulp and pith removed and discarded, and rinsed again

1 garlic clove, coarsely chopped

¼ cup white wine vinegar

¼ cup grapeseed or canola oil

2 tablespoons freshly squeezed lemon juice (from 1 medium lemon)

1 tablespoon honey

½ cup extra-virgin olive oil

Kosher salt and freshly ground black pepper

TONNATO

Makes about 1½ cups

1. Combine the mayonnaise, tuna, anchovies, garlic, capers, and lemon zest and juice in the bowl of a food processor. Puree until smooth. Season to taste with salt and pepper.

1 cup mayonnaise

2 ounces oil-packed tuna, preferably albacore

2 to 3 oil-packed anchovy fillets, according to taste

1 small garlic clove, finely grated on a Microplane

1½ tablespoons capers, rinsed and drained

1½ teaspoons coarsely chopped lemon zest

1 tablespoon freshly squeezed lemon juice

Kosher salt and freshly ground black pepper

SALTED CUCUMBERS
with Ricotta, Red Onions, and Basil

JOSHUA MCFADDEN, EXECUTIVE CHEF/PARTNER, AVA GENE'S

Salting slices of cucumber has the same effect that salting zucchini or eggplant does; it draws out moisture (cucumbers are about 95 percent water) and bitterness, softening the vegetable into something that asks to be coated with a creamy dressing. This recipe recalls old standbys like *mizeria*, a Polish salad that combines cucumbers, sour cream and dill, or the Southern version that adds sweet onion and caraway or celery seed. But it is very much its own glamorous and delicious rendition.

Makes 4 servings

2 pounds cucumbers, several varieties if possible

2 teaspoons kosher salt

¼ cup loosely packed fresh mint leaves

¼ cup loosely packed basil leaves, preferably opal basil

½ cup Homemade Ricotta Cheese (page 174) or store-bought

2 tablespoons extra-virgin olive oil

½ small red onion, thinly sliced (about ¼ cup)

1 to 2 tablespoons red wine vinegar

1 teaspoon red pepper flakes, or to taste

Kosher salt and freshly ground black pepper

1. Slice the cucumbers ¼ inch thick, making an effort to keep them the same thickness. In a large bowl, mix them with the salt, then refrigerate the cucumbers for about 1 hour.

2. Meanwhile, pick through the mint and basil leaves, hand-tearing any that are overly large into smaller pieces. Place the herbs in a small bowl, cover them with a damp paper towel, and refrigerate them until the cucumbers are ready. Put the ricotta in a small bowl and drizzle in the oil while whisking, to make a smooth creamy dressing that looks like sour cream. Set the ricotta dressing aside until the cucumbers are ready.

3. Remove the cucumbers from the refrigerator, pouring off any excess water before adding the red onion and some of the ricotta dressing. Add the vinegar and pepper flakes, and season with salt and pepper to taste. When the amount of ricotta and other seasonings are to your liking, add the herbs, toss gently to combine, and serve.

HOW TO CHOOSE AND STORE CUCUMBERS

English, Kirby, Lemon, Persian, pickling—cucumbers are a prolific summer crop that can become bitter if the weather turns cold. Choose firm, green cucumbers without yellowing, shriveling, or soft spots. Their high water content makes cucumbers somewhat perishable, so don't buy more than you can use within a few days, and keep them in the refrigerator, lightly wrapped in paper towels.

GREEN BEAN SALAD

with Blackberries and Creamy Sweet Onions

ADAM SAPPINGTON, CHEF/CO-OWNER, THE COUNTRY CAT DINNERHOUSE & BAR

This salad contains a medley of summer colors and flavors, and pleasing textures: soft, warm blackberries; crunchy green beans; creamy sweet onions; and toasty almonds. The vinaigrette can be made up to three days ahead and is delicious on all kinds of summer sandwiches and salads, or as a dip for veggies and potato chips. You'll end up with about one and one-half cups, which should be enough to explore the options.

Makes 4 to 6 servings

1. In a wide sauté pan with a tight-fitting lid, warm 2 table-spoons of the oil over medium-high heat. When the oil is hot, add the onions with 1 teaspoon of the salt and toss to coat. Reduce the heat to medium-low, cover the pan, and continue cooking until the onions give up their moisture, about 7 minutes. Remove the lid and continue to cook, stirring the onions occasionally so they cook evenly without browning. Remove the pan from the heat when the moisture has evaporated and the onions are translucent, about 4 minutes. Transfer them to a bowl to cool completely.

2. Meanwhile, bring a large pot of generously salted water to a boil over high heat. Fill a large bowl with cold water and several handfuls of ice cubes, and put a colander in the sink. When the water comes to a rolling boil, add the green beans and cook for 2 minutes. Drain into the colander and immediately plunge the beans into the ice water. When they are completely cool, drain the beans and set them aside to dry.

3. Put the vinegar in a large nonreactive bowl. Slowly drizzle in the remaining oil while whisking, followed by the sour cream. Add the thyme and the remaining 1½ teaspoons of salt. Season to taste with pepper. Stir in the cooled onions and set the vinai-grette aside for 15 minutes or refrigerate for up to 3 days to allow the flavors to combine and develop.

4. To serve, toss the beans with enough vinaigrette to coat them generously. Arrange half of the beans on a large platter and top with 1 cup of the blackberries and ¼ cup of the almonds. Repeat with the remaining ingredients and serve immediately.

¼ cup plus 2 tablespoons extra-virgin olive oil, divided

1 medium sweet onion, such as Walla Walla, cut in ½-inch dice (about 1¾ cups)

2½ teaspoons fine sea salt, divided

1 pound (about 5 cups) fresh green beans, trimmed

¼ cup apple cider vinegar

¼ cup sour cream

1½ tablespoons fresh thyme leaves, coarsely chopped

Freshly ground black pepper

1 pint (2 cups) blackberries

½ cup lightly toasted sliced almonds

FIRE-ROASTED ARTICHOKES
with Lemon Aioli

PATREECE DENOBLE, OWNER, DENOBLE FARMS

Located in Tillamook on the Oregon coast, DeNoble Farms is a small family-owned and operated farm. The area's mild weather and rich, fertile soil combine to create the perfect conditions for artichokes. They specialize in a beautiful purple Italian variety called Violetta, which is usually available at the farmers' market between June and October.

Some of the best things in life take a little bit of work, and artichokes are no exception. Beneath their jacket of leathery petals and prickly thorns lies the prized, succulent heart. There's pleasure in getting there, peeling away the leaves one by one and dragging them through sweet butter and sea salt, or spike the lemon aioli recipe below with herbs to complement those in your marinade.

Makes 6 servings

1. Bring a large pot of generously salted water to a boil over medium-high heat. Cut the artichokes in half lengthwise and use a spoon to scoop out and discard their fuzzy, inedible chokes (the smaller, prickly purple leaves in the center). When the water comes to a boil, add the artichokes and 3 of the garlic cloves, smashed with the back of a knife. Reduce the heat to a gentle boil and cook the artichokes until they begin to soften, but aren't yet fully tender, about 10 minutes, depending on size. Using a slotted spoon, remove the artichokes and set them aside on a plate lined with paper towels to drain.

2. Meanwhile, prepare a medium-hot fire in a charcoal grill or preheat a gas grill on medium-high.

3. Finely chop the remaining garlic clove. In a small bowl, stir together the oil, chopped garlic, garlic chives, parsley, and shallot. Lay the artichokes on a baking sheet and brush them with the oil mixture on both sides. Season them to taste with salt and pepper.

4. When the grill is hot, oil the grill grate and lay the artichokes, cut side down, directly on the grate. Grill them for 5 minutes, then turn them over and baste with the oil mixture, filling the cavity in the middle. Grill them until lightly crispy and charred, 3 to 5 more minutes. Remove the artichokes to a platter and serve them alongside the lemon aioli for dipping.

6 extra-large Violetta or other artichokes

4 garlic cloves, divided

½ cup extra-virgin olive oil

3 tablespoons finely chopped garlic chives

3 tablespoons chopped parsley

2 tablespoons finely chopped shallot

Kosher salt and freshly ground black pepper

Lemon Aioli (recipe follows)

CONTINUED

LEMON AIOLI

Makes about 2 cups

1 medium lemon

1 large (or 3 small) garlic cloves

1 teaspoon fine sea salt, divided

1 teaspoon Dijon mustard

2 egg yolks

1⅓ cup canola oil or other neutral-flavored oil

⅔ cup extra-virgin olive oil

White pepper

1. Zest and juice the lemon, setting each aside. Trim the end of the garlic clove(s) and cut in half lengthwise. Lay the garlic halves flat-side down on the cutting board. Lay the side of the blade of a chef's knife on each clove and smash it with the heel of your palm. Add 2 teaspoons of the lemon zest to the garlic, sprinkle with ½ teaspoon of the salt, and coarsely chop the mixture, then pile it on one side of the board. Hold the knife at a 30-degree angle to the board and drag it over the mixture, lightly scraping it across the surface of the board. Pile it up again, sprinkle with the remaining ½ teaspoon salt, and scrape again. Repeat until you have a smooth paste.

2. In a small bowl, whisk together the garlic paste, half of the lemon juice, mustard, and egg yolks. Combine the oils in a measuring cup with a spout and, whisking continuously, slowly drizzle in the oil, gradually increasing to a slow, steady, thin stream. If the mixture appears to be separating, stop adding the oil and whisk vigorously to re-emulsify. After adding all of the oil, adjust the seasoning as necessary with more lemon juice and salt, and season to taste with the pepper. If the consistency is too thick, stir in a little water, 1 tablespoon at a time, until it is slightly looser than mayonnaise.

LARGE PLATES

Herbed Tomato and Summer Squash
Galettes with Goat Cheese 82

Sweet Corn Chowder 87

Smoked BBQ Beef Brisket 89

Grilled Lamb Burgers with Feta, Garlic, and Pine Nuts 91

Zucchini Noodles with Dandelion Pesto 92

Peach and Pancetta Pizza with Arugula 93

Olive Oil-Poached Albacore with Summer
Beans and Pickled Peppers 96

HERBED TOMATO AND SUMMER SQUASH GALETTES
with Goat Cheese

SARAH CURTIS-FAWLEY, CULINARY DIRECTOR/OWNER, PACIFIC PIE COMPANY

Savory galettes are perfect picnic fare—a simple, tasty alternative to a classic quiche, less homey than a pie, and less fussy than a tart. A main-course option that showcases the season's offerings all wrapped up in a buttery, free-form crust, galettes can be filled with countless vegetable, meat, and cheese combinations. Because they are improvisational, use this recipe as a template and seek out the market's most stunning produce for the filling. Swap the summer squash for winter squash or pumpkin in cold weather. Kale, Swiss chard, or mustard greens stand in nicely for the tomato. Replace the goat cheese with any soft crumbly cheese you prefer.

The pastry dough is also excellent for sweet or savory hand pies and your favorite pie recipes. If you don't have time to make your own pastry, substitute a high-quality puff pastry.

Makes 8 individual six-inch galettes

3 small summer squash or zucchini (about 1½ pounds), cut into ½-inch cubes

3 tablespoons extra-virgin olive oil, divided

1¼ teaspoons fine sea salt, divided

1¼ teaspoons freshly ground black pepper, divided

1 tablespoon unsalted butter

2 medium yellow onions, thinly sliced

1 pound fresh tomatoes, cut into ½-inch cubes

3 garlic cloves, finely minced

2 tablespoons coarsely chopped fresh herbs, such as basil, parsley, thyme, mint, marjoram, or rosemary

½ teaspoon red pepper flakes

1 tablespoon balsamic vinegar

8 ounces goat cheese

1. Preheat the oven to 375 degrees F.

2. In a medium bowl, toss the squash with 1 tablespoon of the oil, ¾ teaspoon of the salt, and ¾ teaspoon of the pepper. Arrange the cubes in a single layer on a baking sheet and roast them until they are just beginning to brown around the edges, 30 to 40 minutes.

3. Meanwhile, in a shallow, wide sauté pan over medium-low heat, heat the remaining 2 tablespoons of the oil with the butter. Add the onions and cook, stirring occasionally, until deep golden brown, 25 to 30 minutes. Add the tomatoes, garlic, herbs, pepper flakes, vinegar, and remaining ½ teaspoon of the salt and ½ teaspoon of the pepper, and continue to cook until the garlic is fragrant, 3 to 5 minutes. Transfer the contents of the pan to a large bowl to cool slightly before folding in the squash and goat cheese. Refrigerate the filling for 2 hours, or overnight, before forming the galettes.

4. To roll out the pastry, liberally flour a dry work surface. Remove one pastry disk from the refrigerator and break it in half. Gently knead the halves together a few turns or until the dough is pliable. Lightly dust the top of the dough with flour.

5. Using a lightly floured rolling pin, apply pressure down and out as you roll the dough. Push the rolling pin out straight in front of you and across the dough, then lift the dough and rotate it a quarter turn to the right. Continue to roll and turn, always moving your pin in the same direction, and adding flour sparingly if the dough begins to stick to the surface or rolling pin, until it is about ⅛ inch thick. After you've rolled the dough to the desired thickness, mend any tears or cracks by applying a small amount of water to the area—the water will work like glue—or attach small scraps of dough to patch unwanted holes.

6. Use a 6-inch plate or bowl to mark rounds on your pastry, fitting as many as possible and using a sharp paring knife to cut them out. You should be able to get at least 3 dough rounds. Gather the scraps and set them aside. Repeat with the second disk of pastry. Combine both piles of scraps, knead them together gently, and roll them out to cut the remaining 2 rounds. Stack the rounds between squares of parchment paper and refrigerate for 1 hour.

7. To fill the galettes, arrange the rounds on a lightly floured work surface or a sheet of parchment paper. Use a pastry brush or the tip of your index finger to lightly moisten the edge of the dough all around with a small amount of water. Place about ½ cup of the filling in the center of each round and fold the bottom edge up over the filling, allowing the dough to fold over on itself, or pleat, as you lift it. It should pleat 5 to 6 times, leaving you with something resembling an octagon (though it will have more or fewer than 8 sides). Place the filled, folded dough rounds on 2 parchment lined baking sheets 2 inches apart, and refrigerate for 1 hour.

8. Preheat the oven to 375 degrees F.

9. Lightly brush each galette with the melted butter. Bake the galettes until the pastry is deep golden brown, 30 to 40 minutes, rotating the pan halfway through the baking time. Cool the galettes slightly before serving or enjoy them at room temperature.

CONTINUED

1 recipe Pacific Pie Company's All-Butter Pastry (recipe follows)

1 tablespoon unsalted butter, melted and cooled

PACIFIC PIE COMPANY'S ALL-BUTTER PASTRY

Makes pastry for 8 six-inch galettes or 1 nine-inch double-crust pie

2⅔ cups unbleached all-purpose flour

1 teaspoon fine sea salt

¼ teaspoon baking powder

1 cup (2 sticks) unsalted butter, cold, cut into ½-inch cubes

1 tablespoon apple cider vinegar

1. In a large metal mixing bowl, combine the flour, salt, and baking powder and chill the mixture in the freezer for 15 minutes. (The bowl can also be covered with plastic wrap and left in the refrigerator overnight.) Working with well-chilled ingredients at every stage of mixing is critical to a tender, flaky pie crust. If your butter gets warm, it will melt into the flour leaving you with a tough, crispy crust. Don't be tempted to skip this step!

2. When you're ready to make the pastry, fill a liquid measuring cup with a spout with ice water and keep it handy. Add the cold butter pieces to the chilled flour and toss to coat thoroughly. Using your hands or a pastry cutter, break up the butter pieces without squeezing or kneading the butter into the flour. The idea is to keep some larger butter pieces (no bigger than a pea) to ensure a flaky crust. Continue to break up the butter, working it gently into the flour until the mixture is pale yellow and the butter pieces are pea-size and smaller.

3. Add ⅓ cup of the ice water (without the ice) and the vinegar. Gently toss the flour with your fingertips, resisting the temptation to squeeze or knead it. When the liquid is absorbed, gather a small handful of pastry (about the size of a golf ball) and squeeze together gently. If it crumbles, add 1 tablespoon of water at a time until the pastry holds together. It should feel slightly dry—the flour will continue to hydrate while it is resting, so don't add too much liquid.

4. Divide the pastry into 2 equal portions, wrap each one in plastic wrap, and refrigerate for at least 3 hours or overnight. The dough can be frozen for up to 1 month when well wrapped; defrost it in the refrigerator for 24 hours before using.

SWEET CORN CHOWDER

VICKI HERTEL, CO-OWNER, SUN GOLD FARM

On those chilly, late-summer evenings that remind us fall is around the corner, Vicki's mom used to make this delicious chowder for dinner. Fast and filling—two criteria that dinner on a working farm must meet—the chowder doesn't need anything extra, but you could add smoked salmon or another smoked fish, bacon, herbs, roasted chilies, or cheddar cheese. Serve it with a salad and good crusty bread.

Even if getting dinner on the table immediately is your first priority, reserve the cobs for corn stock—you can simmer it while you finish the chowder (see Easy Corn Stock below for the recipe).

Makes 6 to 8 servings

1. Put the potatoes in a large saucepan with generously salted cold water to cover and bring the water to a boil over medium-high heat. Reduce the heat to a gentle simmer and cook the potatoes until they are almost fork-tender, about 10 minutes.

2. Meanwhile, in a sauté pan over medium heat, heat the oil. Add the onions and cook, stirring occasionally, until they are translucent, about 5 minutes. Reserve 1 cup of the potato water and drain the potatoes. Return them to the pot with the reserved water, warm onions, milk, and corn kernels. Heat the milk through over medium-high heat, then reduce the heat and simmer until everything is hot and the flavors have blended, about 5 minutes. Stir in the butter until it melts, and season to taste with salt and pepper.

1 pound (8 to 10 small) Yukon Gold potatoes, cut in 1-inch cubes

3 tablespoons extra-virgin olive oil

1 medium sweet onion, cut in ½-inch dice (about 1½ cups)

3 cups whole milk or half-and-half

4 ears sweet corn, kernels cut from the cob (about 4½ cups), cobs reserved for Easy Corn Stock (see below)

3 tablespoons unsalted butter

Kosher salt and freshly ground black pepper

EASY CORN STOCK

Use corn stock to make risotto and soups, or in any recipe that calls for vegetable stock. Break the **reserved corn cobs** from the Sweet Corn Chowder recipe (see above) in half and put them in a large pot with 8 cups of water. Add **4 peppercorns, 2 sprigs parsley, 1 small thyme sprig,** and **½ small bay leaf.** Bring the water to a boil over high heat, reduce the heat, and simmer for 45 minutes. Makes about 4 cups stock.

HOW TO CHOOSE AND STORE CORN

Just-picked corn tastes best, but if you can't put the water on to boil while you run out to the field to pick some, what you'll find at the farmers' market is the next best thing. Most farmers pick what they bring to market within twenty-four hours of when you buy it. Unshucked corn will keep in the refrigerator for about one week, but as its sugars convert to starch, it becomes less sweet. It's best to buy what you'll eat over 2 or 3 days.

When choosing corn, look for ears that are plump, with bright-green husks and glossy silk with a dark tip. There's no need to pull the husk back—use your hands to squeeze the ear firmly, working your way from the bottom up. Feel for gaps or spaces to indicate that the kernels are missing or underdeveloped. And if you're looking for a worm (did you know each ear can only have one?), simply pull the silk to the side slightly to look for damage. It's usually easily trimmed off the top of the ear.

SMOKED BBQ BEEF BRISKET

CHRISTINE DECK, CO-OWNER, DECK FAMILY FARM

Though it's the undisputed choice for classic barbecued beef, brisket is one of the toughest cuts on a cow, and it isn't well suited to dry heat–cooking methods. When slow-roasted below 300 degrees F for several hours, however, the economical cut falls apart and becomes tender. There are as many rubs and sauces and types of smoke to choose from as there are barbecue lovers—time is the ingredient that all recipes include. If you can't let the meat sit with the rub and want to cook it right away, it will still be extremely flavorful; just don't skimp on the cooking time.

Makes 10 to 12 servings

1. Rinse the brisket under cold running water, pat it dry with paper towels, and set it aside. In a small bowl, use your fingers to combine the paprika, cumin, salt, cayenne, oregano and black pepper. Rub the brisket all over with the garlic, followed by the rub, making sure to cover all sides. Place the brisket, fat side up, in a low-sided pan to catch any juices. Cover it with plastic wrap and refrigerate it for at least 1 hour, or up to overnight.

2. Remove the brisket from the refrigerator 1 hour before you plan to begin cooking. This is a good time to soak the wood chips, which need to sit covered in cold water for 1 hour. Meanwhile, set a charcoal grill up for indirect cooking, with the coals banked to one side. After 1 hour, drain the wood chips and set them aside.

3. When the grill is ready, add 2 cups of the wood chips to the coals. Place the pan in the center of the hot grate, away from the heat. Place a thermometer next to the meat and cover the grill. Keep the temperature inside the grill between 225 and 250 degrees F by adding more coals and wood chips as needed, checking every 30 minutes or so and adjusting the vents at the bottom of the grill. Cook-smoke the brisket, basting it periodically with the fat and juices in the pan, until it is tender enough to shred with your fingers, 6 to 8 hours.

4. Remove the pan from the grill and allow the brisket to rest for 10 to 15 minutes. Transfer the meat to a cutting board and use a sharp knife to thinly slice it across the grain. Place the sliced meat on a platter and pour the pan juices on top. Serve immediately with your favorite barbecue sauce or as is.

5- to 6-pounds grass-fed beef brisket, with ¼-inch-thick layer of fat

¼ cup paprika, smoked or sweet

1 tablespoon toasted, ground cumin seed, toasted

1 tablespoon kosher salt

2 teaspoons cayenne pepper

1 teaspoon dried oregano

1 teaspoon freshly ground black pepper

1 tablespoon finely chopped garlic

———————————

6 to 8 cups hickory or mesquite wood chips

———————————

Barbecue sauce, for serving (optional)

GRILLED LAMB BURGERS
with Feta, Garlic, and Pine Nuts

RACHEL REISTER, CO-OWNER, REISTER FARMS

Sheep that graze on a mixture of nutrient-dense natural grasses, forage, and legumes (Reister Farms feeds peas to its sheep) produce succulent, tender lamb. Add lamb to your regular grilling rotation if it isn't already: it's quick, easy, and delicious.

Rosemary, mint, marjoram, and oregano are all good matches for lamb. Add them to mayonnaise or a spread for the burgers, use them in a *chimichurri*-type sauce, or add the herbs to the burgers themselves. The combination of marjoram, mint, and feta cheese is particularly pleasing. Serve these burgers with or without buns, and a spinach or kale salad on the side.

Makes 6 burgers

1. In a large bowl, use your hands to gently mix the lamb, garlic, Worcestershire, ½ teaspoon of the salt, and ½ teaspoon of the pepper, breaking up the lamb slightly and distributing the seasonings. Add the feta and pine nuts, mixing just until well combined. Lightly season both sides of the burger with the remaining ½ teaspoon salt and ½ teaspoon pepper.

2. Form the lamb mixture into 6 (1-inch-thick) patties. Heat a grill to medium-high heat (350 to 375 degrees F) and lightly oil the grill. Add the patties, being careful not to crowd them, and cook for 4 to 5 minutes per side, or until an instant-read thermometer inserted into one of the burgers registers 150 degrees F. Let the burgers rest for 5 minutes before serving. (Alternatively, cook the burgers in 2 batches in a large cast-iron skillet. Heat the skillet over high heat for 2 minutes. Add enough oil to lightly coat the pan and continue to heat for 1 minute more. Carefully place the burgers in the pan and cook until a crust forms, 4 to 5 minutes on each side or a total of 8 to 10 minutes.)

2 pounds ground lamb

2 garlic cloves, finely chopped

2 teaspoons Worcestershire sauce

1 teaspoon kosher salt, divided

1 teaspoon freshly ground black pepper, divided

½ cup crumbled feta cheese

½ cup toasted pine nuts

ZUCCHINI NOODLES
with Dandelion Pesto

PAIGE COMMON, CHEF/OWNER, EATIN' ALIVE

Portland is the best possible place to explore and practice a non-traditional diet. Portland Farmers Market in particular has given many of the businesses devoted to alternative diets their start. If you think raw, vegan and gluten-free aren't for you, or will leave you unsatisfied, Paige Common will change your mind. Her company, Eatin' Alive, has been offering delicious, healthy options that inspire eaters to rethink their definition of nutrition since 2010.

Dandelion greens are delightfully bitter, packed full of essential minerals and vitamins, and help to support liver and gall bladder function. One and a half cups of dandelion greens contain more calcium than a glass of milk and more iron than spinach. Even the gorgeous nasturtium flower garnish is good for you!

Makes 4 to 6 servings

1½ cups hazelnuts, divided

1 tablespoon kosher salt

1 bunch dandelion greens
(about 2 cups, loosely packed)

2 garlic cloves

½ cup extra-virgin olive oil

2 tablespoons honey

2 tablespoons freshly squeezed lemon juice (from 1 medium lemon)

4 to 6 medium zucchini
(about 1 per person)

12 to 18 nasturtium blossoms or other edible flowers

1. In the bowl of a food processor, pulse 1 cup of the hazelnuts with the salt until the nuts are finely ground. Transfer them to a small bowl and set them aside. Add the dandelion greens and garlic to the unwashed food processor bowl. With the machine running, pour in the oil, honey, and lemon juice until the mixture is smooth. Add the ground hazelnuts back to the bowl and blend to fully incorporate.

2. To make the zucchini noodles, using a spiralizer, mandoline, or vegetable peeler to peel/spiral the outer layer of the zucchini, discarding the seeded core.

3. To serve, top the zucchini noodles with the pesto. Coarsely chop the remaining ½ cup hazelnuts and use them to garnish the noodles, along with the nasturtiums.

PEACH AND PANCETTA PIZZA
with Arugula

MARK DOXTADER, CHEF/OWNER, TASTEBUD

Mark Doxtader has been hauling his hand-built mobile wood-fired brick oven to area farmers' markets to serve up pizza, Montreal-style bagels, and rustic baked goods for fifteen years.

Though you'd need a wood-fired oven to achieve the blistered crust and irresistible smoky flavor of his pizzas, a (very hot) home oven and a sense of adventure are all you need to make homemade pizza so good you'll crave it on a regular basis. For a vegetarian version of this summer favorite, substitute a similar amount of thinly sliced jalapeño peppers for the pancetta.

Makes 1 fourteen-inch pizza

1. Position a rack with a pizza stone in the center of the oven and preheat the oven to 400 degrees F. (If you don't have a pizza stone, use an inverted baking sheet, but don't put it in the oven yet.)

2. In a medium bowl, toss the peach slices with 1 tablespoon of the olive oil and the salt. Spread them on a baking sheet in a single layer and roast (on the rack above or below the pizza stone) until the slices are slightly softened, about 7 minutes. Remove the peaches from the oven, set them aside, and increase the temperature to 475 degrees F. Dust a peel or a flat baking sheet (without sides) with cornmeal and set aside.

3. In a small sauté pan over medium heat, sauté the pancetta pieces just until they begin to release their fat and crisp very lightly, about 3 minutes. Remove the pancetta from the pan to a plate lined with paper towels to drain.

4. On a lightly floured work surface, roll out or stretch the pizza dough to form a 14-inch round. Transfer the dough to the prepared peel. (You can also form it on a sheet of parchment paper and transfer it directly onto the pizza stone to bake.) Evenly sprinkle the mozzarella over the dough and top with the peaches and pancetta. Scatter small dollops of mascarpone over the top and bake until the bottom crust is crispy and deep brown, and the cheese has melted, 16 to 18 minutes.

5. Meanwhile, in a small bowl, toss the arugula with the remaining 1 tablespoon olive oil and salt to taste. Remove the pizza from the oven and pile the arugula on top. Serve immediately.

2 firm but ripe peaches, sliced ¼-inch thick

2 tablespoons extra-virgin olive oil, divided

¼ teaspoon kosher salt

Cornmeal, for dusting the peel

⅓ cup pancetta, cut in narrow strips

1 (1-pound) ball Tastebud Two-Day Pizza Dough (recipe follows) or other homemade or store-bought pizza dough, at room temperature

1 cup shredded whole milk mozzarella cheese

¼ cup mascarpone cheese

3 cups loosely packed fresh arugula leaves

Flaky salt

CONTINUED

TASTEBUD TWO-DAY PIZZA DOUGH

This is a two-day project that can be shortened into one with similarly spectacular results. The easy steps can be completed in large, flexible windows of time, and the fact that you work with the dough when it's cold makes this recipe a casual commitment with an unquestionably delicious payoff. The most important part is to plan ahead.

Makes 2 one-pound balls

¼ teaspoon dry active yeast

1½ cups plus 2 tablespoons tepid water

4 cups unbleached all-purpose flour, plus additional for dusting

2 teaspoons kosher salt

1. In a large bowl, combine the yeast and water and let the two sit until the yeast has dissolved, about 5 minutes. Using a wooden spoon, stir in the flour and salt, mixing just until the ingredients are well combined. (The dough will be quite sticky.)

2. Remove the dough to a clean, lightly oiled bowl or container with a lid, cover it with a clean tea towel, and let the dough rest at room temperature for at least 2 hours and up to 4. When the dough shows early signs of fermentation and begins to bubble and expand, use your hand to fold it over on itself 3 times. (There's no need to remove it from the container. Simply reach a clean hand in, scoop the dough from underneath on one side, and allow it to settle on itself. Rotate the container slightly and repeat 2 more times.)

3. Cover the container and move it to the refrigerator for at least 6 hours and up to 24. During that time, it should double in volume. Once it has doubled, turn the dough out of the container onto a lightly floured work surface. Divide the dough into 2 equal pieces, roll the pieces into tight balls, and place them on a baking sheet or peel lightly dusted with flour. At this point, you can loosely cover the dough balls with a clean tea towel and allow them to come to room temperature, or return them to the refrigerator, covered with plastic wrap, to rest overnight.

4. Bring the dough to room temperature before shaping it; it should be relaxed enough that it stretches easily. To avoid drying it out, keep the dough covered until you're ready to use it.

PIZZA IS ALWAYS IN SEASON

Try adding these toppings to your dough in the order they are listed.

- **SPRING**: Mozzarella, shaved asparagus, morel mushrooms, and shallots, finished with a whole egg cracked on top during the final 3 to 5 minutes in the oven.

- **SUMMER/FALL**: Cilantro pesto, fresh mozzarella, heirloom tomatoes, bacon, and roasted jalapeños.

- **FALL**: Mozzarella, roasted kabocha squash, and pickled peppers, topped with dollops of fresh ricotta.

- **FALL/WINTER**: Mozzarella; roasted apples, leeks, and cabbage; and spicy sausage.

- **WINTER**: Mozzarella, roasted brussels sprouts, caramelized onions, Parmesan cheese, and parsley.

OLIVE OIL–POACHED ALBACORE

with *Summer Beans and Pickled Peppers*

JASON FRENCH, CHEF/OWNER, NED LUDD

When the Oregon albacore season begins, Portland chefs get whole fish from the coast, which they prepare using a range of cooking methods and techniques. Poaching in olive oil is a traditional treatment, but the method is not. It mimics sous vide but without the expensive equipment; all you need are three heavy-duty, plastic one-gallon ziplock bags.

Apply the rub to the tuna the day before you plan to serve the dish; the fish will have the best flavor if it sits overnight with the spices.

Makes 6 servings

1 tablespoon coriander seeds, lightly toasted and ground

1 tablespoon fennel seeds, lightly toasted and ground

1 tablespoon kosher salt

2 pounds Oregon albacore tuna loin, trimmed

¾ cup extra-virgin olive oil

3 sprigs fresh thyme

3 small bay leaves

1½ teaspoons red pepper flakes

FOR THE GREEN BEANS:

1 pound green beans (about 4 cups), trimmed

2 tablespoons extra-virgin olive oil

1 red torpedo onion, peeled and quartered lengthwise, or a small red onion

2 garlic cloves, finely minced

1 cup loosely packed basil leaves

_____

2 cups warm Spiced Hazelnut Milk (recipe follows)

1 recipe Pickled Peppers (recipe follows)

1. In a small bowl, combine the coriander, fennel, and salt.

2. Using your hands, rub the spice mixture all over the tuna loin. Put the tuna in a shallow glass baking dish, cover it with plastic wrap, and refrigerate overnight.

3. The next day, remove the tuna loin from the refrigerator and cut it into 6 equal pieces. Place a large pot in your sink and fill it with warm water; the pot should be full and the water should register 115 degrees F on an instant-read thermometer. Place 2 pieces of tuna next to one another in the bottom of a heavy-duty, plastic 1-gallon ziplock bag. Repeat with the remaining pieces of tuna in 2 more bags.

4. Add ¼ cup of the olive oil, 1 thyme sprig, 1 bay leaf, and ½ teaspoon pepper flakes to each bag and submerge the bags halfway into the warm water to create a vacuum. Push any excess air out and make sure each of the bags is sealed tightly. When all 3 bags are submerged in the pot, add more hot water to bring the temperature back up to 115 degrees F. Let the tuna sit in the water bath until one of the pieces registers 113 degrees F, 25 to 30 minutes. Check the temperature of the water occasionally, adding more hot water if it dips below 115 degrees F. Keep the tuna pieces warm by leaving them in their bags in the water.

5. Meanwhile, make the green beans while the tuna is poaching. Bring a medium pot of generously salted water to a boil over high heat. Fill a large bowl with cold water and a handful of ice cubes, and put a colander in the sink. When the water comes to a rolling boil, add the green beans and cook them

for 2 minutes. Drain them into the colander and immediately plunge the beans into the ice water. When they are completely cool, drain the beans and set them aside to dry.

6. In a small sauté pan over medium heat, warm the oil. Reduce the heat to low, add the onions and garlic, and cook them slowly until the onions are soft, 15 to 20 minutes, stirring frequently. Add the onions to a large bowl with the green beans and basil leaves.

7. To assemble the dish, ladle about ⅓ cup of the warm hazelnut milk in the bottom of each of 6 bowls. Make a bed of green beans in the milk, remove the tuna pieces from their bags, and place each one on top of a pile of beans. Drizzle a spoonful of poaching oil on the tuna and scatter the pickled peppers on top. Serve immediately.

SPICED HAZELNUT MILK

Makes about 3 cups

1. Place all the ingredients in a large bowl. Cover with 3 cups of water and let the mixture sit overnight at room temperature, covered with a dish towel.

2. Pour the contents of the bowl into a blender and blend until very smooth, 3 to 4 minutes. Strain the milk through a fine-mesh sieve into a small saucepan. Heat the hazelnut milk over medium-low heat and keep it warm until you are ready to serve the tuna.

2 cups hazelnuts

1 tablespoon fennel fronds

1 tablespoon chive blossoms

2 tablespoons curry powder

1 tablespoon kosher salt

PICKLED PEPPERS

Makes about ½ cup

1. Put the peppers in a small glass bowl. In a nonreactive saucepan over medium heat, bring the vinegar to a boil with the sugar, salt, and pepper flakes. Pour the hot liquid over the peppers, cover lightly, and leave overnight at room temperature to pickle.

1 Jimmy Nardello or similar sweet Italian frying pepper, halved, seeded, and thinly sliced

½ cup champagne vinegar or white wine vinegar

2 tablespoons sugar

2 teaspoons kosher salt

1 teaspoon red pepper flakes

SWEETS, SIPS, AND CONDIMENTS

FROMAGE BLANC–PLUM CHEESECAKE

MIO ASAKA, BAKER/OWNER, MIO'S DELECTABLES (RECIPE TRANSLATED BY MAMI RASKE)

Freshly made plum confiture (preserves, or fruit suspended in syrup) is swirled into half of the creamy filling, and topped with the remainder to create a layered effect. Use the same recipe to make the preserves with other seasonal stone fruit and berries. Adjust the amount of sugar according to the sweetness of your fruit.

Makes 1 eight-inch cake

1. Preheat the oven to 350 degrees F.

2. Grind the graham cracker crumbs in the bowl of a food processor or place them in a ziplock bag and use a rolling pin or wine bottle to crush them until the crumbs are the size of sesame seeds. Add 1 tablespoon of melted unsalted butter if you use store-bought graham crackers.

3. Evenly distribute the crumbs over the bottom of an 8-inch springform pan, using the bottom of a glass to press them down. Bake for 5 minutes, remove the pan from the oven, and press the crumbs down again. (The heat softens the butter in the crackers, allowing them to come together to make a dense crust.) Return the pan to the oven for 5 more minutes before removing it and setting the crust aside to cool.

4. In the bowl of a stand mixer fitted with the paddle attachment, mix the cream cheese on low speed until it is soft and smooth, without lumps. Add the sour cream, ¼ cup at a time, mixing after each addition until it is smooth and well incorporated and stopping the mixer occasionally to scrape off any cream cheese that has accumulated on the paddle or the bottom or sides of the bowl. Continue to mix until the mixture is airy, 2 to 3 more minutes.

5. Add the confectioners' sugar to the bowl and mix on low speed until well combined. Add the heavy cream in 3 additions, mixing each one well before adding the next. Add the wine.

1 scant cup of Honey Graham Cracker Crumbs (recipe follows) or store-bought

11 ounces cream cheese, at room temperature

¾ cup sour cream

1 cup confectioners' sugar

¾ cup heavy cream

4 teaspoons white wine

2 teaspoons powdered gelatin

1 recipe Plum Confiture (recipe follows)

CONTINUED

6. Remove 1 cup of the cheese mixture to a medium saucepan over low heat to warm slightly; make sure it doesn't boil. Add the gelatin to the pan, and when it has dissolved, take the pan off the heat. Add the rest of the cheese mixture to the pan in 2 batches, mixing with a spatula until smooth.

7. Set aside 1 heaping cup of the filling in a small bowl, and fold in the plum confiture without mixing too thoroughly. Pour the contents of the bowl over the crust in the springform pan and spread it evenly over the crust. Place the pan in the freezer for 15 minutes. Add the remaining filling and refrigerate until firm. Serve cold or at room temperature.

HONEY GRAHAM CRACKER CRUMBS

Makes about 1 cup

⅔ cup unbleached
    all-purpose flour

2 tablespoons plus
    2 teaspoons whole
    wheat pastry flour

¼ teaspoon fine sea salt

⅛ teaspoon ground cinnamon

2½ ounces unsalted butter,
    slightly softened but
    not warm

2 tablespoons plus 1 teaspoon
    packed light brown sugar

2 teaspoons honey

1. Preheat the oven to 350 degrees F and line a baking sheet with parchment paper. In a small bowl, whisk together the flours, salt, and cinnamon, and set them aside.

2. In the bowl of a stand mixer fitted with the paddle attachment or by hand, mix the butter on medium-low speed until it is smooth and without lumps. Add the brown sugar, mixing to fully incorporate, followed by the honey.

3. Add the dry ingredients to the butter all at once, mixing on low speed just until the ingredients are crumbly. Spread the crumbs evenly in a thin layer on the prepared baking sheet. Bake until the crumbs are golden brown, checking frequently after about 10 minutes and removing the pan after 15. Set the pan aside to cool.

PLUM CONFITURE

Makes ½ cup

1. In a small nonreactive saucepan or preserving pot, combine the plums and sugar. Let them sit at room temperature for 2 to 3 hours, or until the plums begin to give up their juices.

2. When the fruit is juicy and the sugar is completely moistened with plum juice, place the pan over medium-high heat and cook, stirring constantly, until the mixture registers 217 degrees F on an instant-read thermometer, 12 to 15 minutes. Remove the pan from the heat, and stir in the lemon juice. The mixture should be thick like jam at this point. Allow the confiture to cool to room temperature.

6 ounces (about 5 small), plums any variety, halved, pitted, and coarsely chopped

¼ cup sugar, or more, according to the fruit's tartness

1 teaspoon freshly squeezed lemon juice

BUMBLEBERRY PEACH PIE

LISA CLARK, OWNER, PETUNIA'S PIES & PASTRIES

When Lisa Clark started Petunia's, her gluten-free and vegan baking business, she knew she would need an irresistible pie to sell at the farmers' market. Inspired by the tremendous local bounty and a desire to include as much of it as possible, this pie was born ("bumbleberry" is an old-fashioned term for mixed berries). Whether you're gluten-free, vegan, or just a fan of pie, this one is sure to please. If you don't have any dietary restrictions, feel free to substitute your favorite pie crust recipe (or Pacific Pie Company's All-Butter Pastry, page 84), butter for the vegan shortening, and equal amounts of all-purpose flour for the millet, rice, and tapioca flours in the streusel topping.

Makes 1 nine- or ten-inch pie

1 cup sugar

¼ cup plus 2 tablespoons cornstarch

¼ teaspoon freshly grated nutmeg

5 cups sliced peaches (about 2½ pounds)

2 cups fresh raspberries (1 pint)

2 cups fresh blueberries (1 pint)

2 cups fresh blackberries or marionberries (1 pint)

2 tablespoons freshly squeezed lemon juice (from 1 medium lemon)

FOR THE STREUSEL:

1 cup hazelnuts, toasted and skinned

1 cup unsweetened shredded coconut

⅔ cup sugar

¼ cup millet flour

¼ cup white rice flour

3 tablespoons brown rice flour

3 tablespoons cup tapioca flour (or tapioca starch—it's the same thing)

½ teaspoon ground cinnamon

1. In a small bowl, combine the sugar, cornstarch, and nutmeg. In a large bowl, gently toss the peaches and berries with the lemon juice and sprinkle the sugar mixture over the top. Gently mix the ingredients together and set aside to macerate for 10 to 15 minutes, or until juicy.

2. Preheat the oven to 350 degrees F.

3. Meanwhile, make the streusel. Put the hazelnuts, coconut, sugar, flours, cinnamon, and salt in the bowl of a food processor. Pulse to chop the nuts into small pieces. Add the shortening and pulse a few times, until the mixture resembles coarse meal. The streusel can also be made by hand if the nuts are finely chopped first and the shortening is well and thoroughly incorporated.

4. Pour the fruit into the pie shell. It will seem like too much fruit for the crust, but the fruit will flatten out as it cooks down. Place the pie on a baking sheet lined with aluminum foil and bake for 30 to 40 minutes. At this point, the juices should be bubbling. Remove the pie from the oven, top with the streusel, and bake until the streusel is golden brown and the filling bubbles thickly from the sides, like syrup, 30 to 40 more minutes. If the juices are thin or watery, continue baking. If the crust and/or streusel gets too dark, loosely cover them with aluminum foil for the remainder of the cooking time to avoid further browning.

5. Remove the pie from the oven and let it cool for at least a few hours, or up to overnight. Serve as is, or with a scoop of your favorite vanilla ice cream.

¼ teaspoon sea salt

¼ cup vegan shortening, such as Earth Balance, very cold, cut into ¼-inch cubes

_____

1 recipe Petunia's Basic Gluten-Free, Vegan Pie Crust (recipe follows)

PETUNIA'S BASIC GLUTEN-FREE, VEGAN PIE CRUST

Makes a single crust for 1 nine- or ten-inch pie

1. In a large mixing bowl, combine the flours, xanthan gum, sugar, and salt until combined. Add the cold butter and shortening cubes and crumble them by hand until the pieces are the size of peas. Drizzle the ice water (without the ice) over the mixture and mix by hand just until the dough comes together and forms a ball. Flatten the dough into a disk and place it between 2 pieces of plastic wrap.

2. Use a rolling pin to roll the dough to ¼-inch thickness and remove the top piece of plastic wrap to expose one side of the dough. Pick up the dough and flip it upside down into a 9- or 10-inch pie plate so that the side with the plastic wrap is facing up. Center the dough in the dish and press gently into the sides and corners of the dish. Peel the plastic wrap off slowly and rejoin any dough that breaks off by pressing gently. Roll the edges under to form a smooth, even edge and use your fingertips to create a fluted edge.

½ cup plus 1 tablespoon white rice flour

½ cup minus 1½ teaspoons brown rice flour

½ cup minus 1½ teaspoons tapioca flour

¼ cup plus 2 tablespoons millet flour

¾ teaspoon xanthan gum

1 tablespoon plus 1½ teaspoons sugar

¾ teaspoon fine sea salt

¼ cup plus 1½ teaspoons vegan butter sticks or spread, such as Earth Balance, very cold, cut in ¼-inch cubes

¼ cup plus 1½ teaspoons organic palm shortening, such as Spectrum, very cold, cut in ¼-inch cubes

¼ cup plus 2 tablespoons ice water

BUTTERMILK PANNA COTTA
with Raspberries and Red Currants

KATE MCMILLEN, OWNER, LAURETTA JEAN'S

Panna cotta is the quintessential summer dessert: a super-simple, barely sweet creamy foil for the season's fresh fruit. Because it requires so little effort and makes an enormously elegant statement, you're likely to find yourself making it throughout the season, to showcase whatever fruit you bring home from the market.

The panna cotta can be infused with other flavors too: lavender, lemon verbena, rose geranium, and basil each add their own fresh, floral notes to the understated cream. For these and other flavors, follow the instructions below, substituting a small handful of the leaves of your herb of choice, or about one tablespoon lavender buds for the vanilla bean. If the flavor isn't as strong as you'd like after the cream has cooled to room temperature, remove the herbs and reheat the ingredients in the pan with fresh herbs.

Makes 8 six-ounce panna cotta

2 cups buttermilk

2 cups heavy cream

¾ cup sugar, divided

1 vanilla bean, split, seeds scraped, and pod reserved

2¼ teaspoons (one ¼-ounce package) powdered gelatin

1 pint (about 2 cups) red raspberries

1 cup fresh red currants

2 tablespoons sparkling dry wine, such as prosecco

1. In a large nonreactive saucepan, combine the buttermilk, cream, ½ cup of the sugar, and vanilla bean seeds and pod. Heat the mixture over medium heat until it is steaming, stirring occasionally until the sugar dissolves and you see bubble start to form around the edges and on top. Remove the pan from the heat before it comes to a boil, cover it, and let the vanilla infuse the cream until its flavor is pronounced, about 30 minutes.

2. Meanwhile, measure 2 tablespoons of cold water into a large bowl and sprinkle the gelatin over the top. Return the pan with the cream mixture to low heat and begin to warm it. After the gelatin sits for 5 minutes, slowly whisk the warm cream mixture into the bowl in a steady stream. Strain the mixture through a fine-mesh sieve into a container with a spout, such as a large measuring cup or a pitcher.

3. Lightly coat 8 (6-ounce) ramekins or small dishes with a neutral-flavored oil such as canola. Evenly divide the cream mixture among the ramekins. Loosely cover the ramekins with plastic wrap and refrigerate them for at least 3 hours, for a soft-set panna cotta, or up to 1 day.

4. Before serving, put half of the raspberries in a small bowl with the currants. In a small nonreactive pan, gently heat the rest of the raspberries with the remaining ¼ cup sugar and the sparkling wine. Once the sugar dissolves and the berries have burst, about 5 minutes, pour the mixture over the berries in the bowl and stir gently. Allow the berry sauce to cool briefly while you unmold the panna cotta.

5. Using a thin paring knife, run the blade around the sides of the dish to loosen the panna cotta. Place a small plate or bowl over the ramekin, flip it over, and shake vigorously to loosen. Spoon some berries around the base of each panna cotta.

BLUEBERRY HAND PIES

with Toasted Hazelnut Ice Cream

HELENA ROOT, PASTRY CHEF, IRVING STREET KITCHEN

Since the women of Irving Street Kitchen have Southern roots, it was only a matter of time before fried pies showed up on the menu. The abundance of summer fruit offers many options for filling the pie dough (executive chef Sarah Schafer's mother's recipe), but Oregon blueberries are the favorite among staff and customers. The recipe calls for cooking some of the berries until they are saucy and folding the rest in raw. Frozen berries work just as well if you let one cup thaw slightly to start the filling. And since you can't have pie without ice cream, look no further than local hazelnuts for an unbeatable match. The ice cream custard must chill overnight before it can be frozen, so plan accordingly.

The pies fry up best when they have been assembled and frozen beforehand. Make some now and store the rest in ziplock bags in the freezer for whenever you get a hankering.

Makes 24 small hand pies

4 cups fresh or frozen blueberries, divided

¾ cup sugar

3 tablespoons cornstarch whisked with 3 tablespoons water

1½ teaspoons finely chopped lemon zest

¼ teaspoon ground mace

Pinch of fine sea salt

1 recipe Hand Pie Dough (recipe follows)

FOR THE CINNAMON SUGAR:

2 cups sugar

1 tablespoon ground cinnamon

¼ teaspoon ground mace

1 teaspoon salt

———————————

Soy or vegetable oil, for frying

1 recipe Toasted Hazelnut Ice Cream (recipe follows), for serving

1. In a nonreactive saucepan over low heat, combine 1 cup of the blueberries with the sugar. Using a wooden spoon, stir the mixture vigorously and frequently, crushing some of the berries with the back of the spoon, until the berry juices begin to bubble and the sugar has dissolved, about 5 minutes. Add the cornstarch slurry to the pan and increase the heat to medium high. Bring the contents of the pot back to a boil, stirring continuously to prevent the filling from scorching. Continue to cook for 1 minute after the mixture comes to a boil, then remove the pan from the heat and scrape the contents into a large bowl. Stir in the remaining 3 cups blueberries, the lemon zest, mace, and salt, loosely cover the bowl, and refrigerate the filling to cool completely.

2. To roll out and cut the hand pies, begin by removing 1 disk of dough from the refrigerator and, using as little flour as possible, lightly flour a dry work surface and roll the dough ⅛ inch thick. Use a 4-inch round cutter to stamp out circles. Transfer the dough circles to a baking sheet, cover it with plastic wrap, and refrigerate until all three disks of dough have been rolled and cut. Reroll any dough scraps from one disk by adding them to the next.

3. Assemble the pies 6 at a time. Arrange 6 rounds on a piece of parchment paper or lightly floured work surface. Put 1 tablespoon of filling in the center of each and, using your index finger

or a small brush, lightly moisten the outside edge of the rounds with cold water. Fold the dough over the filling, lightly pinching the edges together before using a fork to crimp them firmly closed. Transfer the hand pies to a baking sheet lined with parchment paper and freeze them for at least 3 hours. Transfer any pies you don't plan to fry right away to a ziplock freezer bag.

4. To make the cinnamon sugar, in a wide, shallow bowl, combine the sugar, cinnamon, mace, and salt. Set the cinnamon sugar aside while you fry the pies.

5. To fry the hand pies, heat the oil in a tabletop fryer until it registers 330 degrees F, or heat a pot with 2 to 3 inches of oil on the stove until it reads 330 degrees F on an instant-read thermometer. Fry the pies a few at a time until they are lightly browned, 2½ to 3 minutes per side, or about 5 minutes total. Remove the pies to a plate lined with paper towels to drain. When they have drained, add the warm hand pies to the cinnamon sugar and toss to coat thoroughly. Repeat until all of the pies are fried and coated with sugar. Serve warm with a scoop of toasted hazelnut ice cream.

HAND PIE DOUGH

Makes enough dough for 24 small handpies

1. In the bowl of a stand mixer fitted with the paddle attachment, mix the flour, shortening, and salt on low speed until they are crumbly. Stop mixing before they come together to form a cohesive ball of dough. Add the cold water and mix just until combined. The dough will form a ball around the paddle and look like other pie dough.

5 cups all-purpose flour

1½ cups vegetable shortening

2 teaspoons kosher salt

1 cup plus 3 tablespoons
   cold water

2. Divide the dough into three disks, wrap each one with plastic wrap, and refrigerate them for at least 30 minutes, or up to overnight. If you make this dough more than one day in advance, wrap it tightly and store it in the freezer to prevent oxidization and discoloration—it will keep up to 3 months. Defrost overnight in the refrigerator.

CONTINUED

Summer

TOASTED HAZELNUT ICE CREAM

Makes about 1 quart

1. Preheat the oven to 275 degrees F.

2. Spread the hazelnuts in a single layer on a baking sheet with sides and toast them until the nuts are aromatic and golden brown, about 20 minutes. Set them aside to cool slightly. Once they are cool enough to handle, place a handful of nuts in a clean kitchen towel and gently rub them together to remove as much of the skin as possible. Repeat with the rest of the nuts. When the nuts have been skinned, finely chop them by hand or pulse them in the bowl of a food processor. Be careful not to overprocess the nuts; you don't want to make a paste.

3. Fill a large bowl with ice water, set a slightly smaller metal bowl inside it, and keep it handy while you make the custard.

4. In a 2-quart saucepan over medium heat, warm the cream, milk, sugar, corn syrup, salt, and vanilla. Using a wooden spoon or heat-resistant rubber spatula, stir the mixture as it heats, until the sugar dissolves. Add the hazelnuts and bring the mixture to a low simmer.

5. Meanwhile, in a large bowl, whisk the egg yolks together. When the cream mixture has come to a simmer, slowly ladle it into the egg yolks, about ½ cup at a time, while whisking constantly. After you've added half of the hot cream, scrape the yolk mixture back into the saucepan.

6. Continue to cook over low heat, stirring the mixture constantly until the custard coats the back of the spoon, or registers 180 degrees F on an instant-read thermometer. Pour the mixture into the prepared bowl in the ice bath to stop the custard from cooking. When it is completely cool, remove the bowl from the ice bath, cover it with plastic wrap and refrigerate it overnight to chill thoroughly.

7. The next day, strain the custard through a fine-mesh sieve, pressing on the nuts to remove all of the liquid. Freeze it in an ice-cream maker according to the manufacturer's instructions.

1 pound (about 3½ cups) hazelnuts

3 cups heavy cream

1 cup whole milk

¾ cup sugar

¼ cup light corn syrup

¼ teaspoon fine sea salt

½ teaspoon pure vanilla extract

9 egg yolks

CHOCOLATE-APRICOT-HABANERO TRUFFLES

MELISSA BERRY, OWNER/CHOCOLATIER, MISSIONARY CHOCOLATES

Many of Melissa's truffles rely on coconut milk to replicate the mouthfeel of heavy cream—which it does very successfully. Choose the coconut milk with the highest fat content (check the label) and don't skimp! The habaneros' floral notes enhance the delectable combination of apricots and chocolate; adjust the number of chilies according to your tolerance for heat.

The ganache, sealed tightly and refrigerated, will keep for up to two weeks. The finished truffles will keep 3 to 4 months in an airtight container in a cool, dark spot or in the refrigerator.

Makes 4½ dozen truffles

1 cup full-fat coconut milk

⅔ pound fresh, ripe apricots (about 6)

2 to 3 fresh habanero chilies

4 cups (about 1¼ pounds) finely chopped bittersweet chocolate, around 65 percent

Unsweetened cocoa powder, for rolling the truffles

1. Pour the coconut milk into a large nonreactive saucepan over low heat. Use a rubber spatula to scrape out all the fat lining the inside of the can. Slowly heat the coconut milk.

2. Meanwhile, halve, pit, and roughly chop the apricots; you should have about 1½ cups. Put them in the bowl of a food processor. Wearing disposable gloves, wash and dry the habaneros. Cut off and discard the stems, and add the whole chilies to the apricots. Pulse the apricots and chilies together until finely chopped and well blended, stopping occasionally to scrape down the sides of the bowl.

3. Still wearing your gloves, scrape the contents of the food processor bowl into the warm coconut milk. Increase the heat to medium-high and continue to cook at a low boil, stirring occasionally, until the mixture has reduced by about half or measures approximately 1⅓ cups, 20 to 30 minutes.

4. Remove the pan from the heat and allow the mixture to cool slightly before straining it through a fine-mesh sieve into a large, clean pot. Warm the mixture over low heat. When it is hot, add the chocolate in 2 batches, stirring until it melts and resembles frosting—this is your ganache, or the center of the truffle. Pour the ganache into a 1½-quart loaf pan, cover loosely with plastic wrap, and cool in the refrigerator for at least 6 hours.

5. After it has set up, use a scoop or melon baller to form the ganache into 1-inch balls. Roll them in cocoa powder or, for a true truffle, dip each ganache ball in tempered chocolate.

MARIONBERRY FRANGIPANE TART

EMILY STONE, PASTRY CHEF,
AND ALICE SWEENEY, ASSISTANT PRODUCTION MANAGER, PEARL BAKERY

Pearl Bakery's farmers' market stall is lovely. Filled with plates of flaky pastries, baskets brimming with baguettes, and jars of cookies displayed on French blue linens, it's hard to pass it without making a purchase. In the summer months, when there's no more wonderful way to enjoy Oregon's sweet berries than in a tart, the bakers at Pearl make this one. It combines a thin layer of raspberry preserves under rich almond filling studded with fresh marionberries. Substitute blackberries if you can't find them, and try the tart with peaches, apples and mascarpone, or fresh cranberries as the seasons roll by.

Makes one 9-inch tart

1. To make the tart dough, in a small bowl, sift the flour and baking powder together and set the dry ingredients aside. In the bowl of a stand mixer fitted with the paddle attachment, mix the butter, sugar, and salt on low speed until the ingredients are well combined, but not fluffy (beating in too much air will cause the tart shell to bubble). Scrape down the bottom and sides of the bowl with a spatula and add the egg, mixing just to combine. Add half of the dry ingredients and mix just to combine. Add the orange juice and vanilla, mix to combine, and add the remaining dry ingredients, mixing until the dough starts to come together into a ball.

2. Turn the dough out onto a lightly floured work surface and shape it into a disk not more than 1 inch thick. Wrap the disk with plastic wrap and refrigerate it for at least 1 hour or as long as overnight.

3. To assemble the tart, remove the dough from the refrigerator. On a lightly floured work surface, roll the dough into a 10- to 11-inch circle approximately ⅛ inch thick. Carefully transfer the dough to a 9-inch fluted, false-bottom tart pan and gently press it into the bottom. By placing your thumb along the top edge as you press the dough into the sides, you can trim any excess dough while keeping the top edge flat. (The top edge should be approximately ¼ inch thick.) Use a fork to prick the dough on the bottom of the pan. Freeze the tart shell until it is firm, about 15 minutes. Preheat the oven to 350 degrees F.

FOR THE TART DOUGH:

1⅓ cups cake flour

⅛ teaspoon baking powder

1 cup (2 sticks) unsalted butter, at room temperature

¼ cup sugar

⅛ teaspoon fine sea salt

1 egg

1¾ teaspoons freshly squeezed orange juice

¾ teaspoon pure vanilla extract

———————————

1 cup almond meal or finely ground toasted almonds

¾ cup cake flour

½ cup (1 stick) unsalted butter, at room temperature

½ cup sugar

1½ teaspoons finely chopped lemon zest

1 egg

1 egg yolk

⅛ teaspoon pure vanilla extract

¼ cup raspberry preserves

CONTINUED

Summer

4. When the tart shell is firm, remove it from the freezer and line the inside with a piece of aluminum foil that has been lightly coated with cooking spray and is large enough to overhang the pan. Press the foil smoothly against the bottom and sides of the shell and wrap it over the edge of the pan so that the entire shell is covered. Fill the shell with beans or pie weights and place it on a baking sheet.

5. Bake the shell for 20 minutes, remove it from the oven, and let it sit for 10 minutes. Carefully pull the corners of the aluminum foil straight up and away from the edges of the tart shell leaving the foil and weights sitting in the middle, but not touching the sides. Let the shell cool for 5 more minutes before removing the foil and the weights completely. Return the shell to the oven for 5 more minutes, then remove it and set the shell aside to cool completely. Leave the oven on.

6. To make the filling, put the almond meal in a small bowl, sift the cake flour on top, stir them together, and set the bowl aside. In the bowl of a stand mixer fitted with the paddle attachment, beat the butter, sugar, and lemon zest on medium speed until light and pale. Thoroughly scrape down the sides of the bowl and add the egg, mixing it in completely. Add the egg yolk and vanilla and mix until fully combined and fluffy. Reduce the speed to low and mix in the dry ingredients, or fold them in by hand, until they are fully combined and the almond mixture is smooth.

7. Spread the raspberry preserves across the bottom of the tart shell. Scrape the almond mixture from the mixer bowl into the shell and distribute it evenly with a spatula. Gently press the marionberries halfway down into the mixture, spacing them evenly around the tart. Sprinkle the crushed almonds evenly over the top.

8. Bake the tart in the middle of the oven until the center is set and the edges have browned, 35 to 40 minutes. Let the tart cool to room temperature before removing it from the pan. Lightly sprinkle the top of the tart with confectioners' sugar just before serving.

1 pint (about 2 cups) fresh marionberries

¼ cup lightly crushed blanched almonds (optional)

Confectioners' sugar, for serving

WATERMELON-JALAPEÑO-VODKA SIPPER

EVA SIPPL, OWNER, EVA'S HERBUCHA

A friend of Eva's brought the inspiration for this cocktail back from his trip to Thailand. The original recipe called for 7Up, but Eva saw an opportunity to substitute her kombucha for a tangier, tastier, better-for-you tipple that refreshes on a summer evening and purportedly prevents hangovers for those who are prone to suffering nasty morning-after headaches.

Makes 4 to 6 servings

1 medium seedless red watermelon

1 small jalapeño pepper, seeded and thinly sliced

¾ cup good-quality small-batch vodka such as Bull Run, House Spirits, or New Deal

Kombucha, as a mixer (see DIY Kombucha, opposite page, if you want to make your own)

1. Cut the top third off the watermelon and reserve it for another use. Put the remaining melon in an appropriately sized bowl with sides that will hold it upright and support its weight. Use a large spoon to scoop out the flesh and set it aside in a large bowl.

2. Put the jalapeños, vodka, and some of the watermelon flesh in the watermelon "punch bowl." Top it off with kombucha (the amount will vary depending on the size of your melon), stir everything together, and refrigerate the melon for 4 to 5 hours to allow the flavors to combine.

3. Serve with straws and long-stemmed spoons for scooping out the watermelon pieces.

SUNGOLD TOMATO AND GIN ZINGER

HOUSE SPIRITS DISTILLERY

The unexpected combination of gin and sweet Sungold tomatoes is wonderfully refreshing and likely to earn a spot in your summertime cocktail rotation. This guaranteed crowd-pleaser blows everyone away with its deliciousness!

Makes 1 cocktail

1. In a cocktail shaker or a pint glass, muddle 4 of the tomatoes. Add the gin, lemon juice, simple syrup, and salt, fill the glass with ice, and shake vigorously. Strain into a chilled cocktail glass garnished with the remaining tomato on the rim.

5 Sungold tomatoes, divided

1½ ounces small-batch gin, such as Aviation American

½ ounce (1 tablespoon) freshly squeezed lemon juice

½ ounce simple syrup, or 1 tablespoon agave nectar plus 1 tablespoon water

Pinch of kosher salt

DIY KOMBUCHA

We brew our own beer (sometimes from hops we've grown), roast our coffee beans, and faithfully feed our (vinegar) mothers and (bread) starters—no wonder Portland DIYers who have acquired a taste for kombucha, the fizzy health drink, are making it at home.

Kombucha is a fermented beverage made by adding a SCOBY (an acronym for "symbiotic colony of bacteria and yeast," which initiates the fermentation) to tea (most commonly a mix of green and black, though either can be used alone) and sugar (from sources including fruit, honey, and sugarcane). The SCOBY eats the sugar and the tea's tannic acids and caffeine to create a cocktail of microorganisms that continue to grow and reproduce much like a bread starter. Like kefir and other cultured foods, kombucha is a good source of the beneficial bacteria that help heal and maintain gut health.

For homemade kombucha, brew about 1 gallon of oolong, green, or black tea (start with 2 tablespoons of tea leaves and add up to 4 tablespoons total, or enough to make a strong brew), add 1 cup of sugar, and pour the mixture into a gallon glass jar. Allow the tea to cool to room temperature, add a kombucha culture and starter liquid (purchase them online, at home-brewing stores, or at Eva's Herbucha in Portland), and let everything ferment at room temperature for about 1 week. Make sure to cover the top of the jar with a piece of cheesecloth or a thin dish towel, to prevent fruit-fly infestation.

CANTALOUPE-CUCUMBER JAM
with Vanilla Bean

AMANDA FELT, BUSHEL & PECK BAKESHOP

Melons and cucumbers may seem an unlikely pairing, but they're close cousins in the botanical world. Their muted pastel tones and refreshing complementary flavors come together beautifully in this jam, flecked with aromatic vanilla-bean seeds. Or you could go in another direction this recipe: substitute honeydew for the cantaloupe and fresh mint or jalapeño for the vanilla bean. Persian and English cucumbers are too dry for this recipe; stick with the usual garden—also called American slicing—cucumbers.

Pomona's Universal Pectin is an easy way to make jams, jellies, and preserves with less sugar. Before you start the jam, make the calcium water called for in the recipe—in a small bowl or jar with a lid, combine one-quarter teaspoon calcium powder and one-quarter cup water. This makes enough calcium water for a few batches of jam, or use liquid pectin and follow the manufacturer's recommendation for the ratio of sugar to fruit for adequate thickening.

Makes 4 half-pint jars

1. Sterilize your jars, prepare your bands and lids, and have your canning equipment ready.

2. In a wide, shallow nonreactive pot, combine the cantaloupe, cucumber, 3 tablespoons of the sugar, the vanilla bean seeds and pod, lemon juice, salt, and calcium water.

3. In a small bowl, combine the remaining 3 tablespoons of sugar and the pectin powder and set it aside.

4. Bring the fruit mixture to a boil over high heat. Boil, uncovered, for 1 minute and then add the pectin-sugar mixture to the fruit in the pot while stirring vigorously; the jam should thicken quickly.

5. After the jam sets up, continue to cook for 1 minute. Don't be tempted to boil the jam longer because it looks thin; cooking the jam too long may cause the pectin to break down and your jam not to jell. Taste for sweetness and add more sugar as needed. Remove and discard the vanilla bean pod and pour the jam into the hot, sterilized jars. Process the jars in a water bath for 10 minutes according to the manufacturer's instructions. Let the jars sit in the water 1 minute and remove. Again, overexposure to heat may cause the pectin to break down, so stick closely to the cooking and boiling times.

1 (2½- to 3-pound) cantaloupe cut into ½-inch cubes (about 4½ cups)

12 ounces cucumbers, peeled, halved, and seeded, then cut into ¼-inch cubes to yield 1¼ cups

6 to 8 tablespoons sugar depending on preference, divided

1 vanilla bean, split, seeds scraped out with a paring knife, and pod reserved

3 tablespoons freshly squeezed lemon juice (from 1 medium lemon)

½ teaspoon kosher salt

4 teaspoons Pomona's calcium water

1 tablespoon Pomona's pectin powder

MICHOACÁN-STYLE SALSA FRESCA

NIKKI MARIA GUERRERO, OWNER, HOT MAMA SALSA

Nikki Guerrero makes this salsa—inspired by the classic Michoacán *salsa de chile manzano* frequently served with meat and tortillas—with different varieties of "not-hot habaneros" grown by Grey Horton of Morgan's Landing Farm on Sauvie Island. The chilies have all the uniquely floral and fruity qualities of the notoriously hot habanero without its searing heat. If you can't find "not-hot habaneros," substitute a combination of habanero, Güero, and Fresno chilies; remove the seeds and ribs, but still expect some heat.

Makes 3 cups

1 pound fresh "not-hot habaneros," any variety

1 small sweet white onion, cut into 1-inch chunks

1 cup freshly squeezed lemon juice (from 5 to 6 medium lemons)

1 small bunch cilantro

Fine sea salt

White balsamic vinegar, for seasoning, if needed

1. Stem the peppers and coarsely chop them, either by hand or in the bowl of a food processor. (If you're using hot chilies, wear disposable gloves.) If you use a food processor, pulse the chilies in quick bursts, occasionally scraping down the sides of the bowl, and taking care not to puree them. The finished salsa should have an irregular, chunky texture.

2. Remove the chopped chilies to a large nonreactive bowl and add the onions to the food processor bowl. Pulse the onions like the chilies, in small bursts, to coarsely chop them. Add the onions to the bowl with the chilies. Pour the lemon juice over chilies and onion, loosely cover the bowl, and refrigerate it for at least 1 hour and up to a day.

3. When the chilies have marinated, finely chop the cilantro, add it to the bowl, and season to taste with salt. Taste the salsa: if it needs a bit of sweetness, add some white balsamic vinegar, 1 tablespoon at a time, tasting after each addition. Don't add too much—the flavor of the salsa depends on the strength of the chilies' floral, fruity qualities, so be sure they are dominant.

AUTUMN

FOLLOWING SUMMER'S ASTONISHING PLENTY IS the arrival of autumn: harvest, a return to school, and the anticipation of the dark, damp, and drizzle for which Portland is famous. The gradual approach of the season in the Pacific Northwest means a gentle easing into its rich flavors and cool, crisp temperatures. Wine grapes hang heavy on the vine and turning leaves shower down on market-goers, a confetti of copper and gold, flaming red and ocher. Apples appear in August, to share space with summer stragglers such as nectarines and plums, and summer and winter squash are displayed side by side in market stalls. Such overlap offers the fleeting opportunity to combine ingredients on the cusp between summer and fall, such as corn, chanterelles, and yellow tomatoes.

One day we wake up, see our breath in the air, don flannel and fleece, and decide to embrace the change of season. But given the choice, most of us would draw out the summer as long as possible. Even in the face of autumn's opulence, a taste for the memory of summer persists and encourages us to keep putting food by as we snatch up gourds, gnarly root vegetables, crisp pears, and intensely floral quince.

Success in the kitchen demands that cooks learn new techniques for getting the most from the mature versions of vegetables that linger on. Overripe tomatoes and overlarge zucchini that no longer please when prepared as they were in the summer months shine again when turned into sauce and quick bread. Eggplant, peppers, and tomatoes become caponata, and sweet corn meets potatoes in fall chowder. Cooking methods such as roasting and braising bring out the best from every plant, vine, and stalk.

Like hibernators who indulge before the winter, we sit down to longer, larger meals in autumn. Summer's cold salads and quickly assembled meals become soups and stews that simmer on the stovetop, and the smell of baking perfumes our hair, clothing, and homes.

KIYOKAWA FAMILY ORCHARDS

FERTILE SOILS AND GLACIER RUNOFF around the base of Mount Hood's timberline create unique growing conditions for Kiyokawa Family Orchards, who have been farming in the Hood River Valley for more than a century. Run by third-generation orchardist Randy Kiyokawa, the 135-acre parcel includes European cultivars like Gravenstein apples, planted in the mid- to late 1800s, and four acres of Oregon Tilth–certified cherry and peach trees. Kiyokawa also grows twenty-six pear varieties, as well as plums, pluots, strawberries, blueberries, and several other crops. But most market shoppers know Kiyokawa for their hundred-plus varieties of sustainably produced apples.

Randy's grandfather, Riichi Kiyokawa, was a Japanese immigrant who came to the West Coast to work on the railroad. In 1911 he began farming in Dee, Oregon, six miles from the current family orchard. (The land in Dee is still in the family, farmed by Randy's uncle and cousin.) Fast-forward to 1988, Oregon State University graduate Randy returned to the valley after working in Portland. He apprenticed under his father, Mamoru, and was running the family business four years later.

Since then, Kiyokawa has implemented an impressive range of conservation-oriented practices. They've reduced water consumption by up to twenty-five percent by monitoring soil moisture and watering with micro-sprinklers. Enormous wind machines that pull warm air down to keep the cell walls of early spring blossoms from bursting have replaced inefficient, polluting smudge pots. Using USDA grant money supplemented with their own funds, a handful of the valley's four hundred orchardists purchased a "burn box" to dispose of tree debris with minimal particulate and smoke. Randy also has plans to certify a portion of his apple trees with Oregon Tilth.

His most significant accomplishment is housing the majority of the orchard's workers and paying employees a fair wage. The markets are what made things click for Kiyokawa. In 1999, a friend offered to sell Kiyokawa apples at the markets where he sold his potatoes. After four years, there was enough demand for Randy to have his own booth. He says farmers markets have been a huge part of their success, making their bounty available to an audience of people who enjoy foraging the markets, rain or shine.

Key to Kiyokawa Family Orchards' survival has been the diversification of operations and their response to market demand over the years. They were Hood River Valley's first U-pick orchard and have expanded their offerings to include heirloom apples, cider apples, organic apples, and smaller apples planted for public schools. Randy has longstanding, committed relationships with chefs and bakers he met at farmers' markets and now supplies. In the end, he points out, it all comes back to the market.

SMALL PLATES

Sautéed Escarole with Peppers, Prosciutto, and Pecorino 127

Roasted Fennel and Herbed Mussels in Vermouth and Cream 128

Grilled Lobster Mushrooms with Oregon Walnut Puree 130

Roasted Eggplant Caponata with Cocoa Nibs 132

Golden Beet, Sunchoke, and Treviso Salad 133

Fall Greens with Delicata Squash, Caramelized
Apples, and Bacon 137

Creamy Cauliflower with Dill and Bread Crumbs 139

Autumn Vegetable Soup with French Lentils 140

Crispy, Buttery Smashed Potatoes 143

Traditional Basque Pipérade 144

SAUTÉED ESCAROLE

with Peppers, Prosciutto, and Pecorino

TED WHITAKER, SPLIT RIVER GROWERS

Easily overlooked in a display of radicchio and other colorful chicories, escarole is a mild endive that looks like a gigantic head of lettuce. Quick-cooking, versatile, and nutritious, it has an appealing bitterness that's transformed with a quick sauté, which tames it into a silky-smooth topping or side dish. "Batavian" is a variety that sweetens, like most chicory, when exposed to a light frost.

Makes 4 to 6 servings

1. Have ready a large pot with a tight-fitting lid and a metal colander or steamer basket that fits inside. Fill the pot with several inches of water and set it over medium-high heat. While you wait for the water to come to a boil, remove and discard the tough outer leaves of the escarole heads. Core the escarole and thoroughly rinse the inner leaves.

2. After the water comes to a boil, put the escarole in the colander and place the colander it in the pot. (You may have to steam the leaves in several batches.) Cover the pot, reduce the heat to a gentle boil, and steam the escarole until it is wilted and slightly tender, 2 to 3 minutes. After all of the greens have been steamed, return them to the colander and squeeze out any remaining moisture. Coarsely chop the greens and set them aside.

3. In a wide, shallow sauté pan over medium heat, warm the oil. Add the prosciutto, onions, and garlic, and cook, stirring constantly, until the prosciutto begins to brown slightly and the onion is translucent, about 5 minutes. Add the peppers and artichoke hearts, and sauté for 2 to 3 more minutes. Add the escarole gradually, stirring in the greens until the ingredients are well combined and evenly distributed. Continue to cook until the greens are satiny, 5 to 6 more minutes. Season to taste with salt and pepper.

4. Reduce the heat to low and add half of the bread crumbs and half of the cheese. Stir constantly until the ingredients come together and bind to one another, about 2 minutes. Remove the greens to a serving platter and top with the remaining cheese, bread crumbs, and more pepper to taste.

2 large heads escarole, preferably Batavian

2 tablespoons extra-virgin olive oil

6 to 8 slices prosciutto, finely chopped

1 medium white onion, cut into ¼-inch dice

6 garlic cloves

6 pickled Italian peppers, sweet or hot, finely chopped (about ¾ cup)

1 cup artichoke hearts, cut in half

Kosher salt and freshly ground black pepper

½ cup bread crumbs, divided

1 cup grated Pecorino Romano cheese, divided

ROASTED FENNEL AND HERBED MUSSELS
in Vermouth and Cream

GREG DENTON AND GABRIELLE QUIÑÓNEZ DENTON,
CHEFS/CO-OWNERS, OX RESTAURANT

Mussels are inexpensive, easy to prepare, and plentiful along the Oregon Coast. This recipe has a few more steps than simple steamed mussels, but once you taste the result, you'll be convinced that the few extra minutes is time well spent. The bright, sweetly herbaceous flavor of raw fennel becomes more intensely licorice-y when roasted. In this recipe, it plays a discreet yet critical supporting role, its notes of anise perfectly matched to the savory custard and subtle sweetness of the mussels. Add crusty bread and a salad, and you have a meal for two.

Makes 4 servings

2 medium fennel bulbs (about 1 pound total)

¼ cup extra-virgin olive oil, divided

Kosher salt and freshly ground white pepper

1½ pounds live mussels, washed

1 teaspoon ground piment d'Espelette, Aleppo pepper, or cayenne pepper

2 tablespoons thinly sliced garlic

4 sprigs fresh thyme

⅓ cup vermouth or dry white wine

4 egg yolks

1 tablespoon chopped flat-leaf parsley, for garnish

1 tablespoon thinly sliced chives, for garnish

1. Preheat the oven to 400 degrees F.

2. Reserving 1 tablespoon of chopped fronds for garnish, trim the stalks from the fennel bulbs and the tough base of the root end. Lay the bulb on its side and slice it lengthwise into ½-inch-thick pieces; you should get 5 or 6 slices from each bulb. Lay the slices on a baking sheet, lightly brush both sides with 1 tablespoon of the oil and sprinkle with salt and pepper. Roast the fennel until it is just tender and beginning to caramelize, 25 to 30 minutes. Remove the fennel from the oven and keep warm.

3. To debeard the mussels, pinch the beard (it's found where the two shells meet) between your thumb and first finger, and use a back-and-forth motion to tug it out.

4. Cook the mussels while the fennel is roasting. Warm a medium-size nonreactive lidded pot over medium heat. Add the remaining 3 tablespoons oil, piment d'Espelette, and garlic, stirring frequently to ensure that the garlic cooks evenly and without sticking to the bottom of the pan. When the garlic smells toasty and turns golden brown, add the mussels and thyme sprigs to the pot and give them a stir. Add the vermouth, cover the pot with a tight-fitting lid, and increase the heat to high.

5. Cook the mussels just long enough for them to steam open, 3 to 5 minutes. Once they've opened, remove the mussels from the heat and separate them from the liquid by straining the contents of the pot through a fine-mesh sieve into a smaller pot. Discard any that haven't opened. Strain the liquid one more time to remove any remaining sand or shell fragments. When they are cool enough to handle, remove the mussels from their shells and add them back to the strained liquid in the smaller pot.

6. In a small bowl, whisk the egg yolks for 30 seconds. Set them aside, but keep the bowl and whisk nearby, as well as a heat-resistant spatula. Place the pot with the mussels and their juices over medium heat. As soon as the liquid comes to a simmer, reduce the heat to low. Ladle a small amount of the hot liquid into the egg yolks while whisking. Remove the pot from the heat and slowly add the yolk mixture to the pot while stirring with a heat-resistant spatula. Return the pot to low heat and warm it gently, stirring constantly so that the egg yolks don't scramble or stick to the pot. Continue to stir over low heat until the mixture thickens into a savory custard sauce. Remove the pot from the heat and transfer the contents to a bowl to stop the custard from cooking.

7. To serve, divide the fennel slices among four warm plates, overlapping them slightly. Sprinkle the parsley, fennel fronds, and chives over the mussels and sauce. Taste and check the seasoning, adding more salt and pepper, if needed. Spoon the mussels and sauce over the roasted fennel slices and serve immediately.

HOW TO CHOOSE AND STORE FENNEL

Fennel bulbs should be white and juicy looking, with sprightly green fronds. The round bulbs (the Italians call these "female") are sweeter, while the flat ("male") bulbs have a stronger anise flavor. Fennel keeps well for up to one week in the refrigerator, in an open plastic bag. Use the fronds to garnish salads or to wrap a fish before grilling or roasting.

GRILLED LOBSTER MUSHROOMS

with Oregon Walnut Puree

JOHANNA WARE, CHEF/OWNER, SMALLWARES

Some say lobster mushrooms taste slightly of seafood, but the more likely explanation for the name is their bright-red/orange exterior and creamy white flesh. It is especially common to find them under conifers in the woods of the Pacific Northwest. The mushroom's delicate, salty-sweet flavor is offset perfectly by the crema-like walnut puree and the crunchy, briny shallots and sea beans in this dish.

In the early eighteenth century, English walnuts were a significant commercial crop in Oregon and Washington. Today, the majority of a now-small handful of producers grow a variety known as Persian walnuts, a crop that typically is harvested in the late fall and early winter.

Makes 4 servings

3 tablespoons soy sauce

3 tablespoons extra-virgin olive oil, divided

1 to 2 teaspoons *mitmita*

½ cup Pickled Shallots and Sea Beans (recipe follows)

1 pound lobster mushrooms, cleaned and sliced ½ inch thick

Kosher salt

¼ cup Walnut Puree (recipe follows)

1. In a medium bowl, stir together the soy sauce, 2 tablespoons of the oil, and the *mitmita*. Add the pickled shallots and sea beans and a few tablespoons of their liquid and set aside.

2. Prepare a grill for medium heat. Brush the mushroom slices with the remaining 1 tablespoon oil and season generously with salt. Grill the mushrooms until tender, 3 to 4 minutes per side. Add the grilled mushroom slices to the bowl with the sauce and sea beans and toss to combine.

3. To serve, spread about 1 tablespoon of the walnut puree in a thin layer on the bottom of each of 4 plates. Divide the mushrooms among the plates, placing them on top of the puree. Spoon a little bit of the liquid on top and garnish with the pickled shallots and sea beans. Serve immediately.

ETHIOPIAN MITMITA CHILI SPICE

Mitmita, a fragrant, very hot Ethiopian spice blend, is the country's second most popular, behind *berbere*. You can try asking the chef at your favorite Ethiopian restaurant for some, purchase it at regional Ethiopian grocery stores or online, or make your own by grinding **8 ounces stemmed and seeded dried red chilies**—preferably *piri piri* (also called African bird's eye chili) or Thai—**¼ teaspoon whole cloves; 3 green cardamom pods** and **2 teaspoons fine sea salt** in a mortar, spice grinder, or a clean coffee grinder.

PICKLED SHALLOTS AND SEA BEANS

Makes 1 pint

1. In a clean, dry pint jar with a lid, place the sea beans and shallots. In a nonreactive saucepan over medium-high heat, bring the water, vinegar, sugar, and salt to a boil. Take the pan off the heat and let the pickling liquid cool until it is just warm to the touch before pouring it over the shallots and sea beans.

4 ounces sea beans, cleaned

3 medium shallots, thinly sliced

1 cup water

½ cup rice wine vinegar

¼ cup plus 2 tablespoons sugar

1 tablespoon fine sea salt

WALNUT PUREE

Makes 1¼ cups

1. In a sauté pan over medium-high heat, warm the oil. Reduce the heat to medium-low, add the onions and cook, stirring occasionally, until they are caramelized, 10 to 12 minutes. Remove the pan from the heat and set it aside for the onions to cool slightly.

2. In a blender, combine the warm onions, walnuts, mirin, salt, and water. Blend until very smooth, like peanut butter.

2 tablespoons extra-virgin olive oil

1 small yellow onion, thinly sliced

1 cup walnuts

3 tablespoons plus 1½ teaspoons mirin

1 teaspoon kosher salt

6 tablespoons of water

SEA BEANS 101

Sea beans (aka sea asparagus, saltwort, or marsh samphire), are small, edible succulents of the *Salicornia* genus that grow in protected salt marshes, on beaches, and among mangroves on every continent but Antarctica. They're not related to beans of any kind, but are crunchy and salty when raw, with a snap similar to that of a green bean. The best way to clean them, with their naturally high salt content, is to blanch them for about a minute in plenty of water, after which the fleshy lateral "beans" can be pulled away from the stringy core.

Most of the foragers at Portland Farmers Market sell sea beans. If you can't find them, substitute blanched green beans or asparagus, cut on the diagonal.

ROASTED EGGPLANT CAPONATA
with Cacao Nibs

ROBERT HAMMOND, CHEF INSTRUCTOR, LE CORDON BLEU COLLEGE OF CULINARY ARTS

Caponata is the Italian equivalent of ratatouille, a meltingly soft Provençal stew of eggplant and late summer/early fall vegetables (peppers, tomatoes, and zucchini), cloaked in a syrupy reduction of their communal juices. Cooked *agrodolce*-style (in a sweet-and-sour sauce) with vinegar and sugar, caponata includes other ingredients not found in ratatouille, such as raisins, olives, and capers. This version of the traditional Sicilian relish is made with chocolate in two forms—cocoa powder and cacao nibs—for added depth and mystery. Use young small purple globe eggplants or Asian eggplants that feel firm and heavy for their size. Serve caponata as a side dish, topping for fish, or slathered on crostini.

Makes about 3 cups

1 small eggplant (about 1 pound), ends trimmed, cut into ¾-inch cubes

2 teaspoons kosher salt

¼ cup extra-virgin olive oil, divided

1 medium red onion, thinly sliced

2 tablespoons cocoa nibs

1 teaspoon unsweetened Dutch process cocoa powder

4 ripe Roma tomatoes, peeled, seeded, and coarsely chopped

⅓ cup pitted kalamata olives, coarsely chopped

2 tablespoons capers, rinsed and drained

2 tablespoons golden raisins

2 inner stalks celery with leaves, very thinly sliced

3 tablespoons red wine vinegar

1 teaspoon sugar

Freshly ground black pepper

3 tablespoons coarsely chopped flat-leaf parsley

1. Put the eggplant in a colander, sprinkle it with the salt, and toss to evenly coat it with the salt. Let the eggplant stand for 20 minutes to remove some of its moisture and bitterness. Rinse it under cold running water, drain, and pat it completely dry with paper towels.

2. Preheat the oven to 450 degrees F.

3. In a small bowl, toss the eggplant pieces with 2 tablespoons of the oil and spread them in a single layer on a baking sheet. Roast them for 10 minutes, turn the pieces over, and roast until soft and lightly caramelized, about 10 more minutes. Remove the pan from the oven and set it aside.

4. Meanwhile, in a large lidded sauté pan over medium heat, heat the remaining 2 tablespoons oil. Add the onions, cocoa nibs, and a pinch of salt and cook, stirring, until the onions have softened, about 8 minutes. Stir in the cocoa powder and cook, stirring constantly, for 30 seconds. Stir in the tomatoes, olives, capers, and raisins. Reduce the heat to low, cover the pan, and simmer for 15 minutes.

5. After 15 minutes, increase the heat to medium and add the roasted eggplant, celery, vinegar, and sugar. Cook, stirring occasionally, until the celery begins to soften. Remove the pan from the heat and season the caponata to taste with salt and pepper. Let it cool to room temperature before serving, garnished with the parsley.

GOLDEN BEET, SUNCHOKE, AND TREVISO SALAD

JC MERSMANN, CHEF, GATHERING TOGETHER FARM AND RESTAURANT

Diversity is fundamental to Gathering Together Farm. Certified organic since 1987, the fifty-odd acre farm grows over three hundred varieties of fifty different vegetables and operates a CSA, a farmstand, and a restaurant.

Their sugary earthiness can make beets difficult to pair marry with other ingredients, but this salad gets it just right. Sweet saffron-colored beets and nutty, creamy roasted sunchokes team up with mildly bitter Treviso radicchio and salty olives and cheese to make a salad that embodies the harvest.

Keep in mind that small summer beets can be boiled in twenty minutes or so, and their thin skins will slip right off in your hand. Larger, more mature beets take twice as long and require a small paring knife to remove their tougher skin. The flavors are remarkably similar, however.

Makes 6 servings

1. Remove the beet greens (if attached) and set them aside for another use. Scrub the beets and place them in a pot large enough to hold them in a single layer. Cover them with cold water by 2 inches and bring the water to a boil over medium-high heat. When the water boils, reduce the heat to a simmer and cook the beets until the tip of a small paring knife goes in and comes out easily, about 40 minutes, depending on the size of your beets. Remove the pot from the heat and drain the beets into a colander. When they are cool enough to handle, peel them and cut them in wedges.

2. While the beets are cooking, prepare the sunchokes. Preheat the oven to 425 degrees F. Scrub the sunchokes to remove any dirt, checking carefully between the lobes; they don't need to be peeled. Cut them into ½-inch chunks. In a medium bowl, toss them with 2 tablespoons of the oil and a pinch of salt. Put the sunchokes in a single layer on a baking sheet and roast them until the outsides are brown and they are cooked and creamy on the inside, about 25 minutes. Remove them from the oven and set them aside to cool.

2 bunches golden beets (about 10 small beets)

1½ to 2 pounds sunchokes

¾ cup extra-virgin olive oil, divided

¼ cup red wine vinegar

2 tablespoons finely diced shallot or red onion

½ teaspoon kosher salt

Pinch of sugar

1 tablespoon coarsely chopped flat-leaf parsley

Freshly ground black pepper

3 heads Treviso radicchio, cored and cut crosswise into 1-inch ribbons

1 cup pitted kalamata olives

2 cups diced or crumbled feta cheese

CONTINUED

3. In a small nonreactive bowl, combine the vinegar, shallot, salt, and sugar. Slowly drizzle in the remaining ½ cup plus 2 tablespoons oil, whisking constantly, until the vinaigrette is emulsified. Add the parsley and season to taste with pepper and more salt, if needed.

4. To assemble the salad, in a large bowl, toss the Treviso leaves, beet wedges, and olives with the vinaigrette. Divide the salad evenly among 6 plates and top each with some sunchokes and cheese.

TREVISO

Treviso is a variety of radicchio, shaped like a torpedo and with a more delicate flavor. The tapered heads range in color from pink to dark red, with white ribs. Like radicchio, it can be soaked in ice water for 30 minutes to remove any bitterness, but in this salad, that flavor is welcome.

FALL GREENS

with Delicata Squash, Caramelized Apples, and Bacon

ERIKA REAGOR, CHEF/OWNER, THRIVE SAUCE AND BOWLS

Hearty greens such as kale, mustard, and chicory are necessary to support the weight and bold flavors of the salad's other ingredients: crescents of roasted squash, smoky bacon, sweet caramelized apples and onions, and the slightly sharp acidity of cider vinegar. Search for a mix of the young, smaller leaves of the robust greens rather than the more mature large leaves. If ever a salad smelled and tasted like autumn, this is it!

Makes 4 to 6 servings

1. Preheat the oven to 400 degrees F. Line 2 baking sheets with parchment paper or aluminum foil and set them aside.

2. Cut the squash in half lengthwise and scoop out the seeds with a large spoon. Slice each half into ¼-inch half moons and add them to a small bowl with 1 tablespoon of the oil, the salt, and a few grinds of black pepper. Toss the squash pieces until they're evenly coated, spread them in a layer on one of the baking sheets, and bake them until they are tender and lightly caramelized, but not mushy, 12 to 15 minutes.

3. Meanwhile, lay the bacon slices 1 inch apart on the other baking sheet. Put the sheet in the oven with the squash and cook the bacon for 10 minutes. Rotate the pan front to back and cook the bacon until it is crispy, 3 to 5 more minutes. Remove the bacon to a plate lined with paper towels to drain and cool completely.

4. In a large sauté pan over medium-high heat, melt 2 tablespoons of the butter. When the butter begins to foam and bubble, add the apples and a pinch of salt. Sauté until the apple slices are tender and lightly browned, 5 to 8 minutes. Stir in 1 tablespoon of the vinegar, and remove the apples to a large serving bowl.

1 small (10 to 12 ounces) delicata squash

¼ cup extra-virgin olive oil, divided

½ teaspoon kosher salt

Freshly ground black pepper

4 to 6 ounces thickly sliced bacon

4 tablespoons (½ stick) unsalted butter, divided

1 firm, tart apple, such as Pink Lady, skin on, thinly sliced

3 tablespoons apple cider vinegar, divided

½ large onion, thinly sliced (about 1 cup)

2 teaspoons Dijon or stone-ground mustard

1 teaspoon honey

4 cups hearty greens, such as baby kale, mustard greens, or chicories

CONTINUED

5. Return the sauté pan to the heat, reduce the heat to medium-low, and add the remaining 2 tablespoons butter. When it begins to bubble, add the onions and a pinch of salt. Cook the onions until they're very soft, lightly golden, and sweet-tasting, 20 to 30 minutes. Add 1 tablespoon of the vinegar, toss to coat the onions, and add them to the bowl with the apples.

6. In a small bowl, whisk together the remaining 1 tablespoon vinegar with the mustard and honey. Slowly drizzle in the remaining 3 tablespoons oil, whisking to combine. Season to taste with salt and pepper.

7. To serve, add the greens to the bowl with the apples and onions. Crumble in the bacon pieces and add the squash. Toss the salad with the dressing to coat the ingredients and season to taste with salt and pepper. Serve immediately.

CREAMY CAULIFLOWER
with Dill and Bread Crumbs

TRUDY TOLIVER, EXECUTIVE DIRECTOR, PORTLAND FARMERS MARKET

If the definition of an old family recipe is that it's handwritten, splattered with food, and shared so widely that no one remembers where it originated, then this one from Trudy Toliver's family qualifies. The sumptuous side dish is a popular contribution to Trudy's holiday table or whenever crisp cauliflower is available at the market.

Makes 6 to 8 servings

1. Preheat the oven to 400 degrees F. Butter a 9-by-13-by-2-inch baking dish and set it aside.

2. In a large bowl, toss the cauliflower with 2 tablespoons of the oil. Spread the florets in a single layer on a baking sheet and roast until cooked through, but still firm, 15 to 20 minutes. Remove the baking sheet from the oven and set it aside. Reduce the oven temperature to 350 degrees F.

3. In a wide, shallow sauté pan over medium-high heat, warm the remaining 2 tablespoons oil. Add the onions and sauté until they soften slightly, about 3 minutes. Add the garlic and cook until it is fragrant and the onions are translucent, about 2 more minutes. Remove the pan from the heat and stir in the parsley.

4. Add the roasted cauliflower to the pan, followed by the butter, sour cream, dill, and paprika. Toss to thoroughly combine the ingredients, season to taste with salt and pepper, and turn the contents of the pan into the prepared baking dish. In a small bowl, toss the bread crumbs with the cheese and sprinkle the mixture evenly on top of the cauliflower. Bake until the mixture is bubbly and the bread crumbs and cheese are lightly brown, 15 to 20 minutes.

1 large head cauliflower (about 3 pounds), cut into florets

¼ cup extra-virgin olive oil, divided

1 large onion, preferably a sweet variety such as Walla Walla, cut into ½-inch dice

2 garlic cloves, finely minced

½ cup loosely packed fresh parsley leaves

2 tablespoons unsalted butter, cut into small pieces

½ cup sour cream

1 tablespoon finely chopped fresh dill

1 teaspoon paprika (sweet, hot, or smoked)

Kosher salt and freshly ground black pepper

½ cup fresh bread crumbs

½ cup grated Parmesan, Grana Padano, or Asiago cheese

AUTUMN VEGETABLE SOUP

with French Lentils

DIANNE STEFANI-RUFF, FORMER EXECUTIVE DIRECTOR,
PORTLAND FARMERS MARKET

Hidden beneath celery root's ugly, gnarled exterior is a dignified vegetable, nutty and redolent of celery. A member of the parsley family, celery root (also called celeriac) can be pureed on its own, mashed with potatoes, or used to thicken soup without adding cream.

Here it brings earthy sweetness to a roasted vegetable and lentil soup. This is a forgiving recipe. Substitute or combine root vegetables (carrots, parsnips, yams, rutabaga, etc.), keeping the size of the dice uniform and the overall quantities the same. To make this soup vegan, omit the feta cheese.

Makes 6 servings

2 pounds celery root, peeled and cut into ½-inch cubes

2 pounds butternut squash, peeled and cut into ½- inch cubes

¼ cup plus 3 tablespoons extra-virgin olive oil, divided

2 teaspoons fine sea salt, plus more for seasoning

1 onion, cut into ½-inch cubes

2 leeks, white and light-green parts, cut into ½-inch pieces

1 fennel bulb, cut into ½-inch cubes

2 garlic cloves, finely minced

5 cups vegetable stock, preferably homemade

½ cup dry white wine

2 tablespoons Dijon mustard

2 tablespoons fresh thyme leaves

2 bay leaves

Pinch of red pepper flakes

1 cup French green lentils, rinsed and drained

1. Preheat the oven to 375 degrees F and lightly oil 2 baking sheets.

2. In a large bowl, toss the celery root and squash with 3 tablespoons of the oil and a generous sprinkle of salt. Divide the vegetables between the prepared baking sheets, spreading them in a single layer to ensure they roast and caramelize rather than steam. Roast the vegetables until they are soft and lightly browned, stirring every 15 minutes, for a total of 45 to 60 minutes. About halfway through the roasting time, reverse the baking sheets between the upper and lower racks of the oven.

3. In a large Dutch oven or lidded soup pot over medium heat, warm the remaining ¼ cup oil. Add the onions and leeks with a pinch of salt and sauté until they are soft but not brown, about 5 minutes. Add the fennel and garlic and continue to cook for about 3 minutes. Add the stock, wine, mustard, thyme, bay leaves, pepper flakes, salt, and lentils.

4. Increase the heat to medium-high and bring the soup to a boil, then reduce the heat and simmer it gently, partially covered, until the lentils are tender, about 30 minutes. Watch the lentils closely; you don't want them to break down. When the lentils are cooked, add the roasted vegetables to the pot, along with some additional stock or water if the soup is too thick. Continue cooking for 10 minutes to blend the flavors.

5. Turn the heat off, remove the bay leaves, and add the lemon juice. Season to taste with pepper and additional salt. Adjust the seasoning with more lemon juice, salt, and pepper as needed—the lemon juice is critical to brightening this hearty soup. Ladle the soup into 6 bowls and garnish each with some parsley and feta cheese.

1 tablespoon freshly squeezed lemon juice

Freshly ground black pepper

¼ cup finely chopped parsley, for garnish

Feta or soft fresh goat cheese, crumbled, for garnish

CRISPY, BUTTERY SMASHED POTATOES

GABRIELLE ROSSI, CO-MANAGER, ROSSI FARMS

Joe Rossi's family has been farming in the Portland area since 1800. He and his daughter Gabrielle co-manage Rossi Farms, where they grow eighteen varieties of handpicked heirloom potatoes.

The power of potatoes to satisfy deeply and completely should not be underestimated. The essence of this humble ingredient is most successfully captured with the simplest of preparations. Here, high heat, butter, and herbs transform fingerling potatoes into a crunchy, wildly addictive cross between a French fry and baked potato.

Makes 4 to 6 servings

1. Add the potatoes to a large pot and cover them with cold water by several inches. Generously salt the water and bring it to a boil over high heat. Reduce the heat to a simmer and cook the potatoes until just before they are fork-tender, about 10 minutes. Drain the potatoes in a colander and let them cool for 10 minutes.

2. Preheat the oven to 425 degrees F.

3. Lightly coat a baking sheet with the oil. Evenly space the boiled potatoes out across the sheet and, using a small glass or a fork lightly coated with oil, gently flatten each potato by pressing down until it mashes into an oblong shape. Brush the potatoes generously with 2 tablespoons of the melted butter, sprinkle them with salt and pepper to taste, and bake them for 10 minutes. Add the garlic and herbs to the remaining 2 tablespoons butter, brush the potatoes again, and bake until they are golden brown and crispy, about 8 to 10 minutes more.

2 pounds (20 to 24) fingerling potatoes, any variety, skin on

Kosher salt and freshly ground black pepper

2 to 3 tablespoons extra-virgin olive oil

4 tablespoons (½ stick) unsalted butter, melted, divided

1 teaspoon finely minced garlic

2 teaspoons finely chopped herbs, such as rosemary, thyme, parsley, chives, or a combination

Autumn

143

TRADITIONAL BASQUE PIPÉRADE

LESLIE AND MANUEL RECIO, OWNERS, VIRIDIAN FARMS

In the Basque country, *pipérade* is served as a side dish with tuna or cod, and sometimes as a sauce to accompany chicken or *morcilla*, Spanish blood sausage. Another delicious option is to poach eggs in the *pipérade* during the last few minutes of cooking. If Bayonne peppers aren't available, substitute a sweet oblong Italian variety such as Jimmy Nardello. *On egin!* ("Bon appétit" in Euskera, the Basque language.)

Makes 4 servings

½ cup extra-virgin olive oil

6 red and green piment Bayonne peppers, stemmed, seeded, and julienned

1 large white onion, thinly sliced

5 garlic cloves, crushed

5 red tomatoes about the size of an orange, peeled and chopped

½ teaspoon honey

½ teaspoon piment d'Espelette, Aleppo pepper, hot or smoked paprika, or cayenne pepper

1 bay leaf

Sea salt

1. In a large terra-cotta *cazuela* or nonreactive saucepan with a tight-fitting lid over medium-high heat, warm the oil. Add the peppers, onions, and garlic, and sauté until the onions and garlic are golden brown, about 5 minutes. Add the tomatoes, honey, piment d'Espelette, bay leaf, and salt to taste, and bring the *pipérade* to a boil, stirring occasionally. After it boils, reduce the heat to a simmer, cover the pot, and cook for 20 minutes. Remove the lid and cook until the *pipérade* thickens to your desired consistency, 5 to 10 more minutes. Remove the bay leaf and serve the *pipérade* in the *cazuela*, or transfer it to a serving dish.

LARGE PLATES

Paella Montaña 146

Fresh Shell Bean Minestrone with Parmesan Brodo 149

Wild Mushroom Risotto with Chanterelle Ragoût 152

Dry-Brined Roasted Chicken with Orange,
Paprika, and Smoked Chili Salt 155

Curried Chicken Pilaf with Cilantro Root and Golden Raisins 156

Chanterelle, Corn, and Yellow Tomato Pasta 158

Posole Rojo 160

Chestnut-Tofu Dumplings in Matsutake Mushroom Sauce 162

PAELLA MONTAÑA

SCOTT KETTERMAN, CHEF/CO-OWNER, CROWN PAELLA

Paella is the dish by which Spaniards—cooks and eaters alike—measure one another. As with most national dishes, there are as many variations of paella as there are regions, but the best share several ingredients in common: even heat, the right pan, bomba rice, flavorful broth, and homemade *sofrito*.

This version, from Portland's reigning paella king, is based on the classic paella Valenciana. It brings together the best of fall and some of Scott's favorite Pacific Northwest flavors. Adjust the recipe according to what's available and in season in your region.

Makes 8 to 10 servings

¼ cup extra-virgin olive oil, plus more for serving

1 pound rabbit meat, or chicken thigh meat, cut into 1-inch pieces

Kosher salt

1 pound fresh chanterelles

½ cup thinly sliced dry-cured chorizo

1 pound (about 4 cups) fresh green beans, trimmed

2 cups cooked white beans

1½ cups Sofrito (recipe follows)

1 tablespoon plus 1 teaspoon smoked paprika

2 teaspoons saffron (18 to 20 threads)

9 cups Homemade Chicken Stock (page 157) or store-bought

Freshly ground black pepper

3 cups Bomba rice (see opposite page)

4 sweet red bell peppers, cut into strips

Lemon wedges, for serving

1. In a 17-inch paella pan, or a shallow, wide stainless-steel or aluminum sauté pan with straight sides and a heavy, flat bottom over medium-high heat, heat the oil. When the pan is hot, brown the rabbit pieces on both sides until golden, 1½ to 2 minutes per side. Season them to taste with salt and move the pieces to the edges of the pan. Add the chanterelles, season them with salt, and sauté them, stirring occasionally, until they are lightly browned, about 10 minutes. Add the chorizo and green beans, and stir all of the ingredients together. Add the white beans, *sofrito*, paprika, and saffron. Stir the ingredients again until everything is evenly coated.

2. Add the broth and bring the liquid to a simmer. Season to taste with pepper and taste the broth, adding more salt and pepper as needed. Sprinkle the rice evenly over the top, making sure the grains are completely submerged. Bring the liquid back to a simmer. After 5 minutes, arrange the peppers on top.

3. Cook the paella over medium heat until the rice has absorbed all of the liquid and smells slightly toasted, about 30 minutes. Take the pan off the heat, cover it with aluminum foil, and let the paella rest for 5 minutes before serving it from the pan with lemon wedges and a drizzle of oil.

SOFRITO

Makes about 3 cups

1. In a wide, shallow nonreactive sauté pan over medium heat, warm the oil. Add the peppers, onions, and garlic, and cook, stirring occasionally, until they are soft and translucent, about 10 minutes. Add the tomatoes, season to taste with salt and pepper, and gently simmer over low heat until the mixture has reduced by half, about 10 minutes.

¼ cup extra-virgin olive oil

2 small green bell peppers, stemmed, seeded, and cut in ½-inch dice (about 2 cups)

1 large onion, cut in ½-inch dice (about 2 cups)

4 garlic cloves, thinly sliced

2 cups coarsely chopped stewed tomatoes (from two 14.5-ounce cans)

Fine sea salt and freshly ground black pepper

BOMBA RICE

Rice is the most important ingredient in paella, and Bomba rice is essential to peerless paella. The ancient Spanish rice absorbs three times its volume in broth (versus the normal two) while remaining firm. Look for it in specialty stores, Spanish markets, or online.

FRESH SHELL BEAN MINESTRONE
with Parmesan Brodo

SOPHIE BELLO, CO-OWNER, GROUNDWORK ORGANICS

Gabe Cox began farming on six leased acres planted with a handful of crops, and since then Groundwork Organics has grown steadily. They now farm on 125 acres, sell to several farmers' markets, operate a CSA, and serve numerous Portland restaurants and co-ops.

Traditionally, minestrone is a hearty, thick soup. This lighter version allows the creamy, fresh beans to take center stage. Good *brodo* (broth) is important too, and the addition of Parmesan rinds is an old Italian trick for building big flavor. Parmesan cheese is made in Australia, Argentina, and the United States, but Italy's Parmigiano-Reggiano is considered the finest. Aged between two and four years, its flavor is decidedly more complex than the others. Consider splurging on it for this broth, along with a brightly colored heirloom tomato such as a Marvel Stripe or Persimmon, which gives the broth a lovely golden-orange hue.

Makes 4 to 6 servings

1. In a large pot with a heavy bottom over medium heat, heat the oil. Add the onions, shallot, garlic, and salt, stir to evenly coat with the oil, and cook until the onions soften and color lightly, about 8 minutes. Increase the heat to medium-high and add 5 cups of the broth, the beans, and tomatoes. Bring the soup to a simmer, then reduce the heat to low and cook it for 45 minutes, stirring occasionally.

2. After 45 minutes, add the carrots, celery, and potato, and the remaining 1 cup of broth, if the beans have soaked up too much liquid and are no longer soupy. Simmer the soup over low heat until the vegetables are tender, about another 45 minutes. Season to taste with pepper and more salt, and garnish with freshly chopped basil and gratings of Parmigiano-Reggiano.

CONTINUED

3 tablespoons extra-virgin olive oil

1 small onion, finely chopped

½ shallot, finely chopped

2 garlic cloves, roughly chopped

1 teaspoon kosher salt

6 cups Parmesan Brodo (recipe follows) or Homemade Chicken Stock (page 157) or vegetable stock, divided

2 cups shelled fresh shell beans (see the following page for suggestions on what types to use)

1 large tomato, peeled, seeded, and finely chopped

3 carrots, thinly sliced

2 stalks celery, thinly sliced

1 medium potato, cut into ½-inch cubes

Freshly ground black pepper

Basil or parsley, for garnish

Parmigiano-Reggiano cheese, for garnish

Autumn

149

PARMESAN BRODO

Makes 6 cups

8 cups water

2 tablespoons extra-virgin olive oil

1 rind Parmigiano-Reggiano cheese, about 3 ounces

2 garlic cloves

4 peppercorns

1 bay leaf

1 carrot, cut into chunks

1 stalk celery, cut into 1-inch lengths

Onion trimmings, or ¼ small onion, skin on

1. Add all of the ingredients to a large pot. Over medium-high heat, bring the broth to a simmer, stirring occasionally to prevent the cheese rind from sticking to the bottom of the pot. Reduce the heat to low and cook until the broth has reduced slightly and has a rich, nutty flavor and aroma, 1½ to 2 hours. Strain the broth and store it in the refrigerator for up to 5 days, or freeze it.

SHELL BEANS

Fresh shell beans, such as Borlotti (aka cranberry), Tarbais, and Tongue of Fire, can be found at farmers' markets in Oregon from August through October. Easy to shell and faster cooking than dried beans, fresh shell beans are well worth the effort. You can also freeze raw, shelled beans for use throughout the winter. Note: Like corn and fresh peas, shell beans begin converting their sugars to starch the minute they're picked, so don't let them sit around if you want to capture their natural sweetness.

WILD MUSHROOM RISOTTO
with Chanterelle Ragoût

HENRY OBRINGER, CO-OWNER/HEAD CHEESEMAKER, ANCIENT HERITAGE DAIRY

The Pacific golden chanterelle is Oregon's official state fungus. The wild mushroom grows exuberantly in the Northwest and is among the easiest to find and identify, with its distinctive trumpet-shaped cap, rounded margin, and sunken center. Forked ridges, low and blunt, travel down the mushroom's stalk, in lieu of gills. Its aroma is fragrant, buttery, and tinged with apricots.

The chanterelle ragoût is the crowning glory of this risotto, which also features shiitake mushrooms' satisfying umami and the earthiness of black trumpets, with a drizzle of black truffle oil for good measure. It's decadent and delicious.

Makes 4 servings

¼ cup dried shiitake mushrooms

¼ cup dried black trumpet mushrooms

1 pound fresh chanterelle mushrooms, cleaned and trimmed

2 tablespoons light olive oil or neutral-flavored cooking oil

Flaky sea salt

5 cups Homemade Chicken Stock (page 157) or vegetable stock

4 tablespoons (½ stick) unsalted butter, divided

1 large yellow onion, finely chopped (about 2 cups)

2 garlic cloves, finely minced

1 cup carnaroli rice

1 teaspoon finely chopped fresh thyme leaves

1 teaspoon finely chopped parsley

1. In a small bowl, rehydrate the dried shiitake and black trumpet mushrooms by soaking them in 1 cup of warm water for 30 minutes. After about 15 minutes, preheat the oven to 425 degrees F.

2. In a medium bowl, toss the chanterelles with the oil and a generous pinch of salt. Arrange them in a single layer on a baking sheet with sides and roast them until they are lightly browned, about 10 minutes. Remove the pan from the oven and set it aside in a warm place.

3. Remove the rehydrated mushrooms from the soaking liquid with a slotted spoon. Strain the soaking liquid through a fine-mesh sieve and set it aside for cooking the rice. Gently rinse the mushrooms, chop them in ¼-inch pieces, and set them aside. Put the stock in a saucepan, bring it to a simmer over low heat, and keep it warm while you start the risotto.

4. In a Dutch oven over medium heat, melt 2 tablespoons of the butter. When the butter is foamy, add the onions and garlic and cook, stirring occasionally, until the onions are soft and lightly translucent, about 4 minutes. Add the rice and cook for 1 minute, stirring constantly. Add the mushroom soaking water, ½ cup warm broth, the rehydrated mushrooms, thyme, and parsley. Cook, stirring frequently, until almost all of the stock is absorbed. Add another ½ cup of the stock, and continue to cook, stirring often, until it is absorbed. Repeat this step until the stock is gone or the rice is cooked to your liking.

5. Remove the pan from the heat and stir in the remaining 2 tablespoons butter, cheese, and truffle oil. Taste for seasoning, adding salt and pepper as needed. Cover the pan and let the risotto sit for about 5 minutes to absorb any remaining liquid and "set." To serve, divide the risotto among 4 bowls, top with the chanterelle ragoût, and finish with more grated cheese.

2 ounces hard aged cheese such as Ancient Heritage Dairy's Hannah or Parmigiano-Reggiano, plus more for serving

2 teaspoons black truffle oil

Freshly ground black pepper

CLEANING FORAGED MUSHROOMS

Depending on the conditions when they were picked, some mushrooms require only a dry brushing, while several rinses in cold (or salted) water is necessary with others. When you purchase foraged mushrooms, ask the forager or vendor for recommendations on how to clean them.

You're likely to find dirt, bugs, and debris in the morel's honeycombed cap or, with larger mushrooms, inside their hollow cone. A vigorous brushing with a dry pastry brush usually loosens anything unwanted on the outside. Trim the ends of the stems, particularly if they are woody or dry, and proceed with your recipe.

DRY-BRINED ROASTED CHICKEN
with Orange, Paprika, and Smoked Chili Salt

BEN JACOBSEN, OWNER, JACOBSEN SALT CO.

Most cooks have a favorite method for roasting chicken, one that yields juicy, flavorful meat surrounded by crispy golden-brown skin. The magic in this recipe is dry brining, so you'll want to plan ahead; allow one to two days before you plan to serve the bird. Smoked paprika, smoked salt spiked with ghost chilies, and orange zest give this recipe an autumnal burnish and aroma, with a flavor to match. You could serve it with Crispy, Buttery Smashed Potatoes (page 143), roasted carrots or squash, or braised greens. There isn't much that doesn't go with roasted chicken.

Makes 4 to 6 servings

1. Rinse the chicken well, inside and out, and pat it completely dry with paper towels. (If moisture remains, the chicken will steam rather than turning crisp and golden brown.) Season all over with the salt (1 tablespoon per pound), adding it more liberally on the breast, legs, and meatier areas and saving some for inside the cavity, along the backbone. Tuck the wing tips behind the shoulders and place the bird on a plate or in a glass pie dish. Refrigerate for at least 24 hours and up to 48 hours.

2. When you are ready to roast the chicken, preheat the oven to 425 degrees F and remove the chicken from the refrigerator. Coarsely chop the orange zest and mix it with the paprika and kosher salt in a small bowl.

3. Transfer the chicken breast-side up to a shallow roasting pan, a cast-iron skillet, or a baking dish just slightly larger than the bird. Drizzle the oil all over and rub the skin with the zest mixture. Place the oranges and onion in the cavity.

4. Place the pan in the middle of the oven and roast the chicken for 20 minutes before reducing the temperature to 375 degrees F. Roast until the juices run clear when you cut between a leg and thigh, and an instant-read thermometer registers 160 degrees F, 40 to 55 minutes more, depending on the size of the bird.

1 (4- to 5-pound) pastured chicken, neck and giblets removed

4 to 5 tablespoons smoked chili salt, such as Jacobsen Salt Company's Smoked Ghost Chili Pepper Salt

2 oranges, zested and quartered

1 tablespoon smoked paprika

½ teaspoon kosher salt

¼ cup extra-virgin olive oil

1 medium onion, quartered

CURRIED CHICKEN PILAF
with Cilantro Root and Golden Raisins

ELANOR O'BRIEN, CO-OWNER, PERSEPHONE FARM

Intensely rich, flavorful stock is the basis for this pilaf. This is one of those recipes where there's no substitute for the main ingredient—take the time to make the stock, dividing it up into two days if necessary, but don't bother with store-bought.

If flame or Thompson raisins are what you have on hand, use them. But don't be tempted to leave the raisins out; they're key to the success of the combined flavors and textures of this dish, and golden raisins are particularly good. Likewise, it's worth seeking out cilantro root, for both the stock and the pilaf—see Cooking with Cilantro Root (opposite page).

Brown rice fans, please note: Elanor has tried, and it just doesn't work in this recipe. Stick with organic white basmati rice, which has a texture that is ideal for pilaf.

Makes 8 to 10 servings

1 bunch fresh cilantro with roots attached

3 tablespoons extra-virgin olive oil

2 medium onions, cut into ½-inch dice (about 3 cups)

2 small jalapeño peppers, finely diced with seeds (about 2 tablespoons)

2 tablespoons plus 1½ teaspoons curry powder

½ teaspoon ground cumin

2 cups organic white basmati rice

1 cup golden raisins

2 quarts Homemade Chicken Stock (recipe follows)

2 cups cooked chicken (from making the stock)

2 teaspoons kosher salt, plus more for seasoning

1. Prepare the cilantro root according to the instructions on the opposite page. Separate the roots from the stems and leaves and coarsely chop the leaves, saving the stems for another use, if desired. Set the leaves aside.

2. In a heavy pot or Dutch oven, warm the oil over medium heat. Add the onions and a generous pinch of salt and cook, stirring periodically, until they are soft and translucent, 7 to 9 minutes. Add the cilantro roots, jalapeños, curry powder, and cumin, stirring well to combine and coat the ingredients, and cook until the spices are aromatic, 2 to 3 minutes.

3. Add the rice and raisins. Cook, stirring frequently, until the rice grains are well coated with oil and spices, and the ingredients are well incorporated, about 2 more minutes. Add the stock, chicken, salt, and cilantro leaves, and bring the mixture to a boil. Reduce the heat, cover the pot, and simmer over the lowest heat possible for 30 to 40 minutes, or until the rice is tender. Remove the cilantro roots, which will be whole and easy to identify, and serve immediately.

HOMEMADE CHICKEN STOCK

Though less tender than roasters, stewing hens are dramatically more flavorful and nutrient-filled, and therefore preferred for stock. Depending on the size of your hen, you may get more or less stock and meat than indicated below.

Makes about 4 quarts

1. To make the stock, put the chicken, cilantro roots, onions, garlic, and jalapeño in a 6- to 8-quart stockpot with a generous pinch of salt. Cover completely with cold water and bring it to a boil. Reduce the heat to a simmer and cook, covered, for 4 hours. Check the water level in the pot occasionally, adding more water to cover the bird if needed. After 4 hours, strain the stock, discarding the mushy vegetables and setting the chicken aside until it is cool enough to handle. Remove the meat from the bones, reserving 2 cups for the pilaf. Any remaining chicken can be set aside for another meal.

1 (2½- to 3½-pound) pastured stewing hen

1 bunch cilantro roots, prepared according to the instructions below

2 small onions, unpeeled and quartered

1 head garlic, cloves separated and unpeeled

1 jalapeño

Kosher salt

COOKING WITH CILANTRO ROOT

Cilantro roots are a staple of Thai kitchens, with a milder, more herbaceous aroma and taste than the leaves. They impart a fabulous flavor to Elanor O'Brien's stock and Curried Chicken Pilaf.

At first, Persephone Farm sold the roots on request, but when shopper demand increased, they began direct-seeding cilantro every week in order to bring the roots to market regularly. Chopped stems with a few leaves mixed in can be substituted, but it's well worth the effort to source the real thing. (If your farmers' market doesn't have them, check Asian markets, which often carry frozen cilantro root.)

To prepare cilantro roots for cooking, cut the large, prominent roots and 1 inch of the stem from the rest of the bunch. Set the stems and leaves aside. Lightly scrub the roots if they are dirty. Unused cilantro roots can be frozen if they're wrapped well and used within 2 months, so stock up when you see them.

CHANTERELLE, CORN, AND YELLOW TOMATO PASTA

AMELIA HARD, COOKING INSTRUCTOR AND PORTLAND FARMERS MARKET SHOPPER

When the stars are aligned just so, there are a handful of Saturdays in late summer and early fall when yellow tomatoes, chanterelles, and corn are all available at the farmers' market. Not only do the colors combine happily, but the flavors complement one another like long-lost cousins. If you can't find yellow slicing tomatoes, substitute cherry tomatoes; you won't have to peel or seed them, which is a bonus.

Makes 4 servings

1½ pounds vine-ripened yellow or cherry tomatoes

Kosher salt

6 tablespoons extra-virgin olive oil, divided

1 medium sweet onion, cut in ¼-inch dice

2 garlic cloves, finely minced

Flaky sea salt

2 ears sweet corn, kernels cut from the cob

8 ounces chanterelle mushrooms, bottoms trimmed and thinly sliced

1 pound imported Italian pasta (any shape you prefer)

¾ cup freshly grated Parmigiano-Reggiano cheese, for garnish

1. Bring a large pot of water to a boil and set up a bowl filled with ice water. Stem the tomatoes and use a sharp paring knife to score the blossom ends with a small X. Plunge the tomatoes in boiling water for 30 seconds and, using a slotted spoon, immediately transfer them to the ice bath. When they are cool enough to handle, peel the tomatoes, halve them crosswise, and squeeze out their seeds. Coarsely chop the flesh and set it aside. (If you are using cherry tomatoes, stem and halve them crosswise.)

2. Fill a large pot with water and enough kosher salt that you can taste it. Bring the water to a rolling boil over medium heat. Meanwhile, warm 3 tablespoons of the oil in a saucepan large enough to hold a pound of cooked pasta. Add the onions and sauté them until they are translucent, about 5 minutes. Add the garlic, stir to coat with oil, and cook it slightly, then add the tomatoes and a pinch of sea salt. Cook, stirring frequently, until the tomatoes begin to break down. Add the corn and continue cooking until the sauce thickens. Remove the pan from the heat, and set it aside to keep warm.

3. Warm the remaining olive oil in another pan over medium-high heat. Add the chanterelles with a pinch of kosher salt. Sauté until the mushrooms release their liquid, then add them to the tomato-corn sauce.

4. When the water is boiling, add the pasta all at once. Stir, and cook the pasta al dente, according to the package directions. Drain the pasta and add it to the sauce. Over medium heat, stir the two together until hot and well combined. Remove the pasta to a serving bowl or divide it among 4 plates and garnish with the cheese. Serve immediately.

POSOLE ROJO

JARET FOSTER, FOSTER CRAFT COOKING

Roasting, toasting, and braising give this traditional Mexican soup its well-developed flavors, which really come together when you make it one day ahead. The hearty *posole* is fabulous on its own, but is elevated to an entirely new level by the garnishes. Choose at least five, put them in colorful bowls, and encourage guests to help themselves.

Makes 8 to 10 servings

2 white onions, divided

1 head garlic plus 6 cloves, divided

12 cups Homemade Chicken Stock (page 157), pork stock, water, or a combination

3 small chipotle chilies

2 pounds boneless pork shoulder, trimmed of excess fat and cut into 3 or 4 (1-inch-thick) slices

Fine sea salt

3 ancho chilies (aka dried poblanos), stemmed and seeded

3 California chilies (aka dried Anaheims), stemmed and seeded

4 cups (two 14.5 ounce cans) hominy, rinsed and drained

1 teaspoon dried oregano, preferably Mexican

FOR GARNISH:

Lime wedges

Avocado

Shredded cabbage

Diced sweet onion

Thinly sliced radishes

Crisp fried tortillas

Cilantro leaves

1. Peel and quarter 1 of the onions and peel 6 of the garlic cloves. In an 8-quart stockpot or Dutch oven, bring the stock to a simmer over medium heat. Add the onion, garlic, and chipotle chilies. Generously season the pork pieces with salt and add them to the pot. Simmer the mixture slowly, without letting the stock boil, until the pork is meltingly tender, about 3 hours.

2. Meanwhile, halve the remaining onion, leaving the skin on. Separate the head of garlic into cloves, leaving the skin on. Warm a cast-iron skillet over medium-high heat. When the pan is hot, add the onion and garlic. Roast, stirring occasionally, until the onions soften, the garlic is tender, and the skins of both have darkened and are nearly black, about 15 minutes. When they are cool enough to handle, remove their skins and add the onions and garlic to a blender or the bowl of a food processor. Set it aside.

3. Toast the ancho and California chilies in the same pan over medium-high heat until they are lightly blistered and aromatic, about 5 minutes. Remove them to a small bowl and cover them with hot water. After 10 minutes, or when they're rehydrated and soft, drain the chilies and discard the bitter soaking water. Add the drained chilies to the blender with ½ cup water and puree until smooth, adding more water as necessary to loosen the mixture and make it easy to blend. You should be left with about 2 cups of thick chili paste. Season the paste to taste with salt and strain it through a fine-mesh sieve, pressing on the solids. Set the chili paste aside.

4. Using a slotted spoon, remove the pork pieces from the stock and set them aside on a plate to cool. Strain the stock and discard any solids; you should have about 6 cups.

5. Add the stock back to the pot and adjust the seasoning, adding more salt, if necessary. Add the hominy to the stock and simmer it over medium-low heat for about 20 minutes. When the pork is cool enough to handle, shred it into bite-size chunks and add it and the oregano to the pot with the stock and hominy. Stir in the chili paste, ½ cup at a time, until the posole is the color and flavor you desire. Heat the posole through and serve it accompanied by the garnishes.

CHESTNUT-TOFU DUMPLINGS

in Matsutake Mushroom Sauce

NAOKO TAMURA, CHEF/OWNER, CHEF NAOKO BENTO CAFÉ

This traditional Japanese dish stars local ingredients: tender fried dumplings cloaked in a velvety matsutake mushroom sauce. The deeply flavorful sauce is also wonderful with chicken or freshly caught steamed or deep-fried rock cod, and a small glass of sake.

Chef Naoko uses a traditional Japanese-style tofu made in Southeast Portland by Eileen Ota of Ota Tofu. Her mushrooms come from Roger Allen Konka, of Springwater Farm in St. Helen. Konka sells many different wild mushrooms at the market, and sets aside his nicest matsutakes for Naoko, who loves the fragrant fall mushrooms, which are a delicacy in Japan.

Makes 4 to 6 servings

1 cup loosely packed bonito flakes

1-pound-block firm tofu, such as Ota Tofu

1 egg yolk

1 tablespoon potato starch, or 2 ounces grated *nagaimo* (Japanese long potato)

1 cup fresh chestnuts, boiled until soft and broken by hand into small pieces

Sunflower oil, for deep-frying

FOR THE MATSUTAKE SAUCE:

8 ounces matsutake mushrooms, torn by hand into small pieces

1 small carrot, shredded

1½ teaspoons soy sauce

Sea salt

1½ teaspoons potato starch

¼ cup water

Finely chopped green onions or slivered lime peel, for flavor and garnish

1. To make the dashi, in a small saucepan, boil 2 cups of water. Add the bonito flakes and simmer for 3 minutes. Remove the pan from the heat and immediately strain the dashi through a fine-mesh sieve. Set the dashi aside.

2. To make the dumplings, in the bowl of a stand mixer fitted with the paddle attachment, mix the tofu, egg yolk, and potato starch on low speed for 3 to 4 minutes, until the mixture is well combined and the tofu pieces are like small crumbs. Remove the bowl from the mixer and, using a spatula, fold in the chestnuts. The mixture should be thick and similar in consistency to bread dough. Using your hands, form the mixture into 12 equal-size dumplings.

3. Fill a wok or deep pot with straight sides with several inches of oil and heat it to between 280 and 300 degrees F. Deep-fry the dumplings in batches, without crowding them, until they swell and turn golden brown, approximately 4 minutes per side. Remove to a plate lined with paper towels to drain and keep warm.

4. To make the matsutake sauce, warm the dashi over medium heat. Add the mushroom and carrot. Increase the heat and bring the dashi to a light boil, add the soy sauce, and season to taste with salt.

5. In a small bowl, stir together the potato starch and water until smooth, then slowly stir it into the broth. Continue cooking at a light boil until the sauce thickens slightly and the fragrance of the mushrooms is strong, 1 to 2 minutes.

6. To assemble the dish, place 2 dumplings in 6 small bowls, or 3 dumplings in 4 slightly larger bowls. Ladle the matsutake sauce over the dumplings, sprinkle with some green onion, and serve immediately.

SWEETS, SIPS, AND CONDIMENTS

Apple Cider–Glazed Hazelnut Doughnuts 165

Buttermilk Pie with Honey-Poached Huckleberries 168

Pear Upside-Down Cake with Caramel Cream and Bacon 170

Honey-Glazed Figs with Lemon Ricotta and Almond Cookies 173

Pumpkin Whoopie Pies with Caramel Buttercream 176

Cranberry Sour 179

Heirloom Apple Butter 180

Quince Chutney 182

APPLE CIDER-GLAZED HAZELNUT DOUGHNUTS

ELLEN JACKSON AND BARB FOUKE, OWNER, FREDDY GUYS HAZELNUTS

Apple cider doughnuts are a mainstay in New England, where it's a cider maker's tradition to use freshly pressed juice to create the lightly tangy, apple-scented treats. In this version, reduced cider is replaced with applesauce, and the still-warm doughnuts are dunked in a cider and applesauce glaze. The addition of hazelnut meal to the batter gives them a distinctly Northwest twist.

Makes 1 dozen

1. In a large bowl, thoroughly whisk together the flour, hazelnut meal, nutmeg, baking powder, baking soda, and salt, breaking up any lumps.

2. In a medium bowl, whisk together the applesauce, sugar, sour cream, butter, eggs, and egg yolk. Make a well in the dry ingredients and add the wet ones, gradually pulling in the dry ingredients and stirring just until combined. The dough will be very soft and sticky. Cover the bowl and refrigerate the dough for 1 hour.

3. While the dough chills, make the glaze. In a shallow, wide bowl, whisk together the sugar, applesauce, 2 tablespoons of cider, and a pinch of salt. Add more cider as necessary, whisking to achieve a thick, smooth glaze the consistency of honey. Set the glaze aside while you finish the doughnuts.

4. After 1 hour, turn the dough out onto well-floured work surface and knead it lightly until it is smooth, adding flour as needed. Pat the dough out into ½-inch thickness and cut it out using a floured 2½ inch doughnut cutter or 2 round cutters, one approximately 2½ inches and a smaller one ¾ to 1 inch. Gently knead the scraps together, reroll, and cut again until you have a dozen.

CONTINUED

2¾ cups unbleached all-purpose flour, plus more to knead the dough

1¼ cups hazelnut meal

1 tablespoon freshly grated nutmeg

1 tablespoon baking powder

½ teaspoon baking soda

1½ teaspoons kosher salt

1 cup unsweetened applesauce, preferably homemade

1 cup sugar

½ cup sour cream

¼ cup (½ stick) unsalted butter, melted and cooled

2 eggs

1 egg yolk

Canola or other neutral-flavored oil, for deep-frying

FOR THE GLAZE:

2 cups confectioners' sugar

¾ cup unsweetened applesauce, preferably homemade

2 to 4 tablespoons apple cider

Pinch kosher salt

5. Preheat a deep fryer or heat several inches of oil in a deep pot to 350 degrees F. Fry the doughnuts and holes 2 or 3 at a time, turning them as they rise to the surface. They should be turned no more than 2 times and will take a total of 2 to 3 minutes. When they're ready, they'll be golden brown. Remove to a pan lined with paper towels to drain and glaze while still warm.

6. To glaze the doughnuts, add them to the bowl of glaze one at a time, turning over to coat both sides. Shake off any excess glaze and set aside to dry on a baking rack or a baking sheet lined with parchment paper.

VARIATIONS

Orange Sour Cream: Substitute 4 tablespoons zest (from 2 oranges) and ½ cup puree from whole oranges for the applesauce, increase the sour cream to 1 cup, and decrease the nutmeg to 1 teaspoon. Make a glaze with 2 cups confectioners' sugar and 2 tablespoons orange juice.

Pumpkin: Substitute ½ cup pumpkin puree for the applesauce and increase the sour cream to 1 cup. Reduce the nutmeg to 1½ teaspoons and add 2½ teaspoons ground cinnamon, 1 teaspoon ground ginger, and 1½ teaspoons ground cloves. Make a glaze with 2 cups confectioners' sugar, 2 tablespoons milk, and ¼ teaspoon ground cinnamon.

HAZELNUTS

Also known as filberts, hazelnuts are an ancient nut grown in temperate regions of Europe and the Pacific Northwest—99 percent of the US crop is grown in Oregon. The nuts are processed into meal, paste, oil, and butter, in addition to being roasted and diced. For a new take (and a heart-healthy boost) on baked goods such as muffins and quick breads, replace a third of the flour with hazelnut meal.

BUTTERMILK PIE
with Honey-Poached Huckleberries

MICHELLE MARIE, CHEF/OWNER, BELLA MERCATO

A classic Southern dessert, buttermilk pie is tailor made for fall and can go right into winter by substituting frozen huckleberries for fresh, or with cranberries for a slightly tarter version.

Here in the Northwest, huckleberries grow along the coast and in the mountains. Because they're not cultivated, they're available for a brief window of time in late summer and early fall, typically peaking between mid-July and mid-September. Less sweet and slightly more astringent than blueberries, and with a thicker skin, huckleberries have their own unique flavor. But access to huckleberries is not a requirement for making this pie; tiny wild Maine blueberries or almost any other cane berry will do.

Note: Get the filling ingredients together before baking the pie shell, which should be hot when you fill it.

Makes 1 nine-inch pie

FOR THE CRUST:

1½ cups unbleached all-purpose flour

⅛ teaspoon fine sea salt

10 tablespoons very cold unsalted butter, cut into ⅛-inch slices

3 tablespoons cold water

2 teaspoons sugar

FOR THE FILLING:

¾ cup sugar

¼ cup (½ stick) unsalted butter, softened slightly

⅛ teaspoon fine sea salt

3 or 4 gratings fresh nutmeg

1 teaspoon pure vanilla extract

2 tablespoons unbleached all-purpose flour

2 eggs

5 egg yolks

1¾ cups buttermilk, at room temperature

¼ cup heavy cream

1. To make the crust, in a large bowl, combine the flour and salt. Using your fingers or a pastry blender, work the butter into the flour until the mixture resembles coarse meal, with pea-size pieces of butter scattered throughout. Sprinkle the water over the mixture and toss it with your fingertips until it becomes a shaggy mass.

2. Turn the dough out onto a lightly floured work surface, gather it together, and use the heel of your hand to smear it gently away from you. Repeat this motion 3 to 4 times, or until the dough begins to come together and no dry patches remain. Gather the dough into a ball, wrap it in plastic wrap, and press it into a disk. Refrigerate it for at least 1 hour or up to overnight, or freeze it to use later; the dough will keep for up to 1 month.

3. When you're ready to make the pie, on a lightly floured work surface, roll the dough out into an ⅛-inch-thick round. Carefully transfer it to a 9-inch pie pan and trim the dough to fit, leaving about 1½ inches overhang all the way around. Reserve the dough scraps. Tuck the overhanging edges under and crimp them. Refrigerate the pie shell for 20 minutes and preheat the oven to 350 degrees F.

4. After 20 minutes, line the inside of the pie shell with parchment paper or aluminum foil, and fill it with pie weights or dried beans. Put the shell on a baking sheet in the middle of the oven and bake it until the edges are golden brown and the center appears dry, about 30 minutes. Remove the weights and check the shell for cracks; if you find any, use the reserved dough scraps to patch them. Sprinkle the shell with the sugar and return it to the oven until it is golden brown all over, about 15 minutes.

5. Meanwhile, make the filling; the pie shell should be hot when you fill it. In the bowl of a stand mixer fitted with the paddle attachment, combine the sugar and butter on low speed. Add the salt, nutmeg, and vanilla and mix until smooth. Add the flour, followed by the eggs and egg yolk. Switch to the whisk attachment and mix in the buttermilk, cream, and vinegar until smooth.

6. Carefully pour the filling into the hot pie shell. Reduce the oven temperature to 325 degrees F and bake the pie until it is golden brown and firm around the edges, and a bit jiggly in the center, 35 to 40 minutes. The filling will finish setting up as it cools.

7. Allow the pie to cool to room temperature before refrigerating it to cool completely. Serve it cold, with whipped cream and warm honey-poached huckleberries.

1½ teaspoons apple cider vinegar

———————

Whipped cream, for serving

1 recipe Honey-Poached Huckleberries (recipe follows), for serving

HONEY-POACHED HUCKLEBERRIES

Makes 2 cups

1. If you are using fresh berries, pick them over, removing any leaves or stems. Rinse them well and let them dry on a towel.

2. Put the berries in a heatproof bowl. In a small saucepan over medium heat, bring the honey to a boil. Immediately pour the boiling honey over the berries. Serve them warm or prepare them ahead of time and serve them at room temperature.

2 cups huckleberries, fresh or frozen

½ cup honey

PEAR UPSIDE-DOWN CAKE

with Caramel Cream and Bacon

MELISSA MCKINNEY, PASTRY CHEF, OLYMPIA PROVISIONS

You've heard the old adage: everything is better with bacon. If you're not already a believer, try this decadent cake. Fragrant pears that simmer and soften under a tender cake batter end up on top when the cake is inverted, their buttery, brandy-spiked juices soaking into the cake. Serve topped with salted caramel cream and a slice of bacon.

This seasonal twist on the classic pineapple upside-down cake can also be made in a cast-iron skillet, once more common in kitchens than cake and baking pans.

Makes 1 nine-inch cake

8 ounces sliced smoked bacon (8 to 10 slices), such as Olympia Provisions

FOR THE TOPPING:

¼ cup (½ stick) unsalted butter, cut into small pieces

½ cup packed light brown sugar

¼ teaspoon ground cinnamon

¼ teaspoon freshly grated nutmeg

¼ teaspoon fine sea salt

2 Bosc pears, ripe but firm, peeled, cored, and sliced ¼-inch thick

1 tablespoon brandy

———

1¼ cups unbleached all-purpose flour

3 tablespoons fine cornmeal

1¼ teaspoons baking powder

¾ teaspoon fine sea salt

½ cup (1 stick) unsalted butter, at room temperature

1 cup sugar

1. Preheat the oven to 375 degrees F. Line a baking sheet with parchment paper and line the bottom of a 9-inch cake pan with a circle of parchment cut to fit. Lightly butter and flour the inside of the pan and set it and the baking sheet aside.

2. Lay the bacon slices on a baking sheet with sides, leaving some space in between. Cook the bacon until the slices are golden but not crispy, about 20 minutes. Set the bacon aside, keeping it warm. Reduce the oven temperature to 350 degrees F.

3. To make the topping, in a small saucepan, whisk together the butter, brown sugar, cinnamon, nutmeg, and salt. When the butter has melted, pour the mixture into the cake pan and use a spatula to spread over the parchment paper. Shingle the pear slices in a circle on top of the brown sugar mixture and sprinkle them with the brandy. Set the topping aside.

4. To make the cake, in a small bowl, whisk together the flour, cornmeal, baking powder, and salt, and set it aside. In the bowl of a stand mixer fitted with the paddle attachment, beat the butter and sugar on medium speed until very fluffy, about 3 minutes. Stop the mixer and use a spatula to scrape down the bottom and sides of the bowl. Reduce the speed to low and slowly add the eggs and vanilla, mixing until thoroughly incorporated. Stop the mixer and scrape down the bowl again before adding the dry ingredients in 3 additions, alternating with the milk. Spread the batter over the pears.

5. Bake the cake for 30 minutes, rotate the pan from front to back, and bake until the cake is golden brown, springs back when pressed gently in the middle, and pulls away slightly from the sides of the pan, about 20 minutes more. Remove to a cooling rack for 15 minutes.

6. To unmold the cake, use a small knife with a thin blade to loosen the sides. Place a serving plate over the pan and invert it quickly, shaking it gently to loosen the cake completely.

7. Just before serving, prepare the caramel cream. Clean the stand mixer bowl and briefly chill it, along with the whisk attachment, before whipping the cream. Add the cream and caramel sauce to the chilled bowl and whip on medium-high speed until the cream holds medium stiff peaks. Add the salt and mix for a few more rotations.

8. To serve, cut the cake in 8 to 10 pieces, garnish each piece with a dollop of caramel cream, and lay a slice of bacon across the top. Pass the remaining caramel sauce.

2 large eggs, at room temperature, lightly whisked

1 teaspoon pure vanilla extract

⅔ cup whole milk, at room temperature

FOR THE CARAMEL CREAM:

1 cup heavy cream

¼ cup plus 2 tablespoons Caramel Sauce (recipe follows)

Pinch of coarse sea salt, such as Maldon

CARAMEL SAUCE

Makes about 1 cup

1. In a small lidded saucepan, place the sugar and cream of tartar with enough water to make it feel like wet sand, about 2 tablespoons. Cover the pan and cook the sugar over medium-high heat until it dissolves and large bubbles form, 3 to 5 minutes. Remove the lid occasionally to observe.

2. Reduce the heat to medium-low and continue simmering until the mixture turns pale amber, 8 to 10 minutes. Do not stir during this time. Remove the lid and watch the caramel closely. When it turns darker amber, remove it from the heat and carefully add the butter while whisking. It will bubble and steam enthusiastically, so stand back! Add the cream, vanilla, and salt and whisk well to combine. Cool the caramel sauce completely before using it to make the caramel cream.

½ cup sugar

¼ teaspoon cream of tartar

3 tablespoons unsalted butter

⅓ cup heavy cream, at room temperature

1 teaspoon pure vanilla extract

Small pinch of kosher salt

HONEY-GLAZED FIGS

with Lemon Ricotta and Almond Cookies

KATHRYN YEOMANS, CHEF, THE FARMER'S FEAST

Fresh, ripe figs are a luscious treat on their own. Served warm, embellished with a drizzle of honey, a spoonful of sweet lemon-scented ricotta, and a crisp almond cookie, they become an elegant yet easy dessert.

You can sweeten ready-made ricotta and add a little lemon zest, but making your own ricotta is simple and more satisfying. Its fresh flavor and creamy texture are noticeably superior, plus there's the added bonus of having the leftover nutrient-rich whey to add to soups, smoothies, or bread dough.

Makes 6 servings

1. To make the cookies, preheat the oven to 350 degrees F. Line 2 baking sheets with parchment paper and set them aside.

2. In the bowl of a food processor, pulse the almonds, sugar, and flour until the nuts are finely ground. With the machine running, pour in the cream and butter and process until you have a soft dough.

3. Drop the dough by tablespoons onto the prepared baking sheets, spacing them 2 inches apart. Dip your fingers in a bowl of cold water, shake off the excess water, and flatten the cookies with your fingers. Bake the cookies until they are golden brown, 7 to 9 minutes. Cool them slightly on the baking sheets before using a spatula to remove the cookies to a wire rack to cool completely. Reduce the oven temperature to 325 degrees F.

4. In a small baking dish, add the honey and place the figs on top. Bake for about 5 minutes, until the figs are warm and the honey is syrupy.

5. To make the ricotta, in a small bowl, use a spatula to fold the sugar and lemon zest into the cheese. Taste, and add a little more sugar if desired.

6. To assemble, put a scoop of ricotta on each of 6 plates. Add a fig, whole or halved, and drizzle it with the honey from the pan. Arrange a few almond lace cookies alongside and serve immediately.

FOR THE COOKIES:

1 cup raw slivered almonds

½ cup sugar

3 tablespoons unbleached all-purpose flour

2 tablespoons heavy cream

2 tablespoons unsalted butter, melted and cooled slightly

---

3 tablespoons local honey

6 firm but ripe figs

FOR THE RICOTTA:

1 tablespoon confectioners' sugar

2 teaspoons finely chopped lemon zest, reserved from making the ricotta

1½ cups Homemade Ricotta Cheese (recipe follows) or store-bought

Autumn

CONTINUED

HOMEMADE RICOTTA CHEESE

Makes about 1½ cups

2 medium lemons

2 quarts whole milk

½ cup heavy cream

1. Zest one of the lemons; you should end up with about 2 teaspoons. Finely chop the zest and reserve it for the finished ricotta. Squeeze the juice from both lemons and measure out ⅓ cup (reserve any remaining juice for another use).

2. In a heavy-bottomed nonreactive pan, using a wooden spoon or heatproof spatula, stir together the milk, cream, and ⅓ cup lemon juice for several seconds. Set the pot over low heat and leave until the mixture registers 175 degrees F on an instant-read thermometer; this will take 40 to 50 minutes. Gently stir the milk once or twice during this time. Do not stir too often or too vigorously, or you will break up the curds as they are forming.

3. After the cheese has reached 175 degrees F, increase the heat to medium-high and, without stirring, watch the pot until the temperature reaches 205 degrees F; this should take 3 to 5 minutes. The surface of the milk will look as though it is going to erupt; don't let the milk boil. Remove the pot from the heat and let it sit for 10 minutes. You now have curds and whey.

4. Place a sieve over a large bowl and line it with fine-weave cheesecloth. Scoop the curds into the cheesecloth and let them drain for 10 minutes. Put the ricotta in a covered container and refrigerate for 3 to 5 days. The whey will keep in the refrigerator for about 1 week, or up to 3 months in the freezer.

HOW TO CHOOSE AND STORE FIGS

Figs should be plump and heavy for their size, with skins that are very slightly wrinkled and loose, rather than taut. Their natural sugars can cause them to crack slightly, which is fine, but avoid fruit with bruising. Keep fresh figs in a warm area of the refrigerator and use within two days.

PUMPKIN WHOOPIE PIES
with Caramel Buttercream

ELIZABETH BEEKLEY, CO-OWNER AND HEAD BAKER, TWO TARTS BAKERY

Whoopie pies are a New England phenomenon and Pennsylvania Amish tradition. Most are as large as an English muffin and filled with marshmallow creme. The little bites in this recipe pack the spicy goodness of pumpkin pie into two cookies held together with rich caramel buttercream. They're the perfect antidote to Thanksgiving dessert overload and should be at the top of your list when you have some extra pumpkin puree to use up.

Makes about 3 dozen

1½ cups unbleached pastry flour

½ teaspoon baking powder

½ teaspoon baking soda

½ teaspoon fine sea salt

¾ cup muscovado sugar or light brown sugar, lightly packed

6 tablespoons canola or vegetable oil

2 tablespoons unsalted butter, melted

2 tablespoons unsulphured molasses

1 tablespoon plus 1½ teaspoons ground cinnamon

2¼ teaspoons ground ginger

1½ teaspoons ground cloves

½ teaspoon ground cardamom

¼ teaspoon freshly grated nutmeg

1½ cups Fresh Pumpkin Puree (recipe follows)

1 egg

1. Preheat the oven to 350 degrees F. Line 2 baking sheets with parchment paper. In a small bowl, whisk together the flour, baking powder, baking soda, and salt and set it aside.

2. In the bowl of a stand mixer fitted with the paddle attachment, mix the sugar, oil, butter, molasses, cinnamon, ginger, cloves, cardamom, nutmeg, and pumpkin puree on low speed until thoroughly combined. Add the egg, increase the speed to medium, and beat until it is thoroughly mixed in, about 1 minute. Reduce the speed to low, add the dry ingredients, and mix just until combined.

3. Using a pastry bag with a round tip, or a ziplock bag with one of the corners snipped off to create a ½-inch opening, pipe the pumpkin batter onto the prepared baking sheets in 2-inch circles. Bake until the pies are lightly golden and firm to the touch, about 10 minutes. Transfer the parchment paper with the cookies onto a wire rack to cool.

4. Meanwhile, make the buttercream. Clean the stand mixer bowl and fit the mixer with the whisk attachment. Put the egg whites and salt in the clean mixer bowl and set them aside.

5. In a small saucepan or skillet (preferably nonstick), add the sugar and water and swirl the pan to combine the two (don't use a utensil). Bring the ingredients to a boil over medium heat, swirling the pan occasionally, then reduce the heat to medium

low and continue to boil the mixture, swirling the pan intermittently, until the sugar begins to caramelize (about 3 minutes); it shouldn't be as dark as you'd like the finished caramelized sugar it to be. Immediately remove the pan from the heat and set aside.

6. While the sugar sits, return your attention to the stand mixer. Whisk the egg whites and salt on medium speed until frothy, increase the speed to medium high, and continue to beat until the whites form soft peaks. Meanwhile, if the sugar isn't as caramelized as you'd like, return it to the heat and watch closely until it is deep golden brown or sufficiently caramelized to suit your taste. Reduce the mixer speed to low until the sugar is ready.

7. With the mixer running on low speed, slowly pour the caramelized sugar into the egg whites in a steady stream. Increase the speed to high and beat until the mixture is thick, glossy, and has cooled to room temperature, about 5 minutes. Reduce the speed to medium and, with the mixer running, gradually add the butter pieces. The mixture will seem thin at first, but it will thicken as more butter is incorporated and the mixture continues to cool. Eventually it will be light and fluffy. Keep the buttercream at room temperature until you're ready to assemble the pies.

8. To assemble the whoopie pies, gently remove half of the cookies from the parchment paper and turn them upside down on a cutting board or work surface. Using a pastry bag with a round tip, or a ziplock bag with one of the corners snipped off to create a ¼-inch opening, pipe a circle of buttercream about the size of a quarter onto each upturned cookie. Top with the remaining cookies. Before serving, dust with confectioners' sugar and cinnamon.

9. Store the whoopie pies in an airtight container in a cool place; they will keep for 2 days. Or refrigerate them for 4 days, which will make them a bit sticky, but still delicious.

FOR THE BUTTERCREAM:

3 egg whites

½ teaspoon fine sea salt

½ cup sugar

¼ cup water

1 cup (2 sticks) unsalted butter, cut into ½-inch cubes

———————————

Confectioners' sugar, for serving

Ground cinnamon, for serving

CONTINUED

Autumn

FRESH PUMPKIN PUREE

Makes about 3 cups

1 small sugar pie pumpkin (about 1½ pounds)

1. Preheat the oven to 350 degrees F and line a baking sheet with parchment paper.

2. Cut off the stem and put the pumpkin on the baking sheet. Roast the pumpkin whole until the flesh begins to collapse slightly and holds an indentation when poked with a finger, 30 to 45 minutes.

3. Remove the baking sheet and let the pumpkin cool to room temperature. When it is cool enough to handle, peel it, discarding the skin and seeds (or save the seeds for roasting). Puree the flesh in a blender or food processor until smooth. If made ahead of time, the puree can be stored in an airtight container in the refrigerator.

CRANBERRY SOUR

STONE BARN BRANDYWORKS

Cranberries join rosemary in this beautifully sweet-tart version of a whiskey sour. You can adjust it to your preference to be more or less boozy, or more or less sweet. The cocktail can also be made with one ounce of rye and two ounces of Stone Barn Brandyworks' cranberry liqueur in lieu of the rye and cranberry concentrate below.

Makes 1 cocktail

1. In a cocktail shaker, combine the whiskey, cranberry juice, lemon juice, simple syrup, and bitters. Have a strainer and cocktail glass ready. Add ice to the shaker and shake vigorously for 10 seconds. Strain the cocktail into the glass, and garnish with the rosemary.

1½ ounces rye whiskey, such as Stone Barn's Hard Eight unoaked rye whiskey

1½ ounces pure, unsweetened cranberry juice, such as Starvation Alley Cranberry Concoction

1½ ounces (3 tablespoons) freshly squeezed lemon juice (from 1 medium lemon)

1 ounce Rosemary Simple Syrup (recipe follows)

Dash of bitters, orange or old fashioned (optional)

1 fresh rosemary sprig, for garnish

ROSEMARY SIMPLE SYRUP

Makes about 1¼ cups

1. In a small saucepan over medium-high heat, combine all the ingredients and bring them to a boil. Reduce the heat to low and simmer the syrup gently for 10 minutes. Remove the pan from the heat and let it steep for 45 minutes. Strain the syrup through a fine-mesh sieve and chill it.

1 cup granulated sugar

2 tablespoons fresh rosemary leaves

1 cup water

HEIRLOOM APPLE BUTTER

WENDY JO DOWNING, KIYOKAWA FAMILY ORCHARDS

Available at the farmers' market from late August until early April, apples are a good storage crop and a mainstay, getting us through the winter when fresh fruit is less plentiful. After you've made all the sauce, pies, cakes, and crisps you can possibly eat, make this wonderfully rich apple butter. It's much better than what you find at the store, and combining several apple varieties will elevate it even further (see Variations, opposite page).

Makes about 8 half-pint jars

5 pounds seasonal apples, any variety or combination of varieties, peeled, cored, and quartered

1½ cups water

3 cups vanilla bean sugar (about 3 cups for every 2 quarts apple pulp)

1½ teaspoons freshly grated nutmeg

1 teaspoon ground cinnamon

½ teaspoon ground cloves

1. In a large stainless-steel saucepan or a Dutch oven, combine the apples with the water and bring everything to a boil over medium-high heat. Reduce the heat and simmer the apples, partially covered, stirring often with a wooden spoon, until they are soft, about 30 minutes.

2. Working in batches, transfer the mixture to a large, clean pot with the sugar, nutmeg, cinnamon, and cloves. Cook over medium-high heat, stirring frequently, until the sugar dissolves. Reduce the heat to low and simmer the mixture, stirring occasionally, until the apple butter thickens and holds its shape on a spoon, anywhere from 30 to 60 minutes. If it thickens too quickly, add fruit juice or water with a squeeze of fresh lemon juice for the desired consistency, adding 30 minutes of cooking time for every additional ½ cup of liquid. While the butter is on the stovetop, adjust the seasoning by adding more spice(s) to taste.

3. To caramelize and finish the butter, preheat the oven to 350 degrees F. Ladle the mixture into 9-by-13-inch glass baking dishes at least 2 inches deep. Bake until the butter caramelizes around the edges and on the top of each baking dish, about 30 minutes.

4. Ladle the hot apple butter into hot, sterilized jars, leaving ¼-inch of headspace. Run a nonmetallic knife around the inside of the jars to remove any air bubbles; wipe the rim of the jar with a clean, damp cloth to remove any drips; and secure the lids with rings, tightening just until resistance is met (fingertip tight). Process in a water-bath canner according to the manufacturer's instructions.

5. If you are not canning the butter, let it cool completely before ladling it into jars. Store it, refrigerated, for 3 to 4 weeks.

VARIATIONS

Chunky: Start with a combination of unpeeled, cored Honeycrisp, Braeburn, Ambrosia, and Winesap apples and cut them into ½-inch cubes, and simmered until soft, 20 to 30 minutes. Add an additional ⅛ teaspoon ground cloves and proceed with the basic recipe.

Smooth: Start with a combination of Valstar, Elstar, Mountain Rose, Zestar!, and Tsugaru apples, peeled, cored, and coarsely chopped, and simmered until very soft, 45 to 55 minutes. Puree the apples with a hand blender to achieve a creamy texture with body, being careful not to overblend and liquefy the apples. Add an additional ½ teaspoon ground cinnamon and proceed with the recipe.

Rich: Start with a combination of Criterion, Ginger Gold, Mutsu (aka Crispin), Empire, and Arkansas Black apples, unpeeled, cored, and coarsely chopped. Simmer with several strips of lemon peel (removed with a vegetable peeler) and a few coins of fresh ginger for 30 to 40 minutes. Process the mixture using a food mill. Add an additional ¾ teaspoon ground ginger and ¾ teaspoon finely grated lemon zest and proceed with the recipe.

THE MANY USES FOR APPLE BUTTER

- Spread it on toast, peanut butter sandwiches, and homemade banana-nut bread.

- Mix it with honey and drizzle it over yogurt or vanilla ice cream.

- Add it to bourbon-soaked ribs for sweetness.

- Serve it on the side of a plate of sautéed winter greens topped with a fried egg and hot pickled peppers.

- Brush it on pork loin, as a glaze.

QUINCE CHUTNEY

LOLA MILHOLLAND, FOOD WRITER AND PORTLAND FARMERS MARKET SHOPPER

In addition to being intensely fragrant, quince flesh magically transforms from creamy white to deep rose as it cooks. Look for bright, plump, yellow-green fruit with an aroma that's almost perfumed. Quinces are very hard, making them frustrating to peel and core, so find a friend to help! They'll oxidize and brown slightly after they're peeled, but it won't affect the finished chutney.

This chutney was created specifically to complement Indian dishes, so it's not very sweet. If you prefer, increase the amount of sugar to ¾ cup. In addition to being the ultimate condiment for Indian food, quince chutney is good stirred into yogurt, spooned over ice cream and/or sourdough pancakes, and served alongside rice and a spicy curry.

Makes 2 pints

2 tablespoons ghee or unsalted butter

½ teaspoon cumin seeds

½ teaspoon coriander seeds

½ teaspoon fennel seeds

1 whole dried hot chili pepper, preferably *guajillo*

2-inch piece gingerroot, peeled and grated

1 cup freshly squeezed orange juice (from 3 medium oranges)

⅔ cup sugar

3 pounds quinces, peeled, cored, and thinly sliced

2 teaspoons fine sea salt

¼ teaspoon ground cinnamon

⅛ teaspoon ground cardamom

⅛ teaspoon ground cloves

⅛ teaspoon ground mace

⅓ cup walnuts, toasted and coarsely chopped

⅓ cup unsweetened dried flaked coconut (also called coconut chips), toasted

1. In a large, heavy-bottomed saucepan or Dutch oven with a tight-fitting lid, melt the ghee over medium heat. Add the cumin, coriander, and fennel seeds and the chili, and cook until the butter is foamy and the coriander seeds have darkened slightly, about 2 minutes. Stir in the gingerroot and cook until the ginger begins to turn golden, about 1 minute more.

2. Stir in the orange juice, sugar, quinces, salt, cinnamon, cardamom, cloves, and mace. Bring the mixture to a boil, lower the heat to a simmer, and cover the pan. Cook for approximately 1 hour, stirring frequently but very gently, so as not to break up the quince slices. The chutney is ready when the quince turns a deep shade of pink, and the juice has reduced to a thick glaze that coats the fruit.

3. Remove the pan from the heat and gently fold in the walnuts and coconut. Ladle the chutney into hot, sterilized jars, leaving ½-inch headspace, and process in a water-bath canner according to the manufacturer's instructions for no fewer than 20—and no more than 30—minutes.

4. If you are not canning the chutney, let it cool completely before ladling it into jars. Store it, refrigerated, for up to 1 month.

WINTER

SINCE 2013, WHEN WE BEGAN operating the winter market on Saturdays in downtown Portland, the number of vendors and customers who turn out to sell and shop in waterproof shells, rain pants, and boots has steadily increased. Against a winter landscape of naked trees, driving rain, and flapping tents and canopies, Portlanders continue to shop for everything from storage crops like apples, onions, and potatoes to the leafy greens and root crops that sweeten with each frost. Though every region—and farmer or vendor—is limited in its capacity to grow by the weather, winter's challenges don't lessen our desire to eat locally and seasonally. Now, with our year-round market on Saturdays at Portland State University, increasing numbers of loyal shoppers brave the elements to stock up on winter greens and support growers.

Winter markets began to thrive in Portland when farmers embraced innovations such as hoop houses, a low-tech enclosure of heavy-grade plastic sheets stretched over PVC pipes that make it possible to extend the growing season on either end. Winter is the toughest time of year to keep food dollars local, but a desire by eaters to do just that has resulted in the region's growers working to expand their offerings through experimentation and by adapting seed strains to Oregon's surprisingly large number of microclimates. From hot and relatively dry southern Oregon and the South Coast's "Banana Belt" to the northwest coast's marine climate and the valleys tucked between the Cascade Mountains and the Coast Range, there's always something seasonal and delicious growing. Like persimmons dangling from bare branches like ornaments, winter's jewels can be unexpected and are all the sweeter for it.

Winter demands more time of the cook, but its braises, roasts, and baked goods also warm kitchens, steam windows, and perfume the air with the aromas of roasted chicken, gingerbread, and spiced cider, the ingredients for which intrepid shoppers seek out at their farmers' market, come rain or shine.

ANCIENT HERITAGE DAIRY

WHEN THE FATHER-AND-SON TEAM OF Paul and Hank Obringer moved their cheese-making operation from the high-desert climes of Madras, Oregon, to industrial Southeast Portland in January 2015, the original pasteurizer was the only piece of equipment they brought with them. They left behind the sheep and dairy cows that were the source of milk for their award-winning cheeses to become Portland's first urban creamery in decades.

Their new home, the Weatherly Creamery Building, housed a creamery in the 1920s that manufactured ice cream, butter, and cheese. Today, Paul, Hank, and their staff occupy a bright, 2,200-square-foot facility outfitted with three temperature- and humidity-controlled cheese caves, a shiny stainless steel milk tank, and a cheese-making vat. Their neighbors include Renata, a rustic Italian restaurant owned by the Arnerich family, who originally met Paul at the Portland Farmers Market and eventually became the primary benefactor of the urban creamery. The neighborhood is populated by distillers, coffee roasters, and artisan food producers.

The Obringer family has been making cheese for a decade. Paul and Kathy, his late wife, happened on the idea because their boys were allergic to cow's milk. They kept goats for their milk but weren't sure what to do with the surplus. There were already plenty of good local goat cheese-makers, and Paul and Kathy shared a love of the sweet, creamy, round flavor of sheep's milk, so they acquired ten ewes and a ram.

Paul was no stranger to the food business, having worked in bakeries and restaurants in Chicago. Kathy was an artist, and she and Paul adopted a somewhat unorthodox approach to making cheese: skip the science and go straight to the art. Beginning with recipes and techniques for making classic small-batch French-style cheeses, they experimented and gradually earned a national reputation among chefs, cheesemongers, and eaters. The recipe for their award-winning Hannah, a natural-rind, raw cow and sheep's milk cheese, was Kathy's.

Making cheese in the city offers new challenges and variables. Now that he has a small staff and support from local partners, Paul has more time to focus on marketing efforts—hand-selling his cheeses to local grocery and specialty food shops, as well as cultivating an audience outside the Pacific Northwest. There's also a retail cheese counter to stock and manage, creamery tours to lead, and cheese-making classes to teach.

Perhaps the most exciting part of this new chapter is Paul's continued enthusiasm and the belief that he and Hank, who has been working with his father since he was fourteen years old and is head cheesemaker, are now making some of their best cheese. Some people look for a change of scenery when they retire; Paul just needed a different view from his "office window."

SMALL PLATES

Creamy Turnip Soup with Garlic-Parsley Butter 191

Black Kale and Roasted Beet Salad with Balsamic 193

Carrot, Prune, and Parsley Salad 195

Freekeh Salad with Sweet Potatoes,
Persimmons, and Yogurt Cheese 196

Kabocha Squash Drop Biscuits 198

Leek Gratin with Gruyère 199

Hakurei Turnips with Miso-Butter 200

CREAMY TURNIP SOUP
with Garlic-Parsley Butter

ROBERT REYNOLDS, AS SUBMITTED BY BLAKE VAN ROEKEL, CHEFSTUDIO

Those who cooked or studied with the late Robert Reynolds would likely characterize this recipe as "classic Robert." That something this delicious could be made with just water and a few simple ingredients both shocks and delights those who taste this soup. Robert was a French-trained chef and Portland food icon who mentored and inspired an impressive list of local talent, taught cooking classes in Portland and France, and authored several cookbooks. He was a jovial presence at farmers' markets, where he shopped faithfully and enthusiastically, trading marketplace banter between purchases. We still miss him.

Makes 8 servings

1. In a Dutch oven or large stockpot, warm 2 tablespoons of the butter over medium-high heat. When the butter is foamy, add the onions and sauté, stirring occasionally, until they are soft and translucent, but haven't begun to brown, 5 to 7 minutes. Add the turnips, ½ cup of the water, and a large pinch of salt, stir to combine, and cover the pot. Reduce the heat to low and continue to cook until the turnips begin to fall apart, about 15 minutes.

2. When the turnips are soft, add the remaining 7½ cups water, another pinch of salt, some pepper, and the bouquet garni. Gently simmer the soup for 30 minutes, then remove the pan from the heat to cool slightly. In a blender, puree the soup in batches, straining each one through a fine-mesh sieve into a clean pot. Stir in the cream, season to taste with more salt and pepper, and return the soup to the stove over medium-low heat to warm through.

3. While the soup reheats, in the bowl of a food processor, process the remaining 6 tablespoons butter, garlic, shallots, parsley, and nutmeg until smooth. Season to taste with salt and pepper.

4. To serve, ladle the hot soup into bowls and place a dollop of garlic-parsley butter on top.

½ cup (1 stick) unsalted butter, divided

2 medium onions, cut into ½-inch dice

2 medium (6 to 8 ounces each) yellow turnips (aka rutabagas), trimmed, peeled, and cut into ½-inch dice

8 cups water, divided

Kosher salt and freshly ground black pepper

1 bouquet garni of parsley, bay, and thyme (see Bouquet Garni on the following page)

1 cup light or heavy cream

1 small garlic clove

2 small shallots, finely minced

⅓ cup lightly packed flat-leaf parsley leaves

Several gratings of whole nutmeg

CONTINUED

HOW TO CHOOSE AND STORE TURNIPS

Root vegetables harvested after the last freeze will be noticeably sweeter. When they are exposed to cold weather, they convert their starches to sugars, which prevents the water in their cell structure from freezing. Their survival tactic is our reward.

When shopping for rutabagas or yellow turnips, look for full, meaty-looking roots with their tops intact and no soft spots and cracks. To store, trim all but 1 inch of the top and place the root in an open plastic bag in the refrigerator for up to 2 weeks.

BOUQUET GARNI

An important contribution from the French kitchen, a bouquet garni is a small bundle of herbs, usually tied with kitchen twine or wrapped in cheese-cloth like a sachet, used to flavor stock, soups, stews, and sauces. Parsley, bay, and thyme are the classic trio, to which other herbs can be added to complement the item being flavored.

BLACK KALE AND ROASTED BEET
SALAD *with Balsamic*

KIMBERLY BOLSTER, CO-OWNER, DEEP ROOTS FARM, ALBANY, OREGON

Here is a welcome variation on the raw-kale salads we've come to expect, and maybe even grown weary of. In this recipe, lacinato kale (*cavolo nero*, or "black kale," in Italian) and beet greens are cooked briefly, so they retain a pleasing firmness. Though the simple combination of flavors needs no embellishment, crumbled feta cheese and toasted walnuts would dress it up beautifully.

Makes 4 servings

1. Preheat the oven to 450 degrees F.

2. Trim the beet greens, pick out the nice-looking leaves, wash, and set them aside. Peel the beets and cut them, depending on their size, into 6 or 8 wedges each. Put the beets in a small roasting pan and toss them with 1 tablespoon of the oil and a generous pinch of salt. Add about 2 tablespoons of water to the pan, or enough to just cover the bottom. Tightly cover the pan with aluminum foil and roast the beets until they are tender when pierced with a fork, about 25 minutes.

3. Meanwhile, bring a large pot with several inches of generously salted water to a boil over medium-high heat. Trim and discard the stems from the reserved beet greens and roughly chop the leaves. Stir the chopped kale and beet greens into the boiling water and cook, stirring frequently, until tender, about 3 minutes. Drain the greens into a colander and rinse them with cold water to stop the cooking. When the greens are cool enough to handle, squeeze the excess water from them and transfer them to a large serving bowl.

4. In a small sauté pan over medium heat, heat the remaining 2 tablespoons of oil. When the oil shimmers, add the garlic and sauté until it is golden brown, about 2 minutes. Remove the pan from the heat, add the vinegar, and gently swirl the pan to combine it with the oil.

5. Pour the dressing over the beets, toss to coat them, and add the beets to the greens. Toss again and season to taste with additional salt and pepper. Serve the salad at room temperature or slightly chilled.

1 bunch beets (about 1 pound or 7 small beets), greens attached

3 tablespoons extra-virgin olive oil, divided

Kosher salt

1 bunch black kale

4 garlic cloves, finely minced

2 tablespoons balsamic vinegar

Freshly ground black pepper

CARROT, PRUNE, AND PARSLEY SALAD

KRISTEN D. MURRAY, CHEF/OWNER, MÅURICE

Kristen's aunt—who loved carrots and simply prepared salads that, in her words, "let the garden speak"—was the inspiration for this salad. Kristen's addition of toasted cumin seeds adds a sophisticated touch that makes the salad perfect fare for Måurice, her acclaimed modern pastry luncheonette.

One of the many benefits of buying carrots at the market, is that, unlike their grocery store cousins, they usually come with their greens attached. Don't discard them: the tender tips can be added to the salad like an herb, and the rest can be used to make pesto. Kristen likes to use carrots from Prairie Creek Farm or DeNoble Farms for this salad.

Makes 6 servings

1. Discard any carrot greens that are yellow or dry looking, and trim about 1 inch of the tender tips. Coarsely chop the carrot tips and set them aside. Thinly shave the carrots, using a mandoline or a vegetable peeler to create ribbons. In a large bowl, toss the carrot ribbons with enough oil to coat them, and set them aside.

2. In a small dry skillet over medium-low heat, toast the cumin seeds, stirring them frequently, until they turn several shades darker, smell fragrant, and start to pop, 3 to 4 minutes. Add the warm cumin seeds to the carrots.

3. Thinly slice the prunes into strips. Add them to the carrots with a generous squeeze of lemon juice, a pinch of salt, and pepper to taste. Add more oil if necessary and then the parsley leaves. Gently toss again, sprinkle with the reserved tender tips of the carrot tops, and arrange the salad on a platter or individual plates, twisting the carrots as you would pasta.

10 to 12 carrots (about 2 pounds) in a variety of colors, greens reserved

Extra-virgin olive oil, for tossing the salad

1 tablespoon cumin seeds

⅓ cup pitted prunes

1 small lemon

Kosher salt and freshly ground black pepper

½ cup loosely packed fresh parsley leaves

FREEKEH SALAD

with Sweet Potatoes, Persimmons, and Yogurt Cheese

TIMOTHY WASTELL, CHEF AND PORTLAND FARMERS MARKET SHOPPER

Freekeh (or frikeh) is an ancient grain that's a staple in the Middle East. Try to find whole *freekeh* in specialty stores and well-stocked groceries; when it's crushed, it loses its appealing nuttiness and texture, which this salad highlights. Or substitute farro or wheat berries. Toast the grains prior to simmering at 400 degrees F until they are fragrant and golden brown, three to four minutes. Because they cook a bit more quickly, start checking them after twenty-five minutes.

When you are ready to assemble it, build the salad in layers, to ensure the proper texture and marriage of flavors. The *freekeh* can be made up to three days ahead, and the yogurt cheese can be made up to one week ahead of time. Store both in the refrigerator.

Makes 6 servings

1 cup whole (not crushed) *freekeh*, farro, or wheat berries

1 bay leaf

1 teaspoon kosher salt

1 tablespoon extra-virgin olive oil

FOR THE SWEET POTATOES:

2 to 3 small sweet potatoes, such as Beauregard, peeled

Kosher salt

2 tablespoons extra-virgin olive oil

1 tablespoon apple cider vinegar

———————

½ cup Yogurt Cheese (recipe follows)

6 teaspoons extra-virgin olive oil, divided

Piment d'Espelette or hot or smoked paprika, for seasoning

1. Rinse the grains in several changes of cold water; this will remove any chaff or grit. Drain it well and transfer it to a pot with the bay leaf and salt. Cover the *freekeh* with cold water by 2½ inches and bring the water to a gentle boil over medium-low heat. (Boiling the grains over high heat may result in a gummy texture.)

2. Cook the *freekeh* until the grains are tender but slightly al dente, 30 to 40 minutes. Drain it and transfer it to a medium bowl. Toss the *freekeh* with the oil and season it to taste with salt. Let it cool to room temperature and then refrigerate it for up to 3 days.

3. To make the sweet potatoes, preheat the oven to 400 degrees F.

4. Cut the sweet potatoes into uniform cubes, about 1 inch in size. In a large bowl, toss the potatoes with a generous pinch of salt and the oil and vinegar. Tip the contents of the bowl onto a baking sheet with sides, large enough to hold the potatoes in a single layer. Roast the potatoes until they are cooked through and caramelized along the edges, about 15 minutes. Set the pan aside to cool slightly, or leave at room temperature.

5. To assemble the salad, smear a generous tablespoon of the yogurt cheese on the bottom and up the sides of 6 bowls. Lightly drizzle about 1 teaspoon of the oil over the yogurt in each bowl and sprinkle with piment d'Esplette. Add the sweet potatoes to the *freekeh* and season to taste with salt and pepper, and more vinegar and oil as needed. Gently mix the ingredients until they're well combined and uniformly seasoned. Spoon about ½ cup into each bowl.

6. In a large bowl, combine the persimmons with the mustard greens. Season with a pinch of *fleur de sel*, a squeeze of lemon juice, and a few drops of vinegar. Add the mint and toss to distribute it. Place a small handful on top of the *freekeh* and sweet potatoes in each bowl and serve immediately.

Salt and freshly ground black pepper

Apple cider vinegar

Extra-virgin olive oil

2 small Fuyu persimmons, very thinly sliced

1 bunch (about 6 ounces) mustard greens, preferably Ruby Streaks, stemmed and torn into 1-inch pieces

Fleur de sel or coarse sea salt, such as Maldon

1 small lemon

5 fresh mint leaves, julienned

YOGURT CHEESE

Makes about 1 cup

1. In a small bowl, whisk the yogurt with the salt until the salt dissolves. Transfer it to a fine-mesh sieve lined with cheesecloth and place the sieve over a container to catch the whey that will drain from the yogurt. Refrigerate overnight or until the consistency is similar to cream cheese, up to 3 days.

16 ounces Greek yogurt

1 teaspoon fine sea salt

HOW TO CHOOSE AND STORE FUYU PERSIMMONS

Fuyu and Hachiya are the two main persimmon varieties. Fuyus have a squat profile, like a tomato, and can be eaten raw. (Hachiyas must be cooked.) Their flavor is the essence of a sugar-sweet, freshly cut squash, and is comfortable on either end of the salty-sweet spectrum. Choose Fuyus that are firm but not hard; store them on the counter to ripen for up to 3 weeks.

KABOCHA SQUASH DROP BISCUITS

NATHAN MCFALL, OWNER, CONVERGING CREEKS FARM

These versatile biscuits are easy to put together, especially if you have a cup of leftover squash puree. (You can use grated fresh squash if you don't.) The recipe comes from a traditional McFall family recipe made with leftover sweet potatoes. Substitute olive or coconut oil for the butter, and maple syrup or sugar for the honey. Add roasted garlic and fresh herbs for biscuits that partner nicely with eggs or a bowl of soup. Or try a few gratings of fresh nutmeg or a pinch of cinnamon to transform the savory orange-colored biscuits into something that begs to be slathered with butter and honey.

Makes 1 dozen biscuits

2 cups unbleached all-purpose flour

¾ teaspoon fine sea salt

1 tablespoon plus 1 teaspoon baking powder

¼ cup (½ stick) unsalted butter, cold, cut into small pieces

1 cup cooked, mashed winter squash or packed grated squash

½ to ¾ cup whole milk

2 tablespoons local raw honey

1. Preheat the oven to 425 degrees F. Line a baking sheet with parchment paper, or lightly butter it, and set it aside.

2. In a large bowl, whisk together the flour, salt, and baking powder. Cut the cold butter pieces into the dry ingredients using a pastry blender, two knives, or your fingertips, until the mixture resembles coarse meal.

3. In a small bowl, combine the squash, ½ cup of the milk, and the honey, and stir the mixture into the dry ingredients. Mix gently until a soft, wet dough forms. Add the remaining ¼ cup milk a little at a time, until all of the flour is moistened. The amount of milk you need will depend on the moisture of the squash; you may not need any.

4. Drop large spoonfuls of dough 2 inches apart on the prepared baking sheet. Bake rotating the pan halfway through, until the biscuits are light golden brown and slightly darker on the bottoms and around the edges, 14 to 16 minutes.

SELECTING WINTER SQUASH

No one ever seems to say so, but we all know that winter squash are basically interchangeable (spaghetti squash is the exception). Kabocha, Buttercup Butternut, Red Kuri, Blue Hubbard, Long Island Cheese: they range slightly in flavor, and their textures sometimes diverge, but 1 pound of any winter squash will yield about 2 cups of cooked squash. Substitute one for the other freely, or with sweet potatoes or pumpkin.

Choose heavy squash with a fat, dry stem on top. They will keep, out of direct sunlight, for several months.

LEEK GRATIN
with Gruyère

MARVEN WINTERS, OWNER, WINTERS FARMS

This rich, creamy gratin is made in the original style before the dish became associated with potatoes. Before the eighteenth century, swish chard, cardoons, or leeks, combined with cream, were more usual.

To clean the leeks, trim the roots and peel away the soft outer layer. Remove the dark-green tops (reserve them to make stock) leaving the white and pale-green parts. Slice them in half lengthwise and fan them under cold running water to completely wash away the grit that hides there. Dry them completely before using.

Makes 4 to 6 servings

1. Cut the leeks into ½-inch pieces. You should have about 6 cups, loosely packed. Melt the butter in a heavy skillet over medium heat and add the leeks with a generous pinch of salt and some pepper. Sauté the leeks, stirring occasionally, for 2 to 3 minutes, then add the cream and bring it to a simmer. Reduce the heat to low, cover the pan, and simmer for about 10 minutes.

2. Meanwhile, preheat the oven to 350 degrees F and butter a 2-quart baking dish or gratin pan.

3. When the oven is hot and the leeks are cooked, spoon them into the prepared dish and sprinkle the cheese over the top. Bake until a golden brown crust forms, 10 to 15 minutes.

2 pounds leeks (about 6 to 8 small leeks), trimmed and cleaned

1 tablespoon butter, plus more for buttering the baking dish

Kosher salt and freshly ground black pepper

½ cup heavy cream

4 ounces Gruyère cheese, grated (about 1 cup)

HAKUREI TURNIPS
with Miso Butter

HARRY SHORT, OWNER, MUDJOY FARM

Creamy, white-fleshed Hakurei turnips are a Japanese variety sometimes called "salad turnips." Their tender skin seldom requires peeling, and they are crisp and delicious eaten raw, in a salad or slaw. This preparation is a perfect example of the vegetable version of nose-to-tail eating: cooking the turnips with their peppery greens enhances their sweet flavor and velvety texture, while the buttery, umami-rich sauce enrobing them transforms the vegetable to much more than a side.

Makes 4 to 6 servings

4 tablespoons (½ stick) unsalted butter, slightly softened, divided

3 tablespoons white miso

1 tablespoon extra-virgin olive oil

1 small onion, thinly sliced

2 bunches Hakurei or other small white turnips with greens (about 2 pounds)

½ cup vermouth or dry white wine

⅛ teaspoon kosher salt

1 cup water

¼ teaspoon smoked paprika

1. In a small bowl, mash 3 tablespoons of the butter and the miso together, and set it aside.

2. In a medium sauté pan with a lid, heat the oil over medium-high heat. Sauté the onions, stirring occasionally, until they begin to brown lightly, about 10 minutes. Meanwhile, trim the stems and greens from the turnips; discard the stems and coarsely chop the greens. Trim the taproot from the turnips and cut them in 1-inch wedges.

3. When the onions are brown and fragrant, add the remaining 1 tablespoon butter, the vermouth, salt, turnips, and water to the pan. Bring the contents to a boil over medium-high heat, cover, and simmer for 8 minutes.

4. Remove the lid and add the turnip greens one handful at a time, turning and stirring them with tongs and adding more as the volume in the pan reduces. Cover and cook for 1 minute. Uncover the pan and add the miso butter, stirring to combine. Continue cooking until the turnips are tender and liquid is reduced to a glaze, about 2 minutes. Season to taste with additional salt, if necessary, and sprinkle with the paprika.

LARGE PLATES

Tortilla Casserole with Butternut Squash
and Guajillo Chili Sauce 202

Northwest Halibut Bouillabaisse 204

Braised Beef Short Ribs 207

Dungeness Crab Cakes 209

Southern Squash Casserole 210

Celery Root "Schnitzel" with Brown Butter and Capers 211

Slow-Roasted Pork Shoulder with Carrots Two Ways 212

TORTILLA CASSEROLE

with Butternut Squash and Guajillo Chili Sauce

WENDY DOWNING, THREE SISTERS NIXTAMAL

"Three Sisters" is a reference to the symbiotic trio of corn, beans, and squash, which have been grown together for thousands of years. "What grows together, goes together," they say, and that's certainly true of this tasty, satisfying casserole. Portland Farmers Market shoppers can pick up dried *guajillo* chilies at the Westwind Gardens stall, at the end of summer and tuck them away to make this dish. New Mexico or cascabel chilies can be substituted.

You can prepare this casserole ahead of time, though its textures and flavors are most distinct when it's assembled, baked, and served straight from the oven.

Makes 4 servings

1½ cups butternut squash cut in ½-inch dice

3 tablespoons extra-virgin olive oil, divided

1 teaspoon sea salt, plus more for roasting the squash

8 garlic cloves, unpeeled

8 *guajillo* chilies (about 1¾ ounces), stemmed and seeded

12 black peppercorns

2 whole cloves

2 allspice berries

1 teaspoon agave nectar or sugar

1 teaspoon apple cider vinegar

1 cup Homemade Chicken Stock (page 157), vegetable stock, or water

1 small white onion, cut into ¼-inch dice

2 cups cooked black beans

Freshly ground black pepper

9 blue corn tortillas, such as Three Sisters

1 cup shredded Oaxaca, mozzarella, or Monterey Jack cheese

1. Preheat the oven to 350 degrees F.

2. In a small bowl, toss the squash with 1 tablespoon of the oil and a pinch of salt. Spread the squash out in 1 layer on a baking sheet. Roast the squash until it is just tender, about 20 minutes. Set the roasted squash aside.

3. Meanwhile, in a large cast-iron skillet over medium heat, gently roast the garlic cloves, turning them often so that they cook evenly without burning, about 15 minutes. Remove them to a plate to cool. Toast the chilies for about 30 seconds on each side, so that they blister without blackening. Remove the chilies to a medium bowl and fill the bowl with cold water to cover. Soak the chilies for 15 minutes, then drain them and set them aside.

4. Peel the garlic cloves and put them in a blender, along with the peppercorns, cloves, allspice, agave, vinegar, salt, softened chilies, and ¾ cup water. Blend on high until smooth and strain the sauce through a fine-mesh sieve to remove any seeds.

5. Warm another tablespoon of the oil in a saucepan over medium-high heat. Carefully add the chili sauce, which it will sputter and spit. Cook the sauce, stirring constantly, until it darkens and thickens slightly, about 5 minutes. Add the stock and simmer over medium heat for about 15 minutes. You should have 1½ to 1¾ cups of sauce.

6. Warm the remaining tablespoon of oil in a sauté pan over medium-high heat. Add the onions, reduce the heat to medium low,

and gently brown the onions, stirring occasionally. Add ¼ cup of the sauce and the beans. Simmer until the beans are tender enough that they can be easily mashed with the back of a spoon, about 5 minutes. (You can use a blender to puree them if you prefer, but don't make them too smooth; some texture should remain.) Turn off the heat, add the roasted squash, and season to taste with salt and pepper. Set aside.

7. Soften the tortillas by heating them on each side in a hot cast-iron pan. Pile them in a stack on a plate, lightly covered with a clean towel to keep them warm.

8. To assemble the casserole, spread ¼ cup of the sauce in an 8-by-8-inch baking dish. Tear up 3 tortillas and layer them evenly over the bottom. Cover the tortillas with half of the beans and squash, top with ½ cup of sauce, and add a second layer of torn tortillas. Top the tortillas with the remaining bean and squash mixture, half of the remaining sauce, and half of the cheese. Finish up with a third layer of tortillas and the remaining sauce and cheese. Bake the casserole for 20 minutes, remove it from the oven, and let it sit for 5 minutes before serving. Garnish the casserole with the radishes, avocado, onion, and cilantro.

FOR GARNISH:

Sliced radishes

Avocado

Diced onion

Cilantro leaves

NORTHWEST HALIBUT BOUILLABAISSE

PIPER DAVIS, CO-OWNER AND CULINARY DIRECTOR, GRAND CENTRAL BAKERY

This one-pot meal is a Northwest take on the classic Provençal seafood stew. Instead of the usual assortment of fish and shellfish in the French dish, this version calls for poaching wild-caught halibut in a rich vegetable broth.

You'll be amazed at the dimension broth takes on when the everyday vegetables it contains—carrots, celery, and onions—are purchased from farmers committed to the best flavors and growing conditions. It's also worth breaking out a jar of precious home-canned tomatoes for this recipe. Ladling the stew over thick slices of rustic bread makes for a satisfying meal.

Makes 4 servings

2 tablespoons extra-virgin olive oil, plus more for drizzling the bread

1 medium yellow onion, cut into ½-inch dice (about 1½ cups)

2 small fennel bulbs, cut into ½-inch dice (about 1 cup)

2 carrots, cut into ½-inch dice (about 1 cup)

2 stalks celery, cut into ½-inch dice (about 1 cup)

3 garlic cloves, peeled, divided

½ teaspoon red pepper flakes, plus more for garnish

1 teaspoon kosher salt

½ cup dry white wine

2 cups canned tomatoes, preferably home-canned

1½ pounds halibut

Freshly ground black pepper

1 loaf rustic bread or baguette

½ cup loosely packed celery leaves or parsley leaves, for garnish

1 lemon, quartered, for garnish

1. In a large pot or Dutch oven, warm the oil over medium-high heat. Add the onions and fennel, and sauté until lightly translucent, about 5 minutes. Add the carrots, celery, 2 cloves of the garlic, the pepper flakes, and salt. Reduce the heat to medium and continue to cook, stirring occasionally, until the vegetables are cooked through and lightly caramelized, 10 to 15 minutes total. Increase the heat to medium high, add the wine, and cook until the liquid has reduced by slightly more than half. Add the tomatoes and, if needed, enough water to make a rich, slightly thick soup. Reduce the heat and simmer, partially covered, until the broth is deeply flavorful, about 30 minutes.

2. Cut the fish into 4 equal pieces and remove the skin. Lightly sprinkle them with salt and nestle the pieces in the broth; there should be enough liquid to immerse them almost entirely. Cover the pan and gently simmer until the fish is firm but tender, about 15 minutes.

3. Meanwhile, preheat the broiler. Cut the bread into thick slices and arrange them on a baking sheet. Broil the bread 6 inches from the heat for about 1 minute per side, until the slices are golden brown around the edges. Rub each slice with the remaining whole garlic clove and drizzle with olive oil.

4. To serve, lay a piece of toast in each of 4 shallow bowls. Top with a piece of halibut and ladle about 6 ounces of broth into each bowl. Sprinkle with the celery leaves, garnish with a pinch of pepper flakes and a lemon wedge, and serve immediately.

BRAISED BEEF SHORT RIBS

VITALY PALEY, CHEF/OWNER, IMPERIAL, PORTLAND PENNY DINER,
AND PALEY'S PLACE BISTRO & BAR

Vitaley Paley is a recipient of the James Beard Award and one of a handful of chefs responsible for shaping the Portland food scene. Many of the city's prominent chefs passed through Vitaley's kitchen at some point in their careers.

Meaty beef short ribs are braised in this recipe in what might appear to be a large volume of liquid. You'll understand once you've tasted the result that it's only by reducing it significantly that the sauce comes to a wonderfully sweet and sour place. Have some extra stock on hand for replenishing the liquid if the level drops and no longer covers the ribs.

These ribs are especially good with potatoes (see Meat and Potatoes, following page, for ideas).

Makes 6 servings

1. Cut the onion in half and, using tongs or a carving fork, burn the halves over an open flame until they are black all over. In a large nonreactive saucepan, combine the stock, tomatoes, wine, chilies, sherry, carrots, thyme, and bay leaves. Add the blackened onions and bring the liquid to a boil over medium-high heat. Reduce the heat to a gentle simmer and cook until a rich flavor is achieved, about 30 minutes.

2. Preheat the oven to 325 degrees F.

3. While the braising liquid reduces, pat the ribs dry with paper towels and season them generously on all sides with salt and pepper. In a lidded Dutch oven or braising pan, heat the oil over medium-high heat. When the oil is hot, add the ribs, in 2 batches, in a single layer and brown them on all sides, about 8 minutes per batch. Remove the ribs from the pan to a plate and set them aside.

4. Add about 2 cups of the braising liquid to the pan, scraping the bottom to loosen any brown bits. Add the seared ribs back to the pan, along with the remaining braising liquid and vegetables, and the prunes. Bring the liquid back to a simmer over medium-high heat, cover the pan, and put the ribs in the

1 large onion, peeled

2 quarts Homemade Chicken Stock (page 157) or beef stock, or store-bought

2 cups peeled canned tomatoes

1 cup dry red wine

4 *pasilla* chilies, stemmed and seeded

½ cup cream sherry

3 medium carrots

½ bunch fresh thyme sprigs (about 10 large sprigs), tied with butcher's twine

4 bay leaves

5 pounds bone-in beef short ribs

Sea salt and freshly ground black pepper

3 tablespoons extra-virgin olive oil

3 cups pitted prunes

CONTINUED

oven to braise until they are tender, about 2½ hours. Use a pair of tongs to turn the ribs every 45 minutes or so. Test the ribs for doneness by pulling on one of the bones; it should slide out freely from the meat.

5. When the ribs are tender, remove the pan from the oven. Discard the onions and thyme bundle, and remove the whole carrots, cut them into chunks, and add them back to the braise. Return the pan to the oven or stove top to heat through completely and serve immediately.

MEAT AND POTATOES

Whether simply mashed and finished with freshly grated horseradish or layered with onions in a Lyonnaise-style gratin, potatoes are a natural complement to beef short ribs. Chef Paley's favorite preparation is the one they serve at Imperial: potatoes steamed, roasted over a wood fire, smashed by hand, then roasted again (at high heat in the oven with butter) until they're crispy and golden brown around the edges. When they come out of the oven, they're tossed with more butter and fresh dill, and finished with flaky sea salt and a drizzle of olive oil. Sometimes there's even a generous dollop of thick, garlicky aioli on top.

DUNGENESS CRAB CAKES

PATRICIA "RUBY" EDWARDS, LINDA BRAND CRAB

Dungeness crabs are prized in the Pacific Northwest, and an ingredient beloved by Portland native son James Beard. Beard's recipe for Grammie Hamblet's Deviled Crab is one of his best known, and bears a close resemblance to the one for these luscious, unfussy crab cakes.

Dungeness crab season typically starts in the late fall and ends in early spring, peaking during the holidays when splurging is encouraged.

Makes 8 cakes

1. Put the crabmeat in a medium bowl. In a small bowl, whisk together the mayonnaise, eggs, Worcestershire, mustard, lemon juice, salt, and cayenne. Pour the mixture over the crabmeat and, using your hands, gently incorporate it into the crab, being careful not to overmix or break up all of the lumps. Sprinkle the bread crumbs and green onions over the top and fold them in gently. Cover the bowl with plastic wrap and refrigerate until the mixture has firmed up slightly, about 1 hour. Line a baking sheet lined with parchment or wax paper and set it aside.

2. When the crab mixture is chilled and firm, shape it into 8 (1-inch-thick) cakes and place them on the prepared baking sheet.

3. In a large sauté pan, warm the butter and oil over medium heat. When the mixture is foamy, add the crab cakes to the pan and cook until the bottoms are dark golden brown, 3 to 4 minutes. Flip the cakes over, reduce the heat slightly, and cook until well browned, another 4 to 5 minutes. Serve with the lemon wedges and tartar sauce.

1 pound Dungeness crabmeat, drained and picked through for shells

¼ cup mayonnaise

2 eggs, lightly beaten

½ teaspoon Worcestershire sauce

1 teaspoon Dijon mustard

1 teaspoon freshly squeezed lemon juice

½ teaspoon sea salt

¼ teaspoon cayenne pepper

1 cup unflavored cracker crumbs, bread crumbs, or panko

¼ cup finely sliced green onions (green parts only) or chives

2 tablespoons unsalted butter

¼ cup grapeseed or other neutral-flavored oil, for frying

Lemon wedges, for serving

Tartar sauce, for serving

FROZEN FISH: AS FRESH AS IT GETS

All plants and animals are affected by the seasons, and what comes from the sea is no different. Fish caught and flash-frozen at sea is at its peak of its freshness, flavor, and nutrition—and is better for fishermen and the environment, not to mention more economical. Buying and freezing fish in season prevents the harvest of fish out of season and reduces the pressure on fishermen by encouraging them to go to sea only in the safest conditions.

SOUTHERN SQUASH CASSEROLE

JIM DIXON, OWNER, REAL GOOD FOOD

Typically made with summer squash, this casserole becomes more substantial when winter squash is used instead. Almost any variety will do: butternut, kabocha, red kuri, or hubbard. Thin-skinned varieties such as delicata can be left unpeeled. A handful of chopped cooked bacon, leftover ham, or tasso (a spicy cured pork widely available in Louisiana) will elevate this one-pot meal into something authentic to its roots and extra special.

Makes 8 to 10 servings

¼ cup extra-virgin olive oil, divided

1 medium yellow onion, cut into ½-inch dice

1 green bell pepper, stemmed, seeded, and coarsely chopped (substitute a mix of hot and sweet green peppers if you want more heat)

2 stalks celery, thinly sliced

2 cups winter squash, peeled and cut into ¾-inch cubes

¼ cup water

2 tablespoons apple cider vinegar

1 teaspoon kosher salt

½ teaspoon freshly ground black pepper

¼ teaspoon cayenne pepper or Cajun-style spice blend, preferably without salt

2 garlic cloves, finely chopped

1 cup bread crumbs

2 cups cooked brown rice

1. In a shallow, wide sauté pan with a lid, warm 3 tablespoons of the oil over medium heat. Add the onions, peppers, and celery with a good pinch of salt and cook for about 10 minutes or until slightly softened and translucent. Add the squash, water, and vinegar. Reduce the heat to low, cover, and cook until the squash is tender, about 15 minutes. Add the salt, black and cayenne pepper, and garlic and cook for another few minutes, until fragrant, then remove the from the heat.

2. Preheat the oven to 350 degrees F.

3. In a small skillet, combine the bread crumbs and the remaining 1 tablespoon oil. Cook over medium heat until the bread crumbs have browned, about 10 minutes. Set the bread crumbs aside.

4. Fold the rice into the cooked vegetables and turn the mixture out into a 12-inch cast-iron skillet (or 9-by-13-inch baking dish). Top with the toasted bread crumbs and bake until heated through and bubbly, about 25 minutes.

CELERY ROOT "SCHNITZEL"

with Brown Butter and Capers

MONA JOHNSON, FORMER COMMUNICATIONS MANAGER, PORTLAND FARMERS MARKET

When celery root is plentiful at the farmers' market, this hearty vegetarian entrée is perfect for a chilly winter's eve. The root's delicate flavor shines against the crispy breading, while the brown butter sauce enhances the vegetable's inherent nuttiness. Capers, herbs, and bright notes of lemon add a dash of sunshine to the plate. Nothing is better with this schnitzel than a salad of mixed chicories.

Makes 4 servings

1. Bring a large pot of generously salted water to a boil over high heat. Meanwhile, peel the celery root and slice it into ½-inch-thick rounds. Choose 8 slices that are fairly equal in size and gently boil them until they are cooked through and easily pierced with the tip of a knife, about 10 minutes. Drain and pat the celery root dry with paper towels.

2. Put the flour, eggs, and bread crumbs in 3 separate shallow bowls. Season the bread crumbs with salt and pepper. One at a time, dip the celery root slices into the flour, coating both sides and shaking off the excess, then into the egg, and finally the bread crumbs. Pat the crumbs to adhere them evenly over the surface of each slice.

3. Heat ¼ cup of the oil in each of 2 large skillets over medium heat. Fry half of the celery root slices in each skillet, turning them once, until golden and crispy, about 3 to 4 minutes per side. Transfer the slices to drain on a plate lined with paper towels and sprinkle them with salt.

4. In a small light-colored saucepan that will allow you to see the color of the butter, heat the butter over medium heat, swirling occasionally so that it melts evenly. It will foam and change color from light to golden yellow, and then golden to toasty brown. When it begins to brown and smells nutty, remove the pan from the heat and immediately add the lemon juice and capers. To preserve their color, wait to stir the parsley and chives into the sauce until just before serving.

5. To assemble the dish, arrange 2 celery root schnitzels on each of 4 plates, spoon the brown butter sauce over the top, and serve immediately.

2 medium celery roots
(about 2 pounds)

½ cup unbleached
all-purpose flour

2 eggs, beaten

2 cups panko bread crumbs

Kosher salt and freshly ground
black pepper

½ cup neutral-flavored oil,
such as grapeseed, divided

½ cup (1 stick) unsalted butter,
cut in 8 pieces

2 tablespoons freshly
squeezed lemon juice (from
1 medium lemon)

2 tablespoons capers, drained

1 tablespoon finely chopped
fresh parsley

1 tablespoon finely chopped
fresh chives

SLOW-ROASTED PORK SHOULDER
with Carrots Two Ways

BENJAMIN BETTINGER, CHEF, AND PATRICK MCKEE, SOUS CHEF,
LAURELHURST MARKET

Braised meats and vegetables are especially satisfying in the winter months—comforting, warming recipes that are easily doubled to allow for leftovers and always manage to taste even better the next day. If you have chicken, pork, or even vegetable stock on hand, use it to braise the pork shoulder, instead of water. The leftover braising liquid can be reduced to make a rich sauce that can be served with the pork. (Even if you use water, the leftover liquid will be flavorful enough.) Instead of the pork shoulder, you could also use a whole bone-in pork roast. Try the spice mix on chicken, fish, lamb, and vegetables too.

Makes 4 servings

1½ pounds pork shoulder, cut into 4 equal pieces

Kosher salt

¼ cup Pork Spice Mix (recipe follows)

2 tablespoons grapeseed oil

1 medium onion, cut into ½-inch dice

2 carrots, cut into ½-inch dice

2 cups dry white wine

1 bunch fresh thyme sprigs

FOR THE CARROT PUREE:

¼ cup (½ stick) unsalted butter

1 pound orange carrots, sliced into ½-inch thick rounds

1 tablespoon kosher salt

2 teaspoons sugar

1 teaspoon Pork Spice Mix (recipe follows)

1 tablespoon freshly squeezed lemon juice

1. To make the pork, season the pork pieces with salt, and rub them all over with the spice mix. Refrigerate for 3 to 4 hours, or preferably overnight. Remove the pork from the refrigerator 1 hour before you're ready to begin the braise.

2. Preheat the oven to 300 degrees F.

3. In a large Dutch oven or roasting pan, warm the oil over medium-high heat. When the oil is hot, add the pork pieces and brown on all sides, turning every few minutes until each surface is caramelized, 8 to 10 minutes total. Remove the pork pieces from the pan to a plate and set them aside.

4. Add the onions and carrots to the pan and sauté the vegetables, stirring occasionally, until they begin to caramelize slightly, 5 to 6 minutes. Add the wine to the pan and reduce the heat slightly, scraping the bottom of the pan with a wooden spoon to loosen any brown bits. Continue to cook until the wine loses any sharpness, about 5 minutes. Add the pork pieces back to the pan with the thyme, cover by three-quarters with water or stock, increase the heat to high, and bring the liquid back to a boil. Cover the pan with a lid or wrap it tightly with aluminum foil and place it in the middle of the oven. Cook, checking the level of liquid and stirring occasionally, until the pork is fork-tender, about 3 hours. Add more water or stock as needed, if the level drops no longer covering the pork.

5. Meanwhile, make the carrot puree. In a large saucepan, melt the butter over medium heat. Add the carrots and cook, stirring occasionally, for 5 minutes before adding the salt, sugar, and pork spice. Stir to distribute the seasoning and add water just to cover the carrots. Reduce the heat to medium low and gently simmer the carrots until they are very tender, 8 to 10 minutes. Drain the carrots, reserving the cooking liquid.

6. Add the carrots to a blender or the bowl of a food processor. Add about ½ cup of the cooking liquid to start and blend until the carrots are very smooth. Add more liquid as needed to achieve a puree that's smooth but not too thick. When the consistency is to your liking, add the lemon juice and adjust the seasonings until the flavor is pleasing to you. You may want to add more spice mix. Keep the puree warm.

7. Just before serving, make the carrot salad. Using a vegetable peeler, shave the carrots lengthwise into ribbons. In a large bowl, toss the carrots with the vinaigrette and garnish with the hazelnuts and mint.

8. To assemble the dish, swoosh some carrot puree on each plate, place a piece of pork on or next to it and pile some carrot salad alongside the pork. Sprinkle a little extra mint and/or pork spice around the plate.

CONTINUED

FOR THE CARROT SALAD:

2 carrots, preferably 1 orange and 1 purple

Lemon-Cumin Vinaigrette (recipe follows)

¼ cup coarsely chopped toasted hazelnuts

6 small fresh mint leaves, julienned

Winter

PORK SPICE MIX

Makes about 1 cup

1. Heat a small sauté pan or cast-iron skillet over medium-high heat. When the pan is hot, reduce the heat to medium low and add the peppercorns, coriander, fennel, cumin, and yellow mustard seeds, gently shaking the pan until the spices are fragrant, 3 to 4 minutes. Take the pan off the heat and let the spices cool completely.

2. Finely grind the spices with a mortar and pestle or a spice grinder.

3. In a small bowl, thoroughly mix the ground spices with the salt. Store leftover spice mix in a cool, dry place or with your other spices. It will keep for 6 months.

2 tablespoons black peppercorns

2 tablespoons coriander seeds

2 tablespoons fennel seeds

2 tablespoons cumin seeds

2 tablespoons yellow mustard seeds

¼ cup kosher salt

LEMON-CUMIN VINAIGRETTE

Makes about ¾ cup

1. Measure the lemon juice. You should have 2 to 3 tablespoons from a medium lemon. Put the juice in a small bowl and add the cumin and fennel. While whisking, slowly drizzle in the oil at a ratio of 1 part lemon juice to 3 parts oil. Season to taste with salt and pepper.

2 to 3 tablespoons freshly squeezed lemon juice (from 1 medium lemon)

1½ teaspoons cumin seeds, toasted and ground

1 teaspoon fennel seeds, toasted and ground

6 to 9 tablespoons extra-virgin olive oil (how much you'll need depends on how much juice you get from the lemon)

Kosher salt and freshly ground black pepper

SWEETS, SIPS, AND CONDIMENTS

PARSNIP-PEAR BREAD

PAMELA KRAEMER, FORMER PORTLAND FARMERS MARKET
VENDOR AND OWNER, DULCET CUISINE

Like carrots, parsnips have a naturally sweet side that's right at home in the pastry kitchen. In this quick bread, the pears, which have an affinity for parsnips, don't compete with the root vegetable's delicate flavor. Both ingredients are enhanced with warm baking spices, including cinnamon and ginger, and hazelnuts. Change up the recipe by substituting apples for the pears, walnuts for the hazelnuts, omitting the cardamom, and increasing the ginger to two teaspoons.

Makes one 9-by-3-by-2-inch loaf

1. Preheat the oven to 350 degrees F. Lightly butter a 9-by-3-by-2-inch loaf pan and dust it with flour.

2. In a medium bowl, whisk together the flour, baking powder, baking soda, salt, cinnamon, cardamom, and ginger. Add the parsnips, pears, and hazelnuts, toss well to coat with the flour mixture, and set the bowl aside.

3. In a separate bowl, whisk the sugar and oil together until creamy and slightly lighter in color. Add the eggs and vanilla, continuing to whisk until the ingredients are well combined. Switch to a rubber spatula and gently fold in the dry ingredients until they are well distributed throughout the batter. Do not overmix the batter or your loaf will be tough and dense.

4. Scrape the batter into the prepared pan. Bake until a toothpick inserted in the middle of the loaf comes out clean, about 1½ hours, rotating the pan every 30 minutes. Transfer the pan to a wire rack to cool for 15 minutes before turning out the bread to cool completely.

2 cups unbleached all-purpose flour, plus more for dusting the pan

2 teaspoons baking powder

2 teaspoons baking soda

1 teaspoon fine sea salt

1 teaspoon ground cinnamon

1 teaspoon ground cardamom

½ teaspoon ground ginger

2 medium parsnips, trimmed, peeled, and grated (about 2 cups)

2 small firm but ripe pears, left unpeeled, cored, and grated (about 1 cup)

1 cup lightly toasted hazelnuts, coarsely chopped

1¼ cups sugar

1 cup canola, sunflower, or safflower oil

3 eggs

1 teaspoon pure vanilla extract

HOW TO CHOOSE AND STORE PARSNIPS

Choose parsnips that look plump and full, avoiding those with a stem end more than 1½ inches in diameter, or overly tapered (they'll be less "meaty"). If it's still attached, a parsnip's green top is a good indicator of its freshness. Store parsnips in the crisper drawer of the refrigerator, where they will keep for several weeks in an open plastic bag.

SWEET POTATO-GINGER COOKIE ICE CREAM SANDWICHES

LISA HERLINGER, FOUNDER, RUBY JEWEL ICE CREAM

Lisa Herlinger sold the first Ruby Jewel ice cream sandwich at the Portland Farmers Market, where the distinctly original treats quickly garnered a loyal following. Their ice cream sandwiches include classic combinations like chocolate chip cookies with vanilla bean ice cream, as well as seasonal favorites like this one.

If the Thanksgiving season could be embodied by a pair of flavors and colors, sweet-potato orange and gingersnap brown might be it. Think marshmallow-topped sweet-potato casserole; creamy sweet-potato pie; and gingerbread cake, houses, and people. Or lightly spiced sweet-potato ice cream sandwiched between molasses-rich ginger cookies. Together, the two are pure magic.

Makes about twenty 2½-inch sandwiches

1. Preheat the oven to 375 degrees F.

2. In a small bowl, toss the sweet potatoes with the butter, coating the pieces evenly. Stir in ½ teaspoon of the cinnamon, the cloves, and salt, taking care to distribute the spices thoroughly. Spread the sweet the potatoes in a single layer on a baking pan with sides and roast until they are soft, about 20 minutes. Remove the pan from the oven and let the potatoes cool slightly.

3. After they have cooled, puree the sweet potatoes in the bowl of a food processor until smooth. You should have a generous cup of puree; scrape it into a large nonreactive saucepan and whisk in the milk, cream, sugar, and remaining ¼ teaspoon cinnamon. Over medium heat, bring the mixture to a boil, stirring constantly to prevent it from sticking to the bottom of the pan. Reduce the heat to a gentle boil and continue to cook while stirring for 3 to 4 more minutes. Remove the pan from the heat, strain the mixture through a fine-mesh sieve into a clean metal bowl, and cool it over an ice bath until the base is room temperature. Remove the bowl from the ice bath, cover it with plastic wrap, and refrigerate at least 4 hours or up to overnight. The next day, freeze it in an ice cream maker according to the manufacturer's instructions.

12 ounces sweet potatoes, peeled and cut into ½-inch dice to make about 2 cups

3 tablespoons unsalted butter, melted

¾ teaspoon ground cinnamon, divided

¼ teaspoon ground cloves

½ teaspoon fine sea salt

2 cups whole milk

1½ cups heavy cream

⅔ cup sugar

CONTINUED

FOR THE COOKIES:

3 cups all-purpose flour

½ teaspoon ground cinnamon

½ teaspoon ground ginger

½ teaspoon fine sea salt

¼ teaspoon freshly
  grated nutmeg

¼ teaspoon ground cloves

1 cup (2 sticks) unsalted
  butter, at room
  temperature

1½ cups sugar

⅓ cup molasses

3 eggs

1 teaspoon pure vanilla extract

4. To make the cookies, in a medium bowl, whisk together the flour, cinnamon, ginger, salt, nutmeg, and cloves, and set it aside.

5. In the bowl of a stand mixer fitted with the paddle attachment, or using a handheld electric mixer, beat the butter and sugar on medium speed until smooth, 1½ to 2 minutes. Stop once to scrape down the sides of the bowl with a rubber spatula. Add the molasses and eggs and mix until blended, about 30 seconds. Add the vanilla, reduce the speed to low, and add the dry ingredients, mixing until blended and stopping twice to scrape down the bowl. Wrap the dough in plastic wrap and refrigerate for at least 3 hours, or preferably overnight.

6. When the dough is chilled, preheat the oven to 350 degrees F and line 2 baking sheets with parchment paper.

7. Using a 1-ounce scoop or your hands, form the dough into 1-inch balls and put them on the baking sheets, 2 inches apart. Bake the cookies until the edges have set, but the middles are still soft, 10 to 12 minutes. Remove the pan from the oven and transfer it to a wire rack to cool.

8. To assemble the ice cream sandwiches, place half of the cookies, bottom-side up, on a baking sheet lined with parchment paper. Place a scoop of ice cream on top of each cookie. Top with a second cookie and gently press down on the top cookie. Serve immediately or freeze until ready to serve. Once frozen, wrap the sandwiches well in plastic wrap, or store in an airtight container.

SWEET POTATO OR YAM?

Yes, yams *are* sweet potatoes. "Yam" came out of an early marketing campaign by Louisiana growers who hoped to make a distinction between their sweet, moist tubers and the dry, less flavorful ones grown in Virginia. Look for Garnets, with reddish skin and deep orange flesh, copper-skinned Jewels, and the purplish-skinned Beauregard, with dense, moist orange flesh.

CHOCOLATE-PEAR BREAD PUDDING

SARAH HART, OWNER/CHOCOLATIER, ALMA CHOCOLATE

This bread pudding is a vehicle not only for seasonal fruit, but for Alma Chocolate's delicious line of caramel sauces (Alma's Salted Caramel spiked with a little whiskey is particularly good). If you don't have some on hand, make a batch of the Caramel Sauce (page 171). You can even infuse it with herbs, spices, or spirits to complement the fruit you choose: whiskey caramel with pears and chocolate, lavender caramel with summer berries, vanilla bean caramel with rhubarb, or caramel finished with flaky sea salt for everything else.

Makes 10 to 12 servings

1. In a large mixing bowl, toss the bread and pears with the butter, making certain to evenly coat all of the pieces. Set the bowl aside.

2. In a medium saucepan over medium heat, bring the milk and cream to a simmer. Add the chocolate and whisk until it is completely melted and well combined. In a medium bowl, whisk the egg yolks and sugar together. Add the hot cream mixture to the yolk mixture while whisking constantly, about ½ cup at a time. After you've added half of the cream, scrape the yolk mixture into the saucepan, whisk vigorously to combine, and pour the custard over the bread cubes and pears. Set it aside for at least 1 hour for the bread to soak up the custard.

3. Preheat the oven to 350 degrees F and butter a 9-by-13-by-2-inch baking dish. Pour the custard-soaked bread and pears into the baking dish. Bake until the center of the pudding is just set, about 40 minutes.

4. Drizzle the whole pan generously with caramel sauce and serve warm, with vanilla ice cream or fresh unsweetened whipped cream.

8 cups stale baguette, cubed (or a combination of about 6 cups bread, plus any bits of leftover cake, croissant, rolls, etc.)

4 Anjou or Bartlett pears, firm but ripe, peeled, cored, and cut into ½-inch cubes

½ cup (1 stick) unsalted butter, melted, plus more for buttering the baking dish

3 cups whole milk

1½ cups heavy cream

12 ounces bittersweet chocolate, finely chopped

6 large egg yolks

1 cup sugar

Caramel sauce, for serving

Vanilla ice cream or whipped cream, for serving

PINOT-PLUMPED CHERRY PIE

CELESTE SHADBOLT BONNIKSEN, GENERAL MANAGER, CHERRY COUNTRY

Cherry Country is located in the Eola Hills, a historic cherry growing region west of Salem. What began as a cherry-growing "hobby" slowly evolved into Cherry Country, pulling in other family members and expanding into a line of cherry products including chocolates.

Full disclosure: This pie is a bit of an investment. A decent bottle of pinot noir and a pound of dried cherries will probably set you back more than you normally spend on dessert, but the pie that results from marrying the two ingredients is spectacular and serves a crowd. The rich, concentrated flavor that comes from poaching the cherries in wine means that just a sliver of this pie satisfies, especially if it's served with ice cream, crème fraîche, or a dollop of lightly sweetened whipped cream.

Makes one 9-inch double-crust pie

1 bottle Oregon pinot noir

1 pound (about 4 cups, lightly packed) dried tart cherries

1 cup sugar, plus extra for sprinkling

¼ cup unbleached all-purpose flour

1 large lemon, zest removed in several large strips with a vegetable peeler, and juiced

3 tablespoons cornstarch

1 tablespoon unsalted butter

Pinch of kosher salt

1 recipe Pacific Pie Company's All-Butter Pastry (page 84) or your favorite pie dough, refrigerated

2 tablespoons heavy cream

1. In a large nonreactive saucepan with a tight-fitting lid over medium heat, bring the wine to a simmer with the cherries. Remove the pan from the heat, cover it, and let the cherries steep until they are plump and have absorbed about half of the wine, 2 to 3 hours.

2. Strain the cherries, reserving the wine; you should have about 2 cups. Put the cherries in a large mixing bowl and set them aside.

3. Pour all but ¼ cup of the wine into a small nonreactive saucepan. Add the sugar and flour to the wine, whisking well. Add the lemon zest. In a small bowl, stir the remaining wine with the cornstarch and set aside. Preheat the oven to 425 degrees F.

4. Bring the contents of the pan to a low boil over medium-high heat and cook, stirring occasionally, until bubbly, 4 to 5 minutes. (This initial cooking will remove any flavor from the flour.) Add the wine-cornstarch mixture and continue to cook, stirring constantly, until the filling thickens to the consistency of honey and coats the back of a spoon. Remove the pan from the heat and add 3 tablespoons of the lemon juice, the butter, and the salt. Allow the filling to cool slightly before straining it through a fine-mesh sieve and adding more lemon juice to taste. Stir the filling into the bowl with the cherries.

5. Remove 1 pastry disk from the refrigerator and break it in half. Gently knead the halves together a few turns or until the dough is pliable. On a lightly floured work surface, roll the dough into a 12-inch circle approximately ⅛ inch thick. Carefully transfer the dough to a 9-inch pie pan, and gently press it into the bottom and up the sides. Refrigerate the bottom crust while you roll out the other pastry disk for the top crust.

6. Remove the bottom crust from the refrigerator and add the filling. Center the top crust as you lower it onto the pie. Seal the edges and crimp or flute the border using your fingers or a fork. Cut about 5 steam vents in the crust and brush it all over with the cream.

7. Bake the pie in the middle of the oven until the pastry is deep golden brown and the juices are bubbling from the vents and around the edges, 45 to 55 minutes. Check the pie periodically—if the crust gets too dark, loosely cover it with aluminum foil for the remainder of the cooking time to avoid further browning.

THE DHARMA GREEN JUICE

HEATHER CAPORASO, PORTLAND JUICE COMPANY

This invigorating juice strikes the right balance of sweet and savory, and delivers a wide range of vitamins, minerals, and antioxidants in each portion. Because most of the ingredients are grown year-round, it's an easy way to add more healthy greens or alkalinity to your diet in any season. Portland Juice Company sources as many ingredients as possible from local organic farms and encourages home juicers to do the same.

Makes 4 servings

1. Thoroughly rinse the ingredients. You may also want to coarsely chop them to limit the burden on your juicer, depending on its type and quality.

2. Beginning with the greens, add the ingredients to the juicer, interspersing with the apples and celery to help flush the greens through. Put the lemon through last and fill your container of choice with the juice. Stir or shake well, and enjoy.

½ bunch fresh kale

½ bunch fresh spinach

1 cup lightly packed parsley

1½ apples, quartered

1 bunch celery

1 lemon, peel removed (optional)

JUICING THROUGHOUT THE YEAR

Makes 4 servings (per recipe)

SPRING: Lavender, Lemon, and Ginger

½ tablespoon dried food-grade lavender buds

2-inch piece gingerroot

2½ lemons

½ cup local honey, preferably raw

- Put the lavender buds in a container with a lid, such as a canning jar, and pour 1 cup hot water (preferably filtered) over them. Cover the container and let the lavender steep for 5 to 10 minutes, until the flavor is to your liking. (You can also cover the lavender with cold water and let it steep overnight.)
- Peel the gingerroot, cut it into several small pieces, and put them through the juicer. Peel the lemons, quarter them, and juice them next, to help flush out the ginger. To a container of your choice, add the honey and 1 cup cold water (preferably filtered), along with the ginger and lemon juices. Stir vigorously to dissolve the honey, then strain the lavender water into the container and stir to combine.

SUMMER: Raspberry, Cucumber, and Mint

2 pints raspberries

2 cucumbers

1 bunch mint

¼ cup local honey, preferably raw

- Rinse the raspberries, cucumbers, and mint. Peel the cucumbers, if desired, halve them, and cut them into long, thin strips, according to the size of your juicer's feed tube. Alternate juicing the raspberries and mint, juicing the cucumbers last, to flush out the remnants of the other ingredients. Pour the juice into a container of your choice, add the honey, and stir vigorously to dissolve it.

FALL: Sweet Potato, Carrot, and Apple

½ sweet potato

6 medium carrots

1 apple

2 teaspoons ground cinnamon

- Gently scrub the sweet potato, carrots, and apple. Depending on the size of the sweet potato, cut it into smaller pieces that fit in your juicer's feed tube. Juice the sweet potato, then the carrots. Cut the apple in wedges and juice them last. Pour the juice into a container of your choice, add the cinnamon, and stir well to combine.

HARVEST HOLIDAY PUNCH

KIRSTIN JOHANSSON AND DANLYN BRENNAN, NEW DEAL DISTILLERY

This punch serves up a fizzy version of our favorite holiday flavors: freshly pressed apple cider, spicy ginger liqueur, and bubbly small-batch tonic. Add a festive ice ring studded with cranberries, orange slices, and whole star anise, and raise a glass to celebrate the season.

Note: Keep the ingredients for the punch chilled and mix them just before you are ready to serve it.

Makes 14 servings

FOR THE ICE RING:

1 orange, sliced

1½ cups fresh cranberries

8 to 10 whole star anise

———————————

1 bottle (750 milliliter) gin, such as Portland Dry Gin 33

1 bottle (375 milliliter) ginger liqueur, such as New Deal Ginger Liqueur

1 bottle (8 ounces) tonic syrup, such as Bradley's Kina Tonic

1½ cups local fresh-pressed apple cider

1½ cups sparkling water

1. To make the ice ring, arrange the oranges, cranberries, and star anise in the bottom of an 8-inch ring mold. Add a thin layer of water or juice and put the mold in the freezer. Once the fruit layer is frozen, add enough water or juice to fill the mold three-quarters full.

2. To make the punch, in a large pitcher, thoroughly stir together all the ingredients. Carefully place the ice ring in a punch bowl, pour the punch over the top, and serve.

CRAFT TONIC WATER

Most bottled tonic water is mediocre, which gets in the way of making stellar cocktails. It has become increasingly popular to whip up your own or use one of the small-batch tonic syrups being made around the country. Seattle-based Bradley's Tonic Company makes the only craft tonic—Kina Tonic syrup—in the Pacific Northwest. Typically, 1 tablespoon (½ ounce) of tonic syrup per 3 ounces of soda or seltzer water is the recommended ratio. If you can't find tonic syrup, substitute about 2½ cups of good craft tonic water.

KAMBURY'S CRANBERRY SAUCE

ALANA KAMBURY, CO-OWNER, STARVATION ALLEY FARMS

This is cranberry relish unlike any you've tasted. Cranberries are included in solid and liquid form (juice and fresh berries) for an intensely tart, puckery condiment for your turkey, roast pork, or cheese plate.

Though its market share is relatively small, Oregon's cranberries are the plumpest, juiciest, sweetest, and reddest you'll find. Grown in the temperate climate of the state's South Coast, they have a longer season: Oregon cranberries set fruit in May, when in other growing regions they have just begun to show bloom. The season continues through the fall, when those same regions have completed their harvest.

Makes about 3½ cups

1. Pour the cranberry juice into a large nonreactive saucepan. Core and coarsely chop 1 of the apples, leaving the skin on, and add it to the pan with the brown sugar, ginger, cinnamon stick, cloves, allspice, nutmeg, and pepper. Bring the mixture to a boil over medium-high heat, reduce the heat to a steady simmer, and cook until the volume is reduced by about half.

2. Pass the mixture through a fine-mesh sieve, pressing on the solids. Taste the juice; it should be barely sweet, fairly tangy, and slightly spicy. Return the reduced juice to the pan.

3. Leaving the skin on, core the remaining apple and dice it into ½-inch pieces. Add the apple to the juice with the cranberries, brandy, and vinegar, and return the mixture to a simmer. Cook, stirring occasionally, until the sauce thickens, 15 to 20 minutes. Remove the pan from the heat and transfer the sauce to a bowl to cool slightly. Cover it with plastic wrap and refrigerate it for at least 2 hours. Bring it to room temperature before serving, tasting it first and adding more acid, or some salt, as needed.

4 cups pure unsweetened cranberry juice, such as Starvation Alley Cranberry concoction

2 red-skinned apples, divided

½ cup packed light brown sugar

2 tablespoons finely chopped fresh ginger

1 cinnamon stick

4 whole cloves

1 teaspoon ground allspice

½ teaspoon freshly grated nutmeg

⅛ teaspoon freshly ground black pepper

1 pound fresh cranberries, preferably from Starvation Alley

2 tablespoons brandy or orange liquor, such as Grand Marnier

1 tablespoon balsamic vinegar

NATURALLY FERMENTED WINTER KRAUT

DAVID BARBER, OWNER, PICKLOPOLIS AND BINGO SANDWICHES

Homemade sauerkraut (literally "sour cabbage") is so much tastier than the commercially produced stuff that it's safe to assume those who don't love sauerkraut have yet to try it. And it's easy! If you're new to the process, make sure to read through the recipe and Fermenting Foods (opposite page) before you begin.

Makes about 2 quarts

3 pounds green cabbage (1 medium head), finely shredded

1 pound brussels sprouts, trimmed and finely shredded

1 pound kohlrabi, peeled and julienned or coarsely grated

5 tablespoons kosher salt (do not use table salt or salt containing iodine, which inhibits fermentation)

¼ teaspoon freshly ground black pepper

¼ teaspoon crushed fennel seeds

1. In a large bowl, toss the cabbage, brussels sprouts, and kohlrabi together with your hands and sprinkle the salt over the top. Toss again to incorporate the salt and lightly massage and squeeze the vegetables; they will begin to release liquid immediately. Add the pepper and fennel and transfer the ingredients into an impeccably clean container.

2. Pack the vegetables as tightly as possible. The ingredients must be completely submerged in the liquid for the entirety of the fermentation process; use a weight to ensure this. Lightly cover the container and let it sit undisturbed at room temperature away from direct sunlight.

3. If you are new to fermenting, check your kraut daily to begin to understand the process; if you're fermentation pro, check the kraut after 1 week. Whenever you check it, if you notice scum forming on the surface, use a clean spoon to remove it; this prevents intrusive bacteria and unwanted mold from establishing.

4. After 1 week, carefully wipe the exposed wall of the inside of your container clean of any scum and remove the weight to a sink or clean surface. Take a whiff—it should smell like something you'd enjoy eating. Insert a large, clean spoon down the side of the jar and underneath the "mat" of kraut. Carefully flip it over and taste a bit. The flavor should be more sour than salty at this point, and depending on your preference, it may not be quite ready. As long as it's not stinky or slimy, you're on your way (and if it is, use a clean spoon to remove any slime or scum from the surface). Replace the weight and return the container to the same spot for another week or so, keeping an eye out for scum or off odors.

5. At the end of the second week, switch to a smaller container, reserving the liquid so the contents are completely submerged. The kraut will get crispier and tastier over the course of weeks or months.

FERMENTING FOODS

Cabbage—and every other fruit and vegetable—has naturally occurring, beneficial bacteria on its surface. One of those bacteria, *Lactobacillus* (also found in yogurt and other cultured foods), converts vegetables' sugars into lactic acid when they are submerged in a brine. Lactic acid is a natural preservative that inhibits the growth of harmful bacteria.

Lacto-fermentation, the process used to make sauerkraut, has been used to preserve seasonal fruits and vegetables for centuries. It is easy, reliable, safe, and best of all, it transforms seemingly unsexy foods such as cabbage into something incredibly healthy and delicious.

Only a few pieces of "special equipment" stand between you and your first ferment. Here's a handy checklist:

· Your ingredients

· A tool for shredding them: A food processor or mandoline makes for lightning-quick shredding, but using a sharp knife for the Zen-like task will strengthen your knife skills and prove deeply satisfying.

· A super-clean work environment

· A large, impeccably clean food-grade container to hold the kraut, such as a stoneware crock, food-grade plastic tub, or a few mason jars

· A tool to help pack the kraut: You can buy a commercial kraut or pickle packer—but a well-scrubbed fist works just as well. If you're packing your ferment into mason jars, a canning funnel and clean spoon can be helpful.

· A weight for holding the vegetables down: Depending on the container you're using, the weight can be anything from a ceramic plate that fits snugly inside the container, topped with something heavy like a quart jar filled with water, or a ziplock bag filled three-quarters full with water and placed inside a second bag to guard against leakage. (The bag, when placed on top of the kraut, will naturally fill the opening, settling against the sides of the fermenting container, leaving only enough space for gas to escape but letting nothing in.)

· Something to cover the container: A piece of cheesecloth or other breathable cloth secured with a rubber band or piece of string will work.

· A place to store your ferment that stays at room temperature (no warmer than 70 degrees F) and is away from direct sunlight. An overhead shelf is a bonus: It will save you from inhaling the fumes when your ingredients off-gas methane, a process that lasts a few days and smells like sulfur or rotten eggs.

· A smaller, more appropriately sized container for later on in the process, when your ingredients have collapsed and become more compact.

ACKNOWLEDGMENTS

JUST AS PUTTING ON WEEKLY farmers' markets depends on a shared vision and collective responsibilities, putting together a cookbook is a collaborative effort— an excellent example of the proverb "It takes a village." Of course, all books are shaped by a team, but few more so than a cookbook like this one, which celebrates a place and its bustling crowds of supporters.

Thanks go first to Trudy Toliver, the leader of our village. Your support of me and our vision for this book have been critical, and I am grateful.

I know Trudy joins me in acknowledging the following:

Photographer Alan Weiner, for capturing the spirit of the market. Your photos are filled with moments that communicate real emotions in the way that only someone with your personal dedication to PFM could.

Our one hundred recipe contributors, seasoned vendors, cooks, and shoppers, one and all. Without you, our plates would indeed be empty. Thank you for growing and preparing the food that nourishes us, body and soul.

The vendors we profiled: Christine and John Deck, Elanor O'Brien and Jeff Falen, Randy Kiyokawa, and Paul Obringer and Henry Obringer. We truly appreciate the time you took away from busy days to welcome us to your farms and creamery. We treasure what you grow and create even more having glimpsed a sliver of your world.

John Eveland and Gathering Together Farm, an original PFM vendor. Many thanks for your iconic, abundant, and vibrant display, which inspired the cover of this book.

Portland Farmers Market board members, who have been supportive of both the investment and time it took for this book to come together. Special gratitude to Jeremy Sacks, who was generous and wise as our legal advisor.

Cory Schreiber and Adam Sappington, longtime shoppers and supporters. It's a privilege to see the market through your eyes and to know how important it is to you.

Mona Johnson, one of the original champions for this project. Thank you for kicking us off with your enthusiasm, your commitment to authenticity, and your companionship.

Chief recipe testers Marianne Frisch and Sara Schrager, and the cast of many who gave these recipes another go or two or three!

Photographer Charity Burggraaf, who brought our contributors' delicious recipes to life.

And finally, to the team at Sasquatch: Susan Roxborough, Anna Goldstein, Em Gale, and Gary Luke who helped us to realize the book we imagined, and in doing so celebrate our community.

CONTRIBUTORS

Contributors

INDEX

CONVERSIONS

VOLUME

UNITED STATES	METRIC	IMPERIAL
¼ tsp.	1.25 ml	
½ tsp.	2.5 ml	
1 tsp.	5 ml	
½ Tbsp.	7.5 ml	
1 Tbsp.	15 ml	
⅛ c.	30 ml	1 fl. oz.
¼ c.	60 ml	2 fl. oz.
⅓ c.	80 ml	2.5 fl. oz.
½ c.	125 ml	4 fl. oz.
1 c.	250 ml	8 fl. oz.
2 c. (1 pt.)	500 ml	16 fl. oz.
1 qt.	1 l	32 fl. oz.

LENGTH

UNITED STATES	METRIC
⅛ in.	3 mm
¼ in.	6 mm
½ in.	1.25 cm
1 in.	2.5 cm
1 ft.	30 cm

WEIGHT

AVOIRDUPOIS	METRIC
¼ oz.	7 g
½ oz.	15 g
1 oz.	30 g
2 oz.	60 g
3 oz.	90 g
4 oz.	115 g
5 oz.	150 g
6 oz.	175 g
7 oz.	200 g
8 oz. (½ lb.)	225 g
9 oz.	250 g
10 oz.	300 g
11 oz.	325 g
12 oz.	350 g
13 oz.	375 g
14 oz.	400 g
15 oz.	425 g
16 oz. (1 lb.)	450 g
1½ lb.	750 g
2 lb.	900 g
2¼ lb.	1 kg
3 lb.	1.4 kg
4 lb.	1.8 kg

TEMPERATURE

OVEN MARK	FAHRENHEIT	CELSIUS	GAS
Very cool	250–275	130–140	½–1
Cool	300	150	2
Warm	325	165	3
Moderate	350	175	4
Moderately hot	375	190	5
	400	200	6
Hot	425	220	7
	450	230	8
Very Hot	475	245	9